Steep Turn

"The age-old adage to 'follow your passion' comes to life in this personal and engaging story, as *Steep Turn* convinces us that it's never too late for a course change. I highly recommend this warm and thoughtful book to anyone contemplating major changes in their career or in any other aspect of their life."

Bill Ayer
Chairman, Board of Regents, University of Washington
Chairman, Museum of Flight (Seattle)
Retired Chairman and Chief Executive Officer, Alaska Air Group

✈   ✈   ✈

"*Steep Turn* is a fascinating look at Dr. David Crawley's remarkable career as both physician and pilot. Replete with anecdotes both personal and professional, this book is sure to delight all readers."

Michael J. Collins, M.D.
Mayo-Clinic-Trained Orthopedic Surgeon
Author of "Hot Lights, Cold Steel" and "Blue Collar, Blue Scrubs"

✈   ✈   ✈

"As a professional pilot, I recognized the lure of aviation developing in a successful doctor and his evolving into an airline captain—a great story, and well written."

Captain John M. Cox
Chief Executive Officer, Safety Operating Systems, Washington, D.C.
Aviation Consultant for NBC, ABC, CBS, Associated Press and others
Fellow of the Royal Aeronautical Society
Former Executive Air Safety Chairman, Air Line Pilots Association
Airline Pilot, Retired

✈ ✈ ✈

"*Steep Turn* is the inspiring and amazing true story of David Crawley's journey toward finding happiness by making a most improbable career change. At the age of 13, I took my first flying lesson with Dave and have been in the clouds ever since. It's never too early or too late to follow your dreams."

Captain Chris Curtis
Airline Pilot

✈ ✈ ✈

"Dave's memoir reads like an adventure story written as a letter from an old friend, catching us up on his life of unbelievable adventure with several lifetimes lived in one. Like the author, I had medicine as a career goal, but, when I got my hands on an airplane, my life too made a steep turn that led to an airline career, with my heart also set on flying competition aerobatic airplanes on the side."

Captain Christy Douglas
Airline Pilot, Retired
Captain of the First All-Women B-727 Crew, Alaska Airlines
Advanced Level Air Show and Competition Aerobatic Pilot

✈ ✈ ✈

"*Steep Turn* is a lighthearted and appealing memoir. I found it an intelligent mixture of painful, pleasurable, serious, and unexpected moments. I enjoyed the book very much. I'm a fan!"

Frank McGill
Senior Air Safety Investigator, NTSB, Retired
Investigator of More Than 600 Aircraft Accidents
Former Chief Operating Officer and Board Director of a Major Airline
U.S. Navy Air Combat Pilot, Southeast Asia

✈   ✈   ✈

"I fondly relived my junior flight surgeon days through the author's eyes in *Steep Turn*. Filled with technical precision but with a folksy flavor; you'll applaud this triumphant journey of passion and personal happiness."

Captain Dave "Doogie" Shiveley, M.D. USN
Force Surgeon, Commander Naval Air Forces

✈   ✈   ✈

"An exemplary first-person story of how a successful physician coped with his own midlife crisis and found his true calling in aviation."

Paul Weitz
Deputy Director of Johnson Space Center, Retired
Spacecraft Commander - Maiden Voyage of Space Shuttle Challenger
Pilot – Skylab 2 Space Mission

Steep Turn

THE ROAD NOT TAKEN

Two roads diverged in a yellow wood,
And sorry I could not travel both
And be one traveler, long I stood
And looked down one as far as I could
To where it bent in the undergrowth;

Then took the other, as just as fair,
And having perhaps the better claim
Because it was grassy and wanted wear,
Though as for that the passing there
Had worn them really about the same,

And both that morning equally lay
In leaves no step had trodden black.
Oh, I kept the first for another day!
Yet knowing how way leads on to way
I doubted if I should ever come back.

I shall be telling this with a sigh
Somewhere ages and ages hence:
Two roads diverged in a wood, and I,
I took the one less traveled by,
And that has made all the difference.

Robert Frost

Dedicated to My Grandchildren

Will – Emily – Rowan – Beatrice

Never be afraid to follow the path to your dreams;
it will make all the difference.

David B. Crawley

Steep Turn

A Physician's Journey from Clinic to Cockpit

✈   ✈   ✈

A Memoir

By

David B. Crawley, M.D.

Either write something worth reading,
or do something worth writing.

Benjamin Franklin

Acknowledgements

My biggest supporter in every new endeavor has always been Martha, my wife of 47 years, my partner in life, and my #1 fan. I cannot begin to express my appreciation to her for believing in me and coming along on every twist and turn of this wild ride. She is not only an integral part of the entire story, but she patiently edited and reviewed every word of my manuscript multiple times. Her experience from a lifetime of voracious reading has endowed her with exceptional qualifications as an editor. She consistently provided valuable suggestions for improving my writing by amending and correcting content, grammar, and formatting.

I wish to thank my daughters, Jill and Alice, for their love and for always being there as reminders of what is most important in my life. Their resilience, flexibility and bravery as they accompanied me through several steep turns over the years are a testament to their strong characters.

Several individuals deserve special thanks. Montana author Nona Babcock doggedly reviewed my manuscript with her professional eye and provided expert editing and advice. Our daughter Alice, a talented writer in her own right, taught me the importance of pulling my chapters together to create a coordinated story arc. My sister Helen Drake, an experienced travel writer, applied her artistic talents to the design elements, and, in the process, she taught me what a "wingding" is. Helen has also meticulously edited my entire manuscript; I don't think I could have found a better person to review it and repair my errors. I can't thank her enough. Helen also introduced me to her friend and prolific San Francisco novelist, Josie Brown, who generously provided enthusiastic encouragement and experienced publishing advice.

Finally, I offer sincere thanks to all my friends and family who, after reading my first book, *A Mile of String,* encouraged me to write a second one. Their enthusiasm and support provided me the confidence to tackle this project.

One Christmas, when I was a young boy, my mother's gift to me was a little black doctor's bag. The bag came equipped with a few toy diagnostic instruments, including a plastic stethoscope, a small penlight, and a head mirror. She had also purchased a little white coat for me to wear when I played "doctor." When my younger sister Martha unwrapped her present that same year, she found a little, white nurse's uniform. Of course everyone knew back then only boys grew up to become doctors and girls nurses. I don't believe my mother particularly cared whether or not Martha ever became a nurse, but she did make it crystal clear to me throughout my childhood that she hoped and dreamed her only son would someday make her proud by choosing what she considered the noblest of all professions.

✈   ✈   ✈

July 14, 1971

It was mid-morning in the second week of my internship when the hospital operator paged me to the Emergency Room. I was the intern on call for the Pediatrics Service at Deaconess Hospital in Spokane, Washington. I had graduated from the University of Kansas School of Medicine early in June and was just starting to get used to the title of "Doctor." It felt a bit unnerving when I heard "Doctor Crawley" over the hospital's public address system. Almost in synchrony with the P.A. summons, I heard a beep-beep-beep from the pager on my belt. I silenced the beeper and phoned the hospital operator from the pediatric ward on Three West. I had been sitting at the nursing station desk following rounds as I reviewed the records of my assigned patients and half-listened to the night nurses giving "report" to the arriving day shift crew. The operator informed me that the intern on duty in the Emergency Room needed me to proceed there immediately.

As an intern, I still had many of the same duties I had as a student during the junior and senior years of medical school. The last two years, known as the clinical years, are spent almost exclusively on hospital wards engaging in direct patient care. I dressed the same as I had during those last

1

two years of school—white shirt with tie, white coat, white slacks, white socks, and white shoes. A stethoscope was curled into the right-hand coat side-pocket. The coat's left-hand breast pocket held a couple of ballpoint pens, a mini-flashlight, and a few tongue depressors. In my left coat side-pocket, I carried a miniature loose-leaf notebook containing reference notes I had collected over my past two clinical years and continued to add to. Every medical student, intern, and resident I knew carried one of these books containing what we considered quick-reference items. We referred to this little notebook as "the book of pearls"—meaning pearls of knowledge—or sometimes called it "the peripheral brain." When a student, intern, or resident was at a patient's bedside or in an exam room discussing a case with a colleague, it was common to hear, "Stand by a second; I have to check something in my peripheral brain."

Although my duties as an intern seemed much the same, I recognized one big difference now: when I wrote an order on a patient's chart for a certain test to be performed or a specific medication to be dispensed or prescribed, I did not have to find a medical resident or staff physician to co-sign the order. In medical school, every order we wrote was reviewed and co-signed. We always had to find an "RD" (real doctor) before the nurses actually executed a medical student's orders and instructions. Some of the nurses at the University Hospital addressed us as "Doctor" at times—at least the nicer ones did—even though they knew we were not real doctors yet. Now I was an "RD" and was enjoying the new status, but I found this new level of responsibility sobering.

One of the most exciting moments of medical school came at the end of the two academic classroom years and just before beginning the next two years of clinical rotations. Every student in my class and their spouses received an invitation to a cocktail party and formal dinner hosted by the Eli Lilly Pharmaceutical Company at a fancy hotel banquet room near the medical center. A large table stood at the back of the room with 125 brand-new black doctor's bags neatly lined up on it. The leather bags were engraved in gold leaf with a student's name, followed by an "M.D."—even though we all had two more years of grueling work ahead of us before any of us could legitimately add that to his or her signature. Inside the bags were a Littmann stethoscope, a reflex hammer, and a tuning fork.

After the meal, we listened to a pharmacy lecture with marketing plugs for Eli Lilly, and then we all proceeded to the back of the room to claim our gifts. It was an exciting moment. We each carried the new black bag to the hospital on our first morning of our first day in whites and every day thereafter throughout medical school, internship, and residency. In addition to the instruments supplied in that bag, we were all required to purchase an otoscope (for examining the ear canal), an ophthalmoscope (for eye examinations), and a sphygmomanometer (blood pressure cuff). All of these diagnostic instruments were necessary as we learned physical diagnosis. We had a formal class in which we learned to recognize signs and symptoms of specific diseases, but we also learned physical diagnosis each day, examining real patients with real illnesses in the Emergency Room, on the hospital wards, and in clinic examining rooms. It was on-the-job training in its most intense form.

When we left the banquet that night, black bags and the tools of our trade in hand, we all felt we were crossing the threshold to a new chapter in our medical education. This is what we had been working toward. The grueling classroom part of our training was behind us, and the practical part was beginning.

The pharmaceutical companies have come under fire from time to time for plying physicians with free dinners and various types of gifts as part of lavish marketing campaigns. Physicians who accept such gifts have also been criticized because of the obvious conflict of interest and for adding to the cost of already expensive drugs, but on the evening the members of my class received our black bags and stethoscopes, we all thought the Eli Lilly Company was pretty great.

I carried that same black doctor's bag with me as I walked from our rental house to the hospital that early July morning of my second week of internship. When I got the urgent page to the ER, I dropped off the bag at the nursing station and headed for the elevator.

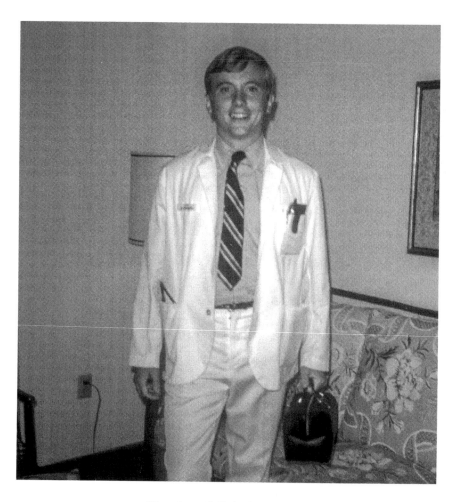

First day of clinical rotations
University of Kansas Medical Center - 1969

The Deaconess Hospital Emergency Room was laid out differently than an emergency room found in a major medical facility today. It was, literally, one large room. The heads of the patient gurneys were pushed up against the outside walls and separated by curtains suspended from rods on the ceiling. A nursing station, from which all activities could be observed and coordinated, occupied a portion of the open central area. This arrangement allowed little privacy and also meant patients with minor illness or trauma were frequently in close proximity to patients being treated for major medical emergencies or severe trauma. Everything going on in an adjacent stall could be heard clearly through the curtain and often even viewed, as medical personnel brushed the curtains aside and swished through. In fact, a patient could easily hear and frequently see what was going on clear across the room. The scent of rubbing alcohol usually permeated the room, and, when major trauma cases were being treated, the smell of blood—often mixed with the foul odor of other various body fluids—could be recognized. So it wasn't a pleasant place to be for the typical athlete who came in for evaluation of a sprained ankle, and it wasn't a particularly efficient setup.

The patient stalls I describe were not equally equipped. They each had some medical supplies and examining tools along the wall at the head of the gurney, and most of the stalls had oxygen dispensers plumbed in, but two patient areas were equipped with items needed for serious medical conditions and severe trauma. This included a "crash cart" equipped with a cardiac defibrillator, a laryngoscope, endotracheal tubes, an Ambu bag, intravenous catheters and fluids, and emergency drugs needed for cardiac resuscitation. Those two "major" areas also had large, bright surgical lights that could be pivoted into position for optimum illumination during procedures. When one or both of these major cubicles were in use, patients in adjacent stalls were frequently moved out and the curtains drawn back to double or triple the size of the area and allow more room for personnel and equipment.

The ER became chaotic at times, particularly late in the evening on Friday and Saturday nights. The floor plan and configuration made it necessary, during those busy times, to constantly rearrange and reconfigure the entire room to accommodate the various levels of severity of patients' problems as determined by triage.

At Deaconess Hospital, one intern was always on duty in the Emergency Room and worked a shift of 24 hours. He (there were no women in our intern class) alternated 24-hour shifts with one other intern for two consecutive months. So, during the ER rotation, it was 24 on and 24 off. Each of the 12 interns was required to spend two months of his 12-month internship in the Emergency Room. This was before the days of the board-certified emergency room physician, and Deaconess did not yet have a residency program. So the hospital had no senior house-staff (residents), and the intern on duty had essentially no supervision or physician assistance during his all-day, all-night shift. He evaluated and treated every patient who came through the door. It was truly a trial by fire.

The ER was buzzing along at a moderate tempo when I entered. I don't think I ever saw it operating at a slow pace, but on this particular morning the patient load did not seem overwhelming. Only two patients waited in the hallway, and neither was in any apparent acute distress. It seemed typical for mid-morning on a weekday. A nurse at the desk directed me to a curtained stall in the corner. Dr. Reg Williams was the intern on duty, and I found him examining a tiny infant who didn't take up much space on the gurney. I had only known Reg for two weeks at that point, but we had quickly connected and already become friends. Reg was a good-looking guy with a thick crop of wavy jet-black hair. He had an affable manner, was obviously well trained, and he seemed unusually self-confident at this early point in his medical career. As the year progressed, I found his confidence to be reassuring when he was working with me and things got a little dicey.

As I stepped into the space behind the curtain, Reg smiled and said, "This one is for you, and she's a sick little tyke." He explained that the infant had been transferred by ambulance from the downtown free clinic. The clinic had been set up by Deaconess and was run by the interns on certain days each week. My partner assigned to the Pediatrics Service for July and August was Gary Wandschneider, and this was Gary's day to run the well-baby clinic. Gary had examined the child and immediately determined she was critically ill with severe dehydration. He had sent the infant to the hospital via ambulance with a scribbled note. The note said he was finishing up and would be back to the hospital shortly, but requested I be paged to start a work-up and treatment as soon as the child arrived. I glanced down at the infant girl on the gurney, and it was obvious we would have our work cut out for us, at least for the next few hours. The baby was pale and barely conscious; her respiration was shallow and rapid. I could see her mucous membranes were parched, and when I pulled up a fold of skin on her chest wall, it stayed tented up after I released it. This indicated at least 15 percent dehydration and that is considered severe. I needed some background information and asked Reg where Mom was. He informed me the child had arrived alone with only the EMTs in the ambulance with her. I could only hope Gary had gotten some background history from the mother at the clinic. In the meantime, I had work to do.

I planned to first collect some specimens for diagnostic lab work and then establish an IV line to start treating the severe dehydration. At that point, we didn't have a name or birth date for our little patient, so her wrist band and the labels on the lab tubes would have to say "Baby Jane Doe" until the mother or some other relative arrived to properly register her. I suspected Dr. Wandschneider had collected at least a minimum of background information and taken some notes, but he was still at the downtown clinic, and Reg didn't know anything more than I did. Gary's brief note, sent with the patient, didn't give me much to go on.

I had no way of knowing why this child was dehydrated. She could have an infectious illness of some sort causing her fluid intake to be inadequate over the past few days, or she could have a severe case of gastroenteritis with vomiting and/or diarrhea—a common cause of pediatric dehydration. The cause was important to determine, but we would likely need to start treatment before a diagnosis was confirmed.

I had a choice of starting my work-up in the Emergency Room or moving her first to the pediatric ward and doing everything there. I decided to begin in the Emergency Room, which was more likely to have all the equipment I needed close at hand, and the ER nurses, who were trained and experienced in critical care, were there to assist me. Reg was there too if I needed another opinion or a second set of hands. Also, I wasn't sure how quickly the admission process would go if I decided to start the work-up on the pediatric floor. The infant needed immediate attention.

My physical exam revealed, in general, a pale, tachypneic, critically ill infant with a rapid, thready pulse. I tried getting a blood pressure reading with a pediatric cuff, on both arms and then the legs, but was unsuccessful. Examination of the ears, nose, throat, chest, and abdomen revealed no obvious signs of infection.

The normal sequence in evaluating a patient for any illness or injury is to first take a complete and thorough medical history, conduct a careful physical exam, and then write this all up to establish a charted record. Orders are then written for any indicated ancillary tests. In this case, as is frequently necessary in emergency situations, I had to alter the sequence to expedite treatment.

I needed to collect blood samples for a CBC, blood sugar, BUN, creatinine, and electrolytes and continue with a septic work-up; this meant obtaining a throat culture, a urinalysis and a culture of the urine, a stool culture, blood culture, and spinal fluid culture. In an infant with severe dehydration, none of these samples would be easy to collect with the exception of the throat culture and probably the spinal fluid.

Reg and I both tried to find a peripheral vein to stick, but all of the superficial veins in the upper and lower extremities were collapsed because of the dehydration. Reg had done external jugular punctures in the neck a couple of times and, as the external jugular was visible on our patient, we decided to use it to obtain the blood samples. I asked Reg to do the stick, as he had done it before, but he thought I should have the experience, and he talked me through it. We had a saying all through our training: "See one, do one, teach one." Reg reminded me of that, but I couldn't find the humor in his quip, and it actually scared me a bit because of the gravity of the situation. As I said, the entire year was "trial by fire." It was like the blind leading the blind at times, and it was a little scary, but it seemed our patients all survived our inexperience. A number of hospital deaths occurred that year, as would be expected, but, thankfully, none were attributed to any errors caused by our inexperience.

My first attempt at a jugular vein puncture was successful, and I got the blood samples I needed. I next performed a supra-pubic needle tap of the urinary bladder, but, as I expected, the bladder was empty due to dehydration. This procedure looks a little gruesome—poking a needle through the lower abdominal wall, in the midline, just above the pubic symphysis of the pelvis. It is a better way of obtaining a sterile specimen than by catheter, which can actually introduce an infection into the urinary tract. I was hoping Baby Jane wasn't already in renal failure. I attached a urine collection bag with adhesive, and I hoped we would see some urine output after pumping some IV fluids into her. The sample for urinalysis and culture would, hopefully, come later.

I was taught to perform a lumbar puncture in infants with the baby in the sitting position and the hips flexed with the forehead held downward toward the knees. This opens up the interspinous spaces between the lumbar vertebrae. I also found it was easier to be sure I was in the midline in that position, as opposed to the patient lying on his or her side. One of the nurses, standing on the opposite side of the gurney, held Baby Jane in a sitting position and flexed her spine by holding her knees and elbows together. I inserted the needle and popped right through the dura mater. I was happy to see clear spinal fluid dripping into the collection tubes. This did not assure me something wouldn't grow on the culture, but it was much better than seeing yellow pus oozing from the hub of the needle.

The last sample was for a throat culture. I inserted a wire swab with a cotton tip through one nostril and sampled mucous from the nasopharynx. With that completed, the next order of business was establishing an IV line. I decided to whisk the baby up to Pediatrics to do that. With all the peripheral veins collapsed, starting the IV was going to be difficult, and after it was running, I didn't want to move her around much and take a chance on it being inadvertently pulled out. I escorted Baby Jane as a nurse and an orderly rushed the gurney down the hall. We stopped in Radiology for a chest x-ray on the way to the ward.

Gary Wandschneider arrived on the pediatric ward, back from the morning clinic, at the same time we got there with our little patient. Gary was a gregarious guy with a cheerful disposition but serious when it came to medicine and his patients. He had a slightly stocky build, curly blond hair, and a neatly trimmed blond mustache. His voice had a Midwest twang with a distinctly Wisconsin accent. When asked where he hailed from, Gary said, "Wis…can…sin."

Gary and I didn't engage in any small talk that morning. I was happy to find he had a name for our patient; her name was Kristin. As the nurses got the infant set up in a crib, I related to Gary what I had done so far in the ER and he gave me a summary of the history of present illness he extracted from the mother. It sounded like a straightforward case of gastroenteritis that should have had treatment started at least three or four days earlier.

We needed to get a line in next. We both looked for a peripheral vein on the scalp and the extremities, but, due to the dehydration, we couldn't find a visible one, even after applying tourniquets around the extremities. We both agreed we were going to have to do a cut-down. I had enjoyed and always looked forward to performing any kind of minor surgical procedure since the first day of my clinical rotations in medical school, so I volunteered to do the cut-down; we chose the greater saphenous vein at the ankle as the site.

When I was on a clinical rotation at Children's Mercy Hospital in Kansas City as a student, I watched the chief pediatrics resident do a couple of these, and then I did one myself under his watchful eye and with his gloved hands right there with mine. This would now be my first solo, and I was happy to have Gary there to assist and give me moral support.

After infiltrating the skin with local, I made a short incision just proximal and anterior to the medial malleolus (the prominent bony knob on the inner aspect) of the ankle. Gary held the extremity firmly for me. I found the vein, teased it up from the surrounding tissues, slipped the tip of a curved probe under it, and pulled a couple of ligatures through. I tied off the vessel distally, made a little nick in the vein, inserted a plastic intravenous catheter into the lumen, and secured it in place with a tie while Gary started some normal saline flowing. I put a couple of interrupted sutures in the skin to close the wound and applied a dressing.

The two of us then sat down and figured the amount of fluid required for maintenance, based on the infant's calculated body surface area, and then added to that the amount needed to correct the estimated 15 percent dehydration. Once we determined the quantity of fluids needed over the next 24 hours, we were able to calculate a drip rate in drops per minute and adjust the flow. Gary and I then went out to the nurses' station where Gary, as this was his patient, began writing up the admitting "H & P" (history and physical) and the admission orders, which included monitoring and recording "I & O" (intake and output).

Dr. Bowen, our staff preceptor for pediatrics, came in from his office to make evening rounds with us at about 6:30 PM. By then little Kristin was already starting to look better. She was perking up, looking slightly alert, and her urine collection bag had a few cc's of concentrated urine in it. That was a good sign.

Dr. Chan Bowen was considered the "granddaddy of pediatrics" in Spokane and was the senior partner of the Spokane Pediatric Group. He was a distinguished-looking physician, always dressed in a suit with the typical pediatrician's bow tie. He had gray hair, was partially bald, and sported a neatly trimmed silver mustache. Dr. Bowen was a true gentleman in every sense of the word. His serene and even manner was effective in keeping his little patients calm and quiet. He had a grueling work schedule, as do most pediatricians, and I could never figure out how he had any time for himself and his own family.

When Dr. Bowen, Dr. Wandschneider and I reached Kristin's room on our rounds, it was "show and tell" time. Gary made the presentation and brought Dr. Bowen up to speed on where we were at that point. The old sage listened thoughtfully, asked a few questions, and then reviewed the results of the lab work reported so far. He finally smiled, looked up from the chart, and said, "If you two handle things this well all the time, we are going to turn over all our cases of severe dehydration to you." Gary looked over at me with a beaming smile on his face and gave me a wink. Dr. Bowen made our day with his nice complement. It meant a lot to both of us.

I had the duty that evening and would be in the hospital all night. It was a typical 36-hour shift that occurred every fourth night. A total of four interns were on duty in the hospital every night: one in the Emergency Room, one in obstetrics, and two to cover surgery, internal medicine, and pediatrics. The two on the emergency room rotation and the two assigned to obstetrics alternated 24 hours on and 24 hours off; the remaining eight interns were each on call every fourth night to cover the other services. Gary had been on duty the night before our little patient came in and had gotten little rest before he took off for the morning clinic earlier that day. So he hadn't seen his pillow for over 36 hours by the time we made our evening rounds with Dr. Bowen.

I couldn't get Gary to go home that night. I assured him we had done everything we could do at that point and the nurses would page me if Baby Kristin's condition deteriorated. I told him I would, in any case, swing by several times during the night to check on her. I then ran down to the interns' lounge, where we had a little kitchenette, and fried myself a hamburger for dinner before things got busy. I hadn't gotten any beeps from my pager by the time I finished my burger, so I ran up to the Emergency Room to see if anything of interest was going on there and to ask Reg if he needed any help. Everything was relatively calm there, so I trolled around the various wards and stopped by the ICU before winding my way back to Pediatrics on Three West. By then it was 9:00 PM, and Gary was still there, hovering over his tiny patient. He looked up at me with a tired half-smile on his face when I walked into the room. He was sitting on a stool next to the crib, and he looked totally exhausted. Baby Kristin was looking better yet; more urine had accumulated in the plastic collection bag, and the IV was running well. I looked at Gary, shook my head, and walked out. I don't know when he finally went home, but he was back the next morning on time for our rounds at 6:00 AM.

Kristin's cultures all came back negative, her diarrhea subsided, we got her on some fluids by mouth after a couple of days, and we pulled the IV. Gary had a long conference with her mother when he discharged Kristin home with instructions to bring her to the clinic the following week. He also scheduled home visits by a social worker whom he instructed to report to him and Dr. Bowen after each of these.

I experienced enormous satisfaction from participating in Baby Kristin's care and sharing with Dr. Wandschneider the personal gratification and contentment that came with the successful outcome of her treatment. The two of us, working together without supervision, saved the life of a critically ill infant during the second week of our internship. Neither of us had much experience under our belts at that point, and I'm not sure either of us working alone could have pulled it off. Although it had been a team effort, this type of personal fulfillment was exactly what I looked for and expected by choosing a career in medicine.

3

Spokane is a relatively small city in Eastern Washington with a population in 1971 of about 165,000 people. It is located 15 miles west of the Idaho state line and is 30 miles from the North Idaho resort town of Coeur d'Alene, which is on the northern shore of the spectacularly beautiful Lake Coeur d'Alene. The Chamber of Commerce and real estate agencies in Spokane boasted a safe, livable city with clean air, clean water, excellent schools, a low crime rate, and unlimited outdoor recreational opportunities. They described a moderate climate with four distinct seasons and a recently revitalized and vibrant downtown with a cold, clear river running through it, generating a magnificent waterfall in the very center of town.

When we arrived in Spokane in June of 1971, the town did indeed seem like an idyllic place to live. The city was a perfect size, having all the quaintness and friendliness of a small town, yet offering most of the cultural and economic opportunities of a large city. Spokane was the boyhood home of Bing Crosby, and what could be more quaint and wholesome than that?

Awful things happen in even the best places, though, and those of us interning at one of the two main hospitals in Spokane didn't miss many of them. Working in a hospital emergency room is like being at the bottom of a funnel, with all the bad stuff being dropped into the wide part at the top and shooting out the bottom right in front of us. The average citizen living in this seemingly idyllic city never saw the things we saw unless they happened to be in the wrong place at the wrong time or something happened bad enough to make the front page of *The Spokesman-Review*. So "Perfectville" was a bit of an illusion for those folks who saw their city exactly as the Chamber of Commerce saw it. The 12 of us got the view from the bottom of the funnel.

Deaconess Hospital was a private hospital, but, as there was no public general hospital in the city or county of Spokane, we received a wide array of medical and surgical illnesses and trauma. Sacred Heart Hospital, just a few blocks away, was a private Catholic hospital of similar size and capability as Deaconess. Those two hospitals fielded almost all the serious medical and surgical illness, as well as the severe trauma, from a large geographical area that extended from Western Montana and North Idaho to the eastern slope of the Cascade Mountains in Washington.

A few of my medical school classmates wanted lots of trauma experience and applied to facilities like Chicago's Cook County Hospital or Denver General Hospital. I didn't want an experience that intense. Interning at either of those hospitals would be like being thrown into a meat grinder. Cook County's ER was referred to as "The Chicago Knife and Gun Club" by the lucky interns and residents assigned there. Surprisingly, we saw our share of stabbings and gunshot wounds at Deaconess, but we probably didn't receive as many of those in one month as Cook County chalked up in one day. We did receive several car accident victims on a daily basis, some of them transported from fairly remote locations. In those days, before widespread seatbelt use and cars equipped with passive restraint systems, the sheer number of severe auto accidents greatly exceeded today's statistics, and the victims often presented on death's doorstep, in hypovolemic shock from severe, multiple trauma. "Multiple trauma" often means ruptured internal organs with massive internal bleeding. These accidents frequently produced several critically injured victims at the same time, and those multiple injuries required rapid triage. These urgent-care scenarios provided a good training ground to enhance my ER skills and were sufficiently intense for me.

The medical internship program at Deaconess Hospital was classified a "rotating" internship because we all rotated through the various services. All 12 interns were required to serve two months in the Emergency Room, two months on obstetrics, two months on surgery, two months on pediatrics, and two months on internal medicine. That left two months for an elective program of choice.

This type of internship is rapidly vanishing, and the existing programs have a difficult time filling their available slots. Most medical school graduates today go directly into a residency specialty program. In this case, the first year of the residency is considered a straight internship, the entire year being spent in the chosen specialty, and it fulfills the internship requirement for state licensure. The straight internship also counts as the first year of the specialty residency program. Graduates today who want to practice general medicine apply for a family medicine residency, which is a three-year program leading to board certification in that field. The family medicine residency is like my one-year rotating internship extended out to three years. At the time I was at Deaconess, family medicine residencies were in their infancy, and only a few of these programs even existed.

Medical interns' pay was referred to as a stipend rather than a salary. Hospitals did not consider the new physicians employees, and therefore did not pay them for their services. The stipend provided was intended to be used for living expenses. Hospitals with the most popular training programs in the country had the lowest stipends since they had no trouble filling all available positions. Some of the most sought-after internships paid as little as $25 per month. Deaconess was more generous. We each received a whopping $300 per month. I had been married since my sophomore year in medical school, and my wife, Martha, was nine months pregnant at the start of my internship. Martha and I both thought my stipend would be adequate for a new little family of three. It worked out for us since our monthly rent was $110, leaving $190 for groceries, utility bills, and other expenses. Our grocery expenses were fairly small since the hospital provided unlimited free meals in the cafeteria for interns and their families. Martha and our new baby, Jill, frequently joined me for lunch and/or dinner when I was on duty. Despite being hospital food, it was generally quite good, and we never complained about the price. This perk helped tremendously to make balancing our family budget possible that year.

The administration and staff at Deaconess Hospital were good to us in a number of other ways as well. When we arrived in Spokane, they provided complementary lodging for us in a nearby Best Western motel while we looked for housing. The hospital administrator's wife supplied us with lists of nearby rental homes and apartments that were available or would soon be available when the previous year's interns moved out. This saint of a woman had slowly, over several years, amassed a collection of used furniture and household items that she stored in her garage and provided to the interns and their families for furnishing their homes or apartments. She solicited donations from the staff doctors and their spouses, and she scoured garage sales and flea markets where she bought items for the interns with her own money. She told all of us to let her know if we didn't find a particular needed household item in her collection, and she would obtain it for us. At the end of my year of internship, Martha and I returned several tables and chairs and a box full of kitchen utensils to her garage for the next year's recruits.

I suspect our contemporaries who were serving at the Cook County "Chicago Knife and Gun Club" would have thought the 12 of us had it pretty soft that year, but I doubt if we were getting any more sleep than they were. In fact, the most difficult aspect of the internship was the lack of sleep and resulting constant fatigue. I consoled myself throughout the year with the fact that, unless I went on to specialty training, it would all be over in one year, and I would never have to stay up all night in a hospital again. I painted a rosy picture of private practice in my mind—days spent in a quiet and comfortable medical office handling interesting and challenging cases, evenings sitting around the hearth at home with my family, and weekends working in the yard and playing with the kids.

4

I had arrived in Spokane from Kansas City in early June, one month before the start of the internship, to find a place for us to live in advance of Martha's arrival. She was almost nine months pregnant and flew to Spokane a few days later. I rolled into town in a 24-foot U-Haul truck with my father-in-law, Bill Scherman, riding shotgun. We were towing my dark blue 1967 Mustang behind us. We had been on the road for four days and had tent camped for three nights.

U-Haul changed their slogan quite a few years ago, but in 1971 every U-Haul truck and trailer had a large sign on the back that read: "Adventure in Moving." This ad had a certain attraction for me, and it was probably intended to appeal to young couples like us, who were just getting started on a first move and wanted to save money by being do-it-yourself movers. Our road trip was a fun adventure in which we got to sleep in a tent and cook over an open fire every night to boot. I think U-Haul realized at some point that some of these moves deteriorated into misadventures, and the slogan might actually be having a negative effect on their marketing. So if you drive up behind a U-Haul truck today it says, "Moving Made Easier." Maybe this catchphrase works better for them. I still like "Adventure in Moving" and I'm happy it said that on the back of our truck. I also think it was a more truthful ploy than the one they are using now.

As we approached Spokane, Bill and I stopped at a service station on the edge of town and talked the owner into using his hydraulic lift to put the drive shaft back into the Mustang. We had taken it out in Kansas City, as Ford Motor Company recommended, to prevent the gears in the transmission from turning while being towed. After we disconnected the Mustang from the tow bar behind the truck, we pushed it onto the lift in one of the station's bays. Twenty minutes later, the sporty little car was ready for the road again. Bill then followed me in the Mustang to the downtown Best Western motel. The motel manager gave us the okay to leave the U-Haul in the parking lot over the next few days while I did my house-hunting in the Mustang.

As it turned out, my search for living quarters was quickly over. I nailed down a great place for us before noon just one day after arriving in Spokane. My find resulted from a hot lead provided by the wonderful wife of the hospital administrator. When she finished describing the place, I felt I was already sold on it before I had even seen it. It was a row house located just three blocks from the hospital. One of the interns from the previous class, Paul Piper, and his wife were currently renting it, but they were in the process of moving out. Paul would finish his internship on June 30, and on the following day he would become an Air Force physician. His first duty assignment was conveniently nearby at Fairchild Air Force Base. On the morning I drove up to take a look at their place, the couple was already packing up to move to new quarters they had found near the base.

It had taken me less than five minutes to drive to the house from the Best Western. I liked the place as soon as I pulled up to the curb. It was a long, white-brick, two-story row house with four units. Each unit had a red-brick chimney towering above the ridgeline of the roof. The old building conveyed a quaint feel of antiquity, but it looked as if it had been recently painted and was otherwise well cared for. The identical two-story apartments each had a large front window facing a small lawn and the street. Concrete steps led to a covered porch and up to an olive-green painted front door with an ornate oval glass window.

I strolled up the concrete walkway and knocked on the door. Bridget Piper, Paul's pretty young wife, answered the door and gave me a tour. I saw they were in the process of packing boxes and close to moving out. The place seemed perfect for us. The first floor had a living room with a wood-burning fireplace, small kitchen, and dining room. On the second floor, there were three bedrooms and a full bath. The basement was accessed by a stairway from the kitchen and opened into an alley behind the building. I got in touch with the landlord that afternoon and signed a one-year lease without even talking to Martha about it; I just made the decision on the spot, and it felt right. I was sure she would be happy with it.

We pulled out of the motel the next morning, headed up to our new home, with me driving the U-Haul and Bill following in the Mustang. We helped Paul and Bridget move their last few things out. They ran their vacuum around the floors and we started moving our stuff in. We had moved all our household items in by late afternoon.

Bill and I ate a free meal in the hospital cafeteria that evening. Before we left the hospital, I called Martha in Kansas City and told her the news. She was excited. Bill and I returned to the house for the night.

The next day I realized I was way ahead of the game; I still had three more weeks before I would start working at the hospital and the pressure was off. I had a lot to do at the house to get us settled in, but it was Bill's sixty-third birthday, and I decided I would give both of us a day off. I asked him what he would like to do on his special day. He said he had seen the peak of Mount Spokane sticking up above the horizon to the northeast of the city and would like to go to the top. We could see it still had snow on it and knew we probably wouldn't be able to go all the way up, but we decided to drive up there anyway and see how far we could get.

Mount Spokane is located 28 miles from the downtown area. It is 5,883 feet above sea level at its summit. The mountain was, and still is, surrounded by a 1500-acre state park with a developed ski area on the upper slopes. In 1971, a gravel road traversed the mountain and led to the base of the ski slope.

June 6 was a beautiful, clear day. Bill and I were at the base of the mountain in less than an hour. We drove up the gravel road until we got to deep, drifted snow about 1,000 feet below the summit. Fresh tire tracks marked the snow ahead, indicating someone had tried to plow through it, but they hadn't made it far before having to back out. We hadn't seen another vehicle from the time we left the highway. I would have to back down the steep road a ways before I could turn the car around. I said, "Well, that's as far as we go, Bill." His immediate response was, "So we'll hike to the top." We did.

We left the Mustang where it was, hoping the road crew didn't pick that day to plow the snow. It was tough going as we post-holed our way through the crusted snow, waist deep in places, but we made it to the top of the mountain in a little over two hours. We discovered a wooden fire lookout tower, which was about 50 or 60 feet tall. It appeared quite old, but it was built with large timbers and looked sturdy and in good condition. I had our old Brownie movie camera with us and filmed Bill climbing to the top and then climbing down. The view from the top was spectacular, especially as we looked toward the Coeur d'Alene Mountains to the east, and the Selkirks to the north, extending along the Idaho-Washington border and into the North Idaho Panhandle.

Our trek back to the car wasn't any easier than the climb up despite trying to stay in our previously made tracks through the drifts. It was late afternoon by the time we got the car turned around and started driving back down the mountain road.

Bill was proud of his accomplishment, and, for the rest of his life, he often told the story of the time he climbed to the top of a mountain on his sixty-third birthday. I was proud of him too, but I postponed his birthday dinner since Martha was scheduled to fly in two days later on June 8, our third wedding anniversary. We both knew Martha would want to be in on her father's birthday celebration, especially since she and I had some things to celebrate ourselves.

By the time my pregnant wife arrived at the Spokane Airport, I was bursting with excitement. Not only had I missed her terribly since Bill and I had left Kansas City 10 days earlier, but I couldn't wait to show her our new home. Her reaction when she saw it was just as I predicted. She thought the place was great. We took her dad out for his belated birthday celebration that night at Stuart Anderson's Black Angus Restaurant in downtown Spokane. The restaurant had a stunning view of Spokane Falls and Havermale Island. The water flow in the Spokane River in late spring and early summer is always at its peak, and Bill was awed at the sight. Martha enjoyed hearing her dad tell proudly about his mountain climbing adventure, and the three of us had a wonderful evening celebrating his birthday and our anniversary. Martha and I were starting our own adventure, having no idea at the time how many twists and turns lay ahead, but that night it seemed all of the stars were aligned.

We took my father-in-law to the airport the next day and got him off to Kansas City. I hated to see him leave. Bill Scherman was not a physician, but he was another mentor for me. He taught me many things, mostly by example. I admired his ability to get pure enjoyment out of the simplest pleasures of life. He also had a wealth of practical knowledge in his head. His career had been as a precision tool inspector at Bendix Corporation, and we shared an interest in all things mechanical. If Bill didn't immediately know the answer to a question I posed (often of a technical nature), he referred to his "little black book" of facts he always carried in his shirt pocket. He called it his "brains." I never got to see what was written in the little leather-bound notebook, but it amused me whenever he pulled it out to search for an answer, just as I did frequently with my little pocket book in the hospital corridors. He had a lot of mathematical formulas in his. I remember one he used to calculate the height of a tree by triangulation. I think everything in the book was written in tiny print so he could cram as much as possible into it. He was nearsighted, so he usually pushed his glasses up on his head and brought the book right up close to his face as he studied his notes. He looked a little comical when he did that, and, if Martha was nearby, we usually gave each other a surreptitious wink.

I wish I could have learned all Bill Scherman had to offer. I was embarking on a career I expected to be arduous and demanding. I trusted my career path was a good decision, but I hoped when I arrived at his stage of life sometime in the future, I would enjoy the same contentment and inner peace he seemed to hold.

✈ 5 ✈

My medical internship began eventfully, two weeks before the Baby Kristin emergency. On Day Three (July 3, 1971) at 1:30 in the afternoon, our first child was born. The event significantly distracted my focus from training, studies, and patients for a few days. A rather unnerving incident also occurred early that morning at about the time my wife, Martha, was settling into her labor room on the fifth floor of Deaconess. Despite the fact my dear wife was in labor and I was soon to become a father, I was on duty for pediatrics that Saturday. I was in the process of helping Martha get settled when one of the nurses came in and asked if I could help out with a problem in the delivery room across the hall. I already had scrubs on, so I just donned a surgical cap and mask as I crossed the corridor.

Dr. Chan Bowen, my pediatrics preceptor, was already there working over a newborn on a table located behind the mother's head, against the wall. The infant was obviously in severe distress. Dr. Royce Van Gerpen, one of my fellow interns, was busy sewing up the mother's episiotomy following the delivery. Dr. Larry Garvin, the obstetrician who would later be delivering our infant, was standing behind Royce and overseeing his suturing job. Meanwhile, Dr. Bowen and I hovered over the infant. The mother could not see us from her vantage point, and I wasn't sure whether she was aware there was a problem.

Dr. Bowen, my newest mentor, whom I had met only two days earlier, did not seem to be the kind of physician who got panicky or excited in emergency situations. I could tell, though, by the grave expression on his face, the newborn was in trouble. I asked him how I could help. The infant was unconscious, cyanotic, and flaccid. Deep tendon reflexes were absent, and there was no spontaneous respiration.

Dr. Bowen glanced at me and said, "Thanks for coming so quickly, but I'm afraid there's nothing either of us can do."

He had tried to insert an endotracheal tube, but, while looking through the laryngoscope, he saw the trachea ended in a blind pouch just below the larynx. I put the bell of my stethoscope on the little chest and listened to a slow, weak agonal heart rhythm. No breath sounds were audible. With no way to inflate the lungs, and the oxygenated blood from the umbilical cord no longer supplied, the tiny infant succumbed quickly after a very short time in this world. The autopsy the next day revealed a

23

tracheo-esophageal fistula, a congenital malformation. There are several different types of T-E fistulas, and not all types are as unmanageable and immediately life-threatening as this type was.

I left Dr. Bowen and Dr. Garvin to convey the heartbreaking news to the new mother, and I returned to Martha's labor room to see how she was doing. I didn't tell her about the sad events in the delivery room across the hall until several weeks later. Martha's labor progressed quickly and uneventfully, and our healthy little daughter, Jill, was born into the world at about 1:30 PM. My joy at the moment of her birth was tempered by the sadness of the morning.

I always knew I would have to face an occasional tragedy as a physician. This one came early in my career and remains etched forever in my memory. Even the birth of our first child on the same day couldn't erase it. How many such heartbreaks would I witness during a lifelong career in medicine? Would there be enough Baby Kristin success stories to provide balance?

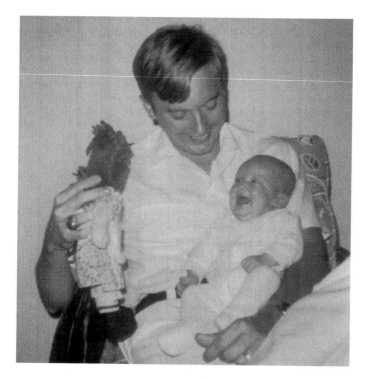

Home from the hospital after a 36-hour shift

While the 12 interns essentially lived at Deaconess Hospital every day and night, honing their skills in the art and science of medicine, the doctors' wives were on their own and quickly united and became friends. Only two of the 12 interns were bachelors. So, there were 10 female spouses, eight of whom had at least one child or who were pregnant that year. Their husbands were essentially absent from their everyday lives for much of those 12 months, and they counted on one another for mutual support.

The new mothers with infants or toddlers often met for "play dates." They formed babysitting pools so they could go to the grocery store and run errands without carting a fussy infant along. They took their babies out in strollers around the neighborhood or went for walks in Manito Gardens, on South Hill, or in one of the other beautiful Spokane neighborhood parks. Sometimes they paired up and came to the hospital to visit us in the interns' lounge or to share a meal in the hospital cafeteria.

Morning coffee and scheduled tea parties were frequent pastimes, and the staff doctors' wives regularly invited them to luncheons. They enjoyed organized sewing and knitting sessions and sharing books and discussing them with one another. The women who were pregnant for the first time received advice about what they should eat, what vitamins they should take, how they would know when they were in labor and what to expect when it came time to give birth. Most important of all, these mothers-to-be shared fashion advice and a pool of maternity clothes; they could trade, "mix and match," and find something to fit their changing forms as the pregnancies progressed.

I don't think our spouses really missed us much that year. Their mutual support group seemed to prevent any loneliness and kept them all mentally balanced.

As I reflect back and consider our brutal work schedule, I wonder how I was able to find any time for entertainment, recreation, or quality time with Martha and our new baby daughter, Jill. I tried to make the most of the little time I had with them; it was just concentrated. During my stints on the obstetrics and emergency room services, the schedule gave me a day off every other day to go out and have fun. The problem was I often felt like a walking zombie from being up 24 hours straight. Every once in a while though, there was a little break between deliveries or I'd have a couple of hours in the ER when I was all caught up. This might occur at 3:00 or 4:00 in the morning, and, whenever it did, I'd lie down in a call room and take a little catnap. Whenever I lucked out and this happened, I wasn't exactly ticking at 100 percent when I got home, but I was "good to go," and the three of us headed out. If I arrived home in the morning with no rest at all, I usually took a two- or three-hour nap, and then we took off in the car for the day.

Martha and I, both native flatlanders from Kansas, were enthralled with the natural environment surrounding Spokane. The nearby mountains, the clean, dry, fresh air, the beautiful clear streams and rivers, and the pristine ponderosa pine forests captivated us. For recreation, we took scenic drives or went on hikes in the national forest or one of the state parks. I'd carry Jill in a Gerry Pack on my back. There were so many wonderful places to explore in Eastern Washington and all around Lake Coeur d'Alene in North Idaho, and we usually packed a picnic lunch and made a full day's excursion of it. Those outings cost us little or nothing, and that was a good thing because we didn't have much money.

When I was on pediatrics, internal medicine, or surgery, I occasionally had a weekend I was not on call. All interns were expected to at least make morning rounds with their preceptors on Saturdays and Sundays, but, after that, we were generally free to get out and play. Occasionally, on one of these much-anticipated holidays, I had to call Martha from the hospital and tell her to put the picnic food back into the fridge because I was going to be delayed a while. Sometimes an unexpected new patient would come in, and I had to do an admission H & P (history and physical examination); other times, the delay was due to a very sick hospitalized patient I couldn't leave. I would have been racked with guilt if I had just left for the day, even when another intern was on call and perfectly willing to check on my patients. Martha rolled with the punches on those occasions, and she changed her plans to coincide with mine.

One Saturday, when Jill was only two weeks old, we decided to drive over to Western Washington to see Mount Rainier, the highest point in the state. We left as soon as I was home from morning rounds on pediatrics. It was a beautiful, clear day and we were excited to be heading out of town on our first family trip. We stuck Jill in her plastic baby carrier and set it on the floor of the Mustang's back seat, right behind the passenger seat. No infant car seats had yet been designed for newborns, so we thought that would be the safest place for her to ride. It's a long way from Spokane to Mount Rainier, and it was a bit ambitious for us to attempt the roundtrip in one day, but that's what we did.

On the way up the mountain, we saw some of the most beautiful mountain scenery we'd ever seen. We stopped at several viewpoints to look at spectacular waterfalls tumbling into precipitous shadowed gorges. At each of these stops, we lifted Jill out of her baby board and took turns holding, hugging, and kissing her, and we stopped a couple of times for bottle feedings.

It was mid-afternoon when we arrived at Paradise Lodge, a popular destination at the 5,400-foot level on the shoulder of the 14,240-foot mountain. The previous winter's snowfall had broken records, and we walked through a snow cave carved out through an enormous drift to reach the front door of the beautiful historic lodge built in 1916. We spent about an hour there, ate a little snack that served as our lunch, and started back toward Spokane.

Our magical day hit a sour note on the trip down the mountain when we encountered a serious auto accident that had just occurred, and I stopped to offer assistance. There was one fatality and three other injured passengers, one of whom was a young boy who appeared to have a critical head injury. I did what I could, which wasn't much, until an ambulance finally arrived more than an hour later from Yakima. It was almost dark when we left the scene, and it was near midnight when we finally got home. Martha and I were completely exhausted.

That accident started me worrying about the safety of our sporty little Mustang, even though the car in the wreck was a full-sized sedan. The following week, I traded the Mustang for a brand new 1971 Oldsmobile station wagon. It was expensive, a little over $2,000, but we were able to get a loan (our first ever), and decided we would need to eat most of our meals at the hospital to fit the payment into our meager budget. I felt my little family was much safer in the new car, and I was happy I'd bought it. Dr. Bowen, my preceptor for pediatrics, was astounded I had purchased such an expensive car on an intern's income. He seemed fatherly and protective toward all the interns, and I think he felt I should have come to him and asked his advice before doing such a crazy thing. The death and injuries I had seen on the mountain highway that day, and the trauma cases that presented daily in the ER, made the purchase of a big new vehicle not seem so crazy to me. I never wanted to see anyone in my family coming through those double doors at the rear of the hospital.

Entrance to Paradise Lodge on Mount Rainier
with two-week-old Baby Jill

July 17, 1971

7

I finished my two-month pediatrics rotation at the end of August, and I spent September and October on the Obstetrics Service. The OB rotation was one of the big attractions of the internship, and I believe each of us had weighed this heavily in selecting Deaconess. The hospital had the most deliveries per month of any of the medical facilities in Spokane; in 1971 and 1972, 300 to 350 babies were born each month there. The interns delivered a large percentage of these. Many of those deliveries were done with the guidance and assistance of a staff physician who was usually the patient's private obstetrician, but quite a few were done "solo," often in the middle of the night or at other times when the staff doctor didn't get there in time. In those solo cases, we weren't really solo, since most of the obstetrical nurses had many years of experience and knew what they were doing. The nurses were, for the most part, tactful and respectful of us as doctors, despite our serious shortage of experience at that point. I think all of us appreciated that token of respect, and we all had a mutual respect for each of them.

The volume of obstetrical admissions every day provided the opportunity to learn about the various stages of labor and to perform a large number of deliveries. It also exposed us to an occasional complication and gave us a chance to learn how to successfully manage them. The birthing process is usually simple and straightforward, but it can, on occasion, become a little scary when everything seems to be going south. I don't think any of us forgot the fact that two lives were at potential risk and, in the case of multiple births, three or four lives. We each witnessed first-hand various complications ranging from a single loop of umbilical cord around the infant's neck to a mother's massive post-partum hemorrhage and everything in between. When one of these dicey moments occurred, it was always nice to have the staff physician there, with years of experience, to guide the intern through. In situations in which the life of the mother or infant was in immediate danger, the staff doctor often took charge and traded places with the intern. The young doctor then learned by assisting and observing.

I had the opportunity to see common malpresentations including occiput posterior, shoulder dystocia, frank breech, and footling breech. We could usually manage these conservatively and perform a vaginal delivery. I encountered a few cases of cephalo-pelvic disproportion in which the mother's pelvis was too small and/or the infant's head too large to deliver vaginally; these resulted in a Caesarian section. The intern served as the surgical assistant in those cases. In 1971, the percentage of deliveries done by Caesarian section was small. That has changed, and today a much higher percentage of births are done by Caesarian section, which is now considered the safer and more conservative approach in the case of fetal distress or any other sign of trouble.

Almost 100 percent of obstetrical patients at Deaconess received an epidural nerve block inserted into the spine by a staff anesthesiologist for the final stages of labor and delivery. It was considered the "Cadillac" of obstetrical anesthesia and was probably the main reason our hospital was so popular for childbirth. With an epidural block, the patient experienced little or no discomfort, and the mothers were left with pleasant memories of the birthing experience. The anesthesia was a local type and did not cause any apparent respiratory depression or other adverse effects in the newborn infant. It did, however, reduce the force of the labor contractions and slow the delivery process somewhat. This meant a fairly high proportion of our deliveries required the use of obstetrical forceps. That provided great experience for us, the interns. There are several different types of forceps with different indications for use, and I got a chance to try all of them.

My partner for the obstetrics rotation was Reg Williams, but we only saw one another when we changed shifts at 8:00 AM each morning. One of us started as the other finished a shift every 24 hours for those two months. If I was just starting, Reg would tell me how many deliveries he had done and relate any particularly exciting moments. He then briefed me on how many women were in labor and gave me an idea of what stage each was in. He normally briefed me right at the bedside as he introduced me to the patient. If Reg was the one starting duty, I presented the patients to him and gave the morning brief before heading for home.

In July and August, before the obstetrics rotation, Reg and I had gone on a couple of outings together when our days off from the hospital coincided. We went fishing in a little stream near the Canadian border north of Spokane and, on another day, we went canoeing on the Spokane River. Reg grew up in a small town on the upper Michigan peninsula and was an avid outdoorsman. He had canoed the Boundary Waters and fished and hunted with his father, who was also an avid outdoorsman. I had enjoyed our manly activities together and wanted to do more, but, now that we were alternating 24-hour shifts with each other, one of us was always at the hospital. It would be at least two months before we could plan another outing.

When I started on the OB service, I was determined to maintain a count of the number of deliveries I performed. Reg and I had an informal competition going and compared numbers each morning, and I hoped to be the winner when we finished our two-month rotation. One day Reg was ahead, and the next day I was ahead, but, by the beginning of the second month, I realized I had lost track of my exact count. That was not surprising at all, since I was, at times, running from one delivery room to another as several mothers were all crowning at almost exactly the same moment. At other times, the deliveries came one at a time and seemed to be spaced evenly throughout the day and night. We'd also occasionally experience a slow time. The hospital had a small on-call room in the department with a bed and desk in it. During those breaks in the action, if I could keep my eyes open, I would sit in that little room and study my *Williams Obstetrics* text.

I remember early one morning I was lying on the bed in the on-call room reading about placenta previa when the phone on the bedside table rang. I had fallen into a deep sleep, and I hadn't even awakened when the heavy *Williams* text fell out of my hands and slid to the floor. When I became conscious, I found myself sitting up in bed with the phone receiver in my hand. The OB nurse said, "Doctor, we have moved your patient into Delivery Room One; we are ready for you." I remember feeling totally confused but answered her with, "Okay. I'll be right there." Then I stared at the black phone base on the table and added, "….but I can't figure out why this phone didn't ring." Her answer was: "Doctor, if it didn't ring, why did you pick it up?" I had no good answer for that. When I came shuffling out in my rumpled green scrub suit, my hair was most likely sticking up in all directions like a madman, and all three nurses on duty were standing in a row laughing at me.

When our time on the service ended on the last day of October, Reg and I estimated we had each done approximately 250 deliveries. We didn't know which of us was the winner in total deliveries performed, but we both felt fairly comfortable and proficient in obstetrics at that point.

I had no idea what I would eventually specialize in or whether I would specialize at all, but I knew I liked obstetrics. Not all deliveries went smoothly without complications, but the vast majority of them did. It was a happy field of medicine. The patient came to the hospital to have a baby—not because she was sick or injured. Delivering an infant provided an

31

opportunity to share in a joyous event, and I always felt privileged to be a part of such a momentous occasion.

8

Ken Gimple and I paired up for internal medicine in November and December. Since all of our experience involved the care of hospital inpatients, it meant taking care of some very sick folks. We spent a lot of time in the Intensive Care Unit analyzing cardiac rhythm strips, treating arrhythmias, and managing cases of pulmonary edema. We treated patients with myocardial infarction, congestive heart failure, chronic obstructive pulmonary disease, acute pancreatitis, liver failure, renal failure, ulcerative colitis, gastrointestinal hemorrhage, malignant hypertension, and stroke—to name a few.

I had known Ken all through medical school at the University of Kansas, and we had actually gone through the interview board together prior to our admission. Ken was a big, kind of goofy-looking guy who reminded me of Gomer Pyle (actor Jim Nabors) on The Andy Griffith Show on TV. He was also very cheerful all the time and acted as if he didn't have a care in the world, just like Gomer. When the other interns and staff doctors at Deaconess met Ken, I suspect many of them wondered how this wacky guy had ever become a doctor, and then, why in the world Deaconess would have selected him. They soon found the answers to both of those questions, just as I had four years earlier.

After taking the MCAT exam during my junior year of college in 1966, I submitted my application for medical school. I was praying I would be selected for a personal interview, and my prayers were answered the following spring. The interviews were a three-step process, and an applicant had to pass each one before advancing to the next. The first of these was conducted before a selection board of physicians that included the Dean of Students of the K.U. Medical Center, Dr. David Waxman. It was at this interview that I first met Ken Gimple.

I arrived about 20 minutes early and found 8 or 10 other candidates sitting in chairs along opposite walls of the waiting area, just outside a conference room on the second floor of the medical center's administration building. No one said a word to me as I walked in and sat down in the last empty chair. I didn't recognize any of the faces. There were no women. All the interviewees were dressed in conservative coats and ties, as was I. Everyone looked quite somber, and, as a couple of them glanced my way, I gave a weak smile and a nod. They seemed to look right through me with glassy stares. The stress was obvious. A few of the candidates gazed down at magazines they had picked up from a table; others just stared straight ahead and fidgeted with their hands. As we sat there, everyone glanced at the closed conference room door every few seconds.

I had talked to several freshman medical students and gotten a pretty good briefing on what kind of questions to expect for this phase of the interview process. I was told the board would consist of three physicians and the only one who was always there was David Waxman, and so I should be prepared to answer all of the questions he was known to ask. The other two interviewers would be "wild cards," and I would have to just wing it with them. I also learned that three students would be interviewed at a time. So as the seconds and minutes ticked by, we were all waiting for the door to open and three names to be called. We each had an appointed time to show up, but none of us sitting there had any idea whether the interviews were moving along on schedule or were behind. No one knew who was scheduled when or who would be called next.

I had arrived plenty early for my show time of 10:15 AM. I glanced at my watch at 10:13, just as I heard someone bounding up the stairway to the waiting area, apparently in a frantic rush. A big guy with a show-stopping grin on his face came swaggering in. He whipped his right arm into the air and made a sweeping wave of his hand with outstretched fingers as he greeted us all in a loud voice with, "How are y'all doin' today? Isn't this great?"

We all just stared at him blankly as he looked around and saw there wasn't a chair available for him. He turned around in the middle of the waiting area a couple of times, still grinning from ear to ear. Before the bizarre atmosphere in the room had time to get too uncomfortable, the door to the conference room opened and three sober-looking young gentlemen walked out and turned toward the top of the stairs. A burly looking doctor in a white lab coat, Dr. Waxman, took a step into the hall and called, "Cranston….Crawley….Gimple."

Dr. Waxman sat down in a chair at the end of a long conference table of polished mahogany with his back toward the door. Another doctor sat at the far end, the third interviewer sat on the right side of the table, and Ken Gimple took the seat next to him. Steve Cranston and I sat across from them on the left side of the table. The table and chairs in the room were fancy, but the room itself was otherwise unremarkable. The walls were plain and painted light beige. A window with a venetian blind at the far end overlooked the main hospital entrance steps and the traffic on Rainbow Boulevard.

Introductions were made all around, but no one stood or shook hands. I made a conscious effort to remember everyone's name, but, except for Dr. Waxman, they were all gone from my head by the time the first few questions started. I knew who Dr. Waxman was. He was a professor in the internal medicine department and also an Air Force Reserve general. He was legendary. I hoped part of the interview didn't include a quiz on the other doctors' names.

The first few minutes were informal and Dr. Waxman seemed to be trying to get the three of us to relax and loosen up a bit. That wasn't necessary for Ken Gimple; he didn't appear to be even the slightest bit nervous and acted as though he was thoroughly enjoying himself. The big smile was bigger than ever.

Dr. Waxman started by asking each of us in turn to just tell a little about ourselves so they could get to know us. I learned both Steve and Ken had grown up somewhere in Central Kansas. I was the only one of the three from Kansas City. As they told about themselves, I wondered how good the schools could be out in those small towns in the middle of farm country.

Then the interview turned more serious. Dr. Waxman started with me and asked why I wanted to be a physician. I thought it best not to tell them my grandmother, mother, and father all wanted me to be a doctor, and that might have provided strong motivation. I knew what they wanted and expected to hear, and I told them how I had always wanted to do something that would help people and really make a difference in the world and blah...blah...blah. My answer wasn't untrue, but I was careful to emphasize only the altruistic motives.

If I had been more truthful, I would have told them I was attracted by the idea of continuing on in school and eliminating a search for employment upon college graduation. I also might have explained I had simply reasoned that any pursuit with such a difficult goal to attain must have a suitable and fulfilling reward at the end. If I had admitted those incentives for choosing a medical career, I might have been advised and corrected, right then and there, that my logic might be faulty and my motives questionable.

When I had completed my answer, Dr. Waxman nodded and asked Steve the same question. Steve was a tall, thin fellow with dark, slicked-down hair, and he wore horn-rimmed glasses. He looked like the quiet, studious type. He spoke in a hesitant manner and did not exhibit a lot of confidence, but he gave an answer along the same lines as mine. He knew what they wanted to hear too.

35

Dr. Waxman then presented the same question to Ken, who grinned at all of us and said, "Oh gosh, I really don't know. I was pretty good in science in school. I guess that's why." Well, that probably wasn't a bad answer, and it was a little different than they were used to hearing. In fact, if I had been completely honest with my answer, I probably would have admitted my strong interest in science had been a major influence on my choice of careers.

Dr. Waxman asked me what I would do if I didn't get accepted to medical school. I was ready for that one too and thought I knew what they would like. "Sir, I will keep trying. I will go to graduate school and do some biomedical research, and then I'll reapply each year for as long as it takes. Being a physician is all I have ever wanted to do in life." That last statement wasn't exactly a blatant lie, but I must admit it was a major overstatement.

Steve's answer to the same question was almost identical to mine, and obviously well thought-out ahead of time. Dr. Waxman gave a satisfied nod, and looked at Ken.

Ken replied, "Well sir, if I don't get into med school it won't be a big deal. I'll probably just try out for pro football." This was followed by another big smile. Dr. Waxman tilted his head forward and put his chin on his chest. He looked down at the pile of papers in a folder on the desk in front of him then put his right hand up on his forehead in front of his eyes. I think he was afraid to look at the other two doctors after hearing Ken's answer.

One of the other interviewers, whose name I had forgotten, quickly picked up the ball and posed a question to Steve. He asked, "Mr. Cranston, what do you think of euthanasia?" Steve got a confused look on his face and asked the doctor to repeat the question. He listened to the question again and still looked befuddled. He then, in a hesitating voice, said, "Gosh, I never thought about it before, but I think they are probably just as nice as the youth in the United States."

Dr. Waxman was still sitting with his head down and his hand over his eyes. At this point I could see he was shaking all over and doing his best to keep from exploding into laughter.

The doctor who had asked the question looked at his watch and then at Dr. Waxman and said, "David, I think our time is up for this group." He looked at each of us and said, "You gentleman should be hearing from us in the next six weeks or so. If you don't receive a letter in that time frame, check back with the dean's secretary." He asked us to close the door behind us as we stood and filed out. I understood that the three of them needed a little time to recompose themselves for the next group.

As we walked back out into the waiting room, all eyes turned toward us. Steve and I headed for the stairs, but Ken stopped and turned back toward the candidates who were all nervously waiting to be called. Making a sweeping wave of his arm, just as he did when he had arrived, he said cheerfully, "See all you guys next year!" I immediately thought to myself, "Yeah...right."

I didn't think Ken had a chance of being admitted to medical school, but there were some things I didn't know about him yet. Ken just happened to be brilliant. He ranked near the top of his class every year in college, and his MCAT test scores were outstanding. It really didn't matter much what he said during his interview. He was "in like Flynn" and likely would have been accepted into any medical school in the country to which he applied.

So now, over four years later, here we were, 1,600 miles from where we had met, and we were partners on the Internal Medicine Service. I had gotten to know Ken well by the time we both received our MD degrees, and I thought a lot of him. His happy, optimistic attitude made him fun to be around, and I was glad he was working with me. I never hesitated to call him to a patient's bedside and ask his opinion when I had a tough case I was scratching my head about.

Steve was a smart fellow too. He was pretty much a shoo-in also. He and I were lab partners throughout the two academic years, since the spots were assigned alphabetically. By the time we met again, he had learned the definition of the word "euthanasia," but I never stopped teasing him about that.

Ken was accepted into an orthopedic surgery residency after internship, and he later had a successful orthopedic practice in Topeka, Kansas, for many years. Orthopedics seemed like a good fit for him with his love for sports, and I suspect treating sports injuries was his favorite segment of the practice. I have no doubt he is a fine orthopedic surgeon and highly respected by his patients and professional colleagues.

In 1971, I was confident I would, sometime in the next few years, find an area of medicine that would be a perfect niche for me too, just as Ken eventually did.

37

9

I started the new year in the Emergency Room, alternating 24-hour shifts with Mike Thompson. Mike was a good doctor, but he was shy and soft-spoken, and I wondered how he would do in the chaotic atmosphere of the ER. I never got to see him in action, since we were on separate shifts, but, from what I heard from the nurses, he did just fine. His thoughtful, reserved manner apparently had a calming influence on the rest of the staff when things got a little crazy.

We took care of everything you can imagine during those two months. Problems ranged from treating minor upper respiratory infections to performing cardiopulmonary resuscitations and managing severe trauma; we saw everything in between. I repaired hundreds of lacerations, reduced and casted a number of simple extremity fractures, treated nosebleeds, removed foreign bodies from almost every body orifice, reduced a few dislocated shoulders, taped sprained ankles, managed drug overdoses, diagnosed and treated cases of VD, and took care of so many other things that I can't remember them all. I quickly learned that a vast majority of car accidents and other types of trauma were associated with alcohol intoxication. That was an eye-opener, since nothing much was said in those days about a possible relationship between the ingestion of excessive alcohol and impaired driving.

Occasionally a procedure was indicated that I had never performed before, and, since no one else was around who was qualified to do it, I had to go it alone. This happened one evening when an older gentleman presented with acute shortness of breath and was in severe distress. After examining him, I felt he had all the physical signs of a tension pneumothorax. He told me, in a gasping voice, that he had emphysema. I knew large blebs form in the lungs of patients with emphysema, and, when blebs spontaneously rupture, air leaks into the space between the lung's pleural covering and the pleural lining of the chest wall. It becomes a tension pneumothorax if the air can flow only one way—into the space, but not back out. As pressure rose in the man's left chest cavity with each breath he took, it restricted movement of the entire chest so that very little air was getting in and out of the functioning right lung. His breathing took great effort, his breaths were shallow and gasping, and he was deteriorating rapidly.

I really wanted to get a chest x-ray to confirm my working diagnosis of tension pneumothorax, but time was running out and I had to do something in the next few minutes if I was going to save the man's life. I hollered at the nearest nurse and told her to see if either Dr. Ellsworth or Dr. Bonvallet, the two thoracic surgeons on staff, were in the hospital. She checked with the operator who said neither of their lights was lit on her panel. I told her to page them anyway—stat to the ER. I heard the speaker in the ceiling almost immediately blare out, "Doctors Ellsworth or Bonvallet—ER stat....Doctors Ellsworth or Bonvallet—ER stat." Since neither of their "in" lights was on, I didn't expect either of them to show up. I told the nurse to call their answering service and tell them I needed one of them to come in as soon as possible.

I then started barking orders. I had already put an oxygen mask on the frightened patient and cranked the flow up to eight liters per minute. "Set me up a chest tube tray, and get an IV going with D-5 Ringers....quickly, quickly, ladies, and page Dr. Reg Williams to the ER stat."

I had never inserted a chest tube before, nor had I ever even seen anyone insert one; I had only studied the procedure in a book—that was all. I gloved up and started prepping the skin with Betadine. I was hoping Reg would come running in and say he had a lot of experience putting in chest tubes, and I would then just step aside. I could feel my heart pounding and my breathing was rapid and shallow—just like my patient's. I filled a 10cc syringe with one percent Xylocaine and infiltrated the skin in the second intercostal space, mid-clavicular line. I went deeper with the needle then and emptied the syringe into the intercostal muscle and along the upper edge of the third rib, just below the area where I planned to insert the tube.

I picked up the scalpel handle from the sterile tray and fixed a Bard-Parker #11 blade to it. I was just getting ready to make a stab wound in the chest wall when Reg rushed in and asked me what was going on.

"Have you ever put a chest tube in?" I asked.

"I watched one of the surgery residents insert one when I was in medical school, but that's it."

"Oh great! Reg, take a listen to his chest, and tell me if you agree that he has a tension pneumothorax."

Reg did a quick evaluation and said, "It sure looks that way to me, but shouldn't we get a chest x-ray?"

"Look at him. No. We need to get a tube in now. As I remember, when you think it is just a pneumothorax and not a hemo-pneumothorax, the preferred location is the second intercostal space, mid-clavicular line."

"That's what I remember too," he replied.

"Okay, here we go then. Get on a pair of gloves and open up the chest tube package for me."

While Reg was doing that, I made a three-quarter inch long horizontal incision in the area I had infiltrated along the top edge of the third rib. The plastic chest tube was a little less than one-half inch in diameter and had a beveled point at the insertion end. There was a solid metal trocar down the center of it with a sharp, pointed tip extending just beyond the beveled tip of the tube.

"I picked a size 24 French; does that look like a good size?"

"I think it's perfect."

I gripped the tube and trocar with both of my gloved hands and attempted to push it through the chest wall. I was pushing hard and I couldn't get it through.

Reg said, "Pull it back out and use a curved hemostat to enlarge the hole. I forgot to tell you about that."

I stuck a hemostat into the hole and spread it in all directions. I was then able to pop the trocar through, but it still took considerable force to penetrate the chest wall. As soon as I got it in, I pulled the trocar back out of the center of the tube. There was a sudden gush of air from the end of the tube as the tension pneumothorax deflated. Reg said, "Wow!"

My patient then took his first full breath. The worried look on his face disappeared, and the terrified look in his eyes changed to calm. I fed a few more inches of the tube into the chest cavity until we both guessed it was about right. I sutured the wound around the tube, put in an anchoring suture to secure the tube from pulling out, fashioned a sterile dressing for the insertion point, and taped the tube down to his chest wall. I then put a one-way flapper valve on the end of the tube. An underwater vacuum apparatus could be hooked up once the patient was in ICU.

Reg took my patient to x-ray to check the position of the end of the tube in the chest. I walked over to look at the film with him. There was not a radiologist in the hospital at that time of evening to give a reading, but it looked good to both of us. If it wasn't okay, it could always be adjusted later, but for the moment it was working. Our patient was exhausted from his ordeal and had fallen asleep on the gurney while in x-ray.

I turned my patient over to Reg, and he moved him upstairs to the ICU and wrote the admission orders.

Several hours later, Dr. Ellsworth, the thoracic surgeon on call, finally got my message and came in to check on the new patient in the ICU. This type of delay in contacting one of the staff physicians happened sometimes. Cell phones hadn't been invented yet, and the beeper system was short-range and only worked within the hospital. This meant a physician in private practice had to advise an answering service of his/her whereabouts when on call and provide the service with a phone number where he/she could be contacted. Dr. Ellsworth had been attending a charity ball at the Spokane Opera House all evening, where the only telephones were pay phones, and no one had been able to reach him.

It was almost midnight when Dr. Ellsworth stopped by the Emergency Room looking for me before he headed home for the night. I was sitting on a stool sewing up a lacerated forehead when he slipped up behind me. "Nice job on that chest tube, Dr. Crawley. Your patient is doing fine. I checked the x-ray, and the tube is positioned perfectly. I didn't change a thing."

I was relieved and happy, and I wanted to say something like, "Well, Doctor, we do these all the time, and it's pretty routine," but instead, I just replied with, "Thanks, Dr. Ellsworth."

I wonder what he would have thought if I had said, "I had no idea what I was doing. I'd really like to watch you put in a chest tube someday, Dr. Ellsworth, since I have never seen it done before."

10

My friend Reg was not only an avid outdoorsman, he was also an all-around natural athlete and sports fan. He loved hockey and volunteered to serve as the physician for the home hockey games of the Spokane team, *The Jets.* One afternoon, in the middle of the winter, he approached me in the interns' lounge and asked if I would cover the hockey game for him on Saturday night that week. Reg's staff preceptor, Dr. Fred Viren, had invited him and his wife Karen to his house for dinner that night. He admitted he would rather be at the hockey game, but he couldn't graciously refuse the dinner invitation with what might sound like a lame excuse.

I wasn't much of a sports fan and had no interest whatsoever in hockey. I had never been to a hockey game in my life or even watched one on TV. I told Reg I wanted him to find one of the other interns to sub for him, but he wouldn't let it go. He kept working on me. He told me I would see what I had been missing and would soon be an avid hockey fan. He thought the big hook for me was the fact the attending doctor got in free. That seemed to him much better than getting paid for this duty. He said Martha and Jill could even go with me and they would get free admission too—another big bonus. In addition to all that, they always gave the attending doctor the puck from the game to keep as a souvenir.

He kept nagging and nagging until I finally agreed to do it. "Okay, okay. I'll cover the hockey game for you, but I'm doing you a big favor. I'm not going to enjoy it."

Reg smiled broadly at me, chuckled, and said, "David, David, you will love it."

"Yeah, I'm sure. So what will I have to do?" I was aware there was no enthusiasm in my voice.

"David, you won't have to do anything. You'll have a reserved seat right behind the team where you will be able to see all the action. Nothing ever happens, but if one of the players does get hurt, it's usually a minor laceration that you'll just have to throw a few sutures in. It's no big deal, I can assure you."

"Where am I supposed to do that?"

Reg replied, "You just take the player back to the locker room and have him lie down on one of the benches. You'll have my kit stocked with gloves, instruments, suture material, dressings, and everything else you'll

43

need. Now, you have to realize these guys are extremely tough, and all they want to do is get back out there and into the game. You won't need to use any local anesthetic. They don't even flinch; they barely feel the needle. Just sew up the wound quickly. It doesn't have to be a fancy, plastic closure. These guys don't care how they look and even enjoy showing off all their scars."

"Okay, give me the kit," I said flatly.

Martha and I got a babysitter for Saturday night. I wasn't going to take our precious baby to an arena filled with screaming, raucous hockey fans. We arrived just a few minutes before the game started and found our seats, right behind the team benches. I identified myself to the team trainer, and he said he would give me a hand signal if he needed me.

I tried to adjust my mood, and Martha kept telling me I might enjoy the game despite myself if I would just get rid of my negative attitude. When the play started, I actually got into it a little, as I watched the skilled skaters slapping the puck around the rink and listened to the excited cheers all around me. Maybe the evening wouldn't be so bad after all, I thought. My cheery feeling didn't last long.

The game had only been going for about five minutes when there was suddenly a big crunch of helmets, knee plates, shoulder guards, and hockey sticks as several players crashed and then started an altercation that every player on the ice was soon participating in. Hockey sticks were cracking and breaking and fists were flying. The officials broke up the melee after a couple of minutes, but there was a player down on the ice. I was on!

It seemed everyone in the arena was looking toward me. *The Jets'* team trainer was on the ice and at the injured player's side. He did a quick evaluation and then started frantically motioning for me to come out into the rink. The coach was also motioning for me, as were several of the players. One of the players opened a gate in the wooden fence around the rink and directed me through it. As I stepped out onto the ice, a skater got on each side of me and supported me by my upper arms to make sure I didn't fall on my face on the slick surface. I shuffled along tentatively, and they finally just lifted me off the ice and cruised over to the downed athlete.

I got down on my knees next to him and asked, "Are you okay?"

"No, I'm not; my head is bleeding. Can't you see that?" he whined pathetically.

I could see he had a small laceration of his left eyebrow. It was probably no more than three quarters of an inch long, bleeding freely, as all scalp and facial lacerations do. I did a quick assessment for other injuries. I examined his neck carefully for any signs of injury to his cervical spine and checked the rest of his body for any other obvious injuries. He had no signs of a concussion. It looked like the minor laceration of his eyebrow was it.

"Okay, get up," I said. "We'll go into the locker room and I'll sew up that little cut for you."

"I can't get up, I'm really hurt," he sniveled.

"Where are you hurt besides the cut on your eyebrow?" I asked.

"My head is bleeding," he sobbed.

I felt a tap on my shoulder. It was the coach. "Doc, we need to get this game going."

"Okay, guys, could two of you pick him up and carry him into the locker room for me? He apparently is not going to get up," I said.

Two of his teammates grabbed him under the arms, lifted him to a standing position, and dragged him to the locker room as he limply stumbled along on his skates. They placed him on his back on one of the long wooden benches in front of a wall of lockers and left the two of us there.

I got all set up, donned a pair of gloves, prepped the skin, and covered his forehead with a fenestrated drape. I opened a package of 5-0 Ethicon suture material and snapped my needle-holder onto the small curved needle. When I poked the needle through on one side of the laceration, my patient let out a blood-curdling scream that could probably be heard by all the fans out in the arena.

"Aren't you going to use any Novocain? That hurt really bad!"

"Okay, Buddy, I'll inject some Xylocaine. I didn't think I would need any. It's a tiny little needle I am using, and I thought you guys were so tough."

I infiltrated the area with local anesthetic, put in three or four tiny interrupted sutures, and put a Band-Aid over the little cut. "Okay, my friend, you're ready to get back out there and make some goals," I said cheerily.

"You aren't going to make me go back out there after this, are you? I can't play anymore tonight." His face was white as a sheet, and his forehead and upper lip glistened with beads of sweat.

I gave him a big, positive smile and an encouraging pat on the back. "I guess that will be up to the coach, but there's no medical reason to bench you. Get on out there now. I'll walk with you."

"What about pain? Aren't you going to give me some pain pills?" I thought he might start crying—he was on the verge. "I hope you did a good job, because I don't want some awful scar on my face," he added.

"Come on, tough guy." I grabbed him by the arm and started toward the door.

I went looking for Reg in the hospital the next morning. He got a big kick out of the story and laughed until he couldn't talk. I made it clear I was not going to cover for him at a hockey game ever again and that he owed me big-time.

"By the way, David, what was the final score of the game?" he asked.

I had no idea.

I used the puck from the game as a paperweight for many years after that. Sitting on my desk, it was a continuous reminder of my stint as a hockey team doctor.

That hockey puck also reminded me of my friend Reg. He was a physician who loved practicing medicine, the number one thing in his life. He was frequently cheerful and smiling, even at the end of a long, sleepless shift. His attitude was infectious, and I remember finding practice more interesting and exciting when he was around. In those early days of our careers, I remember wishing I had his degree of love for the profession. I admired him and wanted to be more like him. He seemed to get joy out of even the simplest diagnosis or procedure. I think I knew then, deep down inside, that we were different.

11

I noticed early signs of spring as I walked down the hill on March 1, the first day of my two-month surgery rotation. A row of colorful primroses had already emerged in the narrow strip of earth between the front porch and lawn. Some trees were showing tiny green buds on the tips of their twigs, and the birds were chirping cheerfully as they seemed to welcome the new day and the approaching new season. It was a blustery day and the air was still chilly, but I no longer felt the bite of winter, and the wonderful fresh smell signaled to me that spring was just around the corner.

I have always loved each change of season, and, on this particular day, it coincided with a new season in my internship. I was past the halfway hump and only had four months left to complete. I felt happy and full of self-confidence as I bounded down the hill toward the hospital in the early morning light. When I reached the back door, I inhaled deeply to enjoy one last breath of the sweet-smelling air before entering the hospital for the day.

I hurried to the interns' lounge, dropped off my windbreaker, grabbed a fresh doughnut from the counter in the kitchenette, and picked up my black bag of instruments. I then headed back to the doctors' entrance door adjacent to the staff parking lot. I had been told to wait by the door for my surgery preceptor, Dr. Everett Coulter, and that he would expect me to meet him there at 6:00 AM sharp. I knew, from talking to my fellow interns, he was virtually never a minute early or a minute late. Also, I had been warned that he didn't wait a second for his assigned intern; if you were not there on time, he would start rounds without you. If this ever happened, he made it clear to his intern he was unhappy about it. I never let it happen.

Since this was my first day with Dr. Coulter, I gave myself plenty of leeway and arrived at the meeting spot at 5:45 AM. The door from the parking lot opened into a long hallway on the first floor and there was no place to sit and wait. I leaned against the wall and stared at the panel of lights on the opposite wall that was arranged in a grid, with each light labeled with a doctor's name—one for each physician on staff. As I stood and waited, I said good morning to several doctors arriving to start their morning rounds, and I watched as each one flipped on the little light switch next to his name. That also turned on a corresponding light on an identical panel at the main switchboard. This system let the operator know which staff doctors were in the hospital at any given time. None of the physicians who arrived that morning appeared to be surprised to see an intern, in his crisp white attire, leaning against the wall just inside the door. They all likely knew I was now Dr. Coulter's intern, since he was the only staff doctor who required a meeting at the back door. His assigned intern was standing there waiting every morning of the year.

Dr. Coulter was the only surgeon who always had an intern assigned to him. He demanded that, and the administration made sure it always happened. The interns considered him the granddaddy of general surgery in Spokane, just as we looked on Dr. Bowen as the granddaddy of pediatrics. He was highly respected by his patients, the nurses, and by his colleagues. He was chief of surgery that year and also chief of staff.

Dr. Coulter had a solo practice, and, therefore, no partner to share call with. Having an intern assigned to him was like having a partner at the hospital all the time, albeit a partner with minimal experience. The intern served as his first assistant in the Operating Room. Surgeons in a group practice usually assisted one another, or the referring general practitioner assisted. The intern assigned to one of those surgeons often only pulled on a retractor throughout the operation, as second or third assistant. Dr. Coulter's intern had a much better experience since he usually served as at least first assistant, and, at times, he even performed the operation under the doctor's watchful guidance.

The practice of one or two physicians assisting on a surgical case is now a rarity. When insurance companies stopped paying physicians for assisting in the OR, the system changed, and today most surgery is performed solo with a salaried operating room technician serving as first assistant. I prefer the old way.

I had previously met Dr. Coulter a couple of times when he had patients in the Emergency Room, but I wasn't sure he knew who I was. At exactly 6:00 AM, the door opened and he walked in, with a cigar sticking out of one side of his mouth and a fedora sitting on his head at a jaunty angle. He was a big man, and I guessed he was about 60 years old. He had a ruddy complexion, but his face had few wrinkles, and he looked healthy and fit. I had heard he was an outdoorsman and an avid downhill skier.

He took off his hat and stubbed his cigar out in an ashbin, which stood inside the door. He said, "Good morning, Dr. Crawley. Let's go up to the doctors' lounge so I can drop off my coat and hat, then we'll make rounds and you can see what we've got on the schedule this week."

He walked in long strides, and I had to practically run to keep up with his pace as we cruised down the hospital corridors. He had several patients he wanted to visit before his first case in the OR, scheduled for 7:00 AM. He spent a minimum of time in each hospital room and spoke very little to his patients. He said "good morning" upon entering the room and answered questions with an economy of words. He poked around on most of the patients' bellies, since the majority of his surgery was abdominal. Several of the patients were post-op, and we checked the surgical wounds and changed their dressings. A nurse was always in the room, ready for him, and, when a dressing change was expected, the tray and supplies were at the bedside. Dr. Coulter treated his nurses with warmth and respect, but he made it clear he expected only the best of care for his patients. The respect he held for the nurses was mutual, and they catered to him.

Each visit lasted only a couple of minutes. If the patient was post-op, he asked him or her about pain, bowel movements, and urination. He queried the nurse about fever. When ordering a new test or medication, instead of sitting down and writing a new order, he simply told the nurse and she entered it in the chart with the notation "per Dr. Coulter." I made notes in my pocket notebook to check that everything he ordered was later accomplished.

While in medical school, I noticed there was a level of efficiency with surgeons I hadn't seen during my time on the Internal Medicine Service. The internists frequently spent all morning on hospital rounds, even when they didn't have many patients hospitalized. They meticulously extracted and digested every last detail of the person's medical history, conducted an exhaustive and time-consuming physical exam, and then walked out into the hall with their students, interns, or residents and discussed the case interminably before finally deciding on a course of therapeutic action. With the surgeons, it was click...click....click. We used to quip that the internists knew everything and did nothing, and the surgeons knew nothing and did everything.

We finished rounds in plenty of time to change into scrub suits for the first case and enjoy a cup of coffee in the surgical lounge. Dr. Coulter told me when it was time to head to the scrub sinks. We each pulled a disposable surgical cap and mask from a box in the locker room, put them on, and I followed him through a door that led from the locker room to the scrub area. The scrub sinks looked like big laundry room sinks. They were lined up in a row along one side of a central vestibule, which had doors leading to each of the Operating Rooms. Several other surgeons were scrubbing at the sinks, discussing various topics in animated conversation. We found two adjacent sinks that were open and began the standard ten-minute scrub. I saw Dr. Coulter casually eyeing me as I began the process, and I'm sure he was checking to be certain I had been taught properly. I had been well trained in medical school on the proper surgical scrub technique, but I nevertheless kept an eye on him to make sure he didn't have his own variation to the routine and expect me to follow. The sinks each had a floor pedal you pressed down on with your foot to start the flow from the spigot. With the water going, I pulled a disposable nail file and scrub brush from a dispenser on the wall and began with my nails, being careful to keep my hands above the level of my elbows the whole time. Dr. Coulter's technique seemed to be the same as mine, and he didn't say anything to me, so I guessed he approved.

We both entered the Operating Room with our hands raised in the air in front of us. The scrub nurse held a gown open for Dr. Coulter, and I stood to one side while she gowned and gloved him. She then gowned and gloved me. The patient was on the table, prepped, draped and anesthetized. Dr. Coulter stepped to the patient's right side and told me to position myself on the left. He gave the skin a pinch with a sharp, curved towel clamp to be sure the patient was fully under and didn't feel any pain. He then made a right subcostal incision in the abdomen for a cholecystectomy (removal of the gallbladder). Before I had a chance to think about it, I was clamping and tying bleeders, snipping the tails off sutures, sponging blood away, operating the suction tip, and repositioning retractors to improve exposure. I tried to anticipate what he needed me to do, and he didn't say anything unless I wasn't doing it right. Several times during the operation, though, he completely stopped operating, laid down his instruments, put his hands on the drapes, looked at me, and said sternly, "David, stand up straight." Toward the end of my two-month stint with him, I finally kicked the habit of hunching like Quasimodo over the surgical site.

We did several more cases that day, back to back. Over the next two months, I performed the admission H & Ps on every one of Dr. Coulter's surgical patients and scrubbed on all his cases. We did appendectomies, vagotomies and pyloroplasties, bowel resections for cancer or obstruction, herniorrhaphies, hemorrhoidectomies, mastectomies, an occasional exploratory laparotomy, and a few more cholecystectomies. Dr. Coulter was an excellent surgeon and, in his able hands, an unsuccessful result or a post-op complication was rare.

I learned a lot during those two months. I discovered the proper way to hold a pair of scissors and cut with only the tips. I improved my knot-tying skills. I learned to cut suture tails so they were not too long or too short, and I learned how to keep the operating field dry and provide good exposure. I learned the art of handling human tissues carefully and gently so as not to add to the trauma of surgery. I learned the skill of anticipating the surgeon's next move and how I might provide the best assistance without him telling me. Finally, toward the end of the rotation, I learned to stand up straight in the Operating Room.

One afternoon in April, I did an admission workup on a woman scheduled for surgery the next morning. Dr. Coulter was going to remove her gallbladder for gallstones. It took me almost two hours to complete her admission history and physical and write it up. This was much longer than normal, due to the fact she had a long and complicated medical history which included five previous abdominal surgeries. At least two of these operations had been for bowel obstruction caused by adhesions from previous operations. I had scrubbed on abdominal cases in which we encountered multiple adhesions from previous surgery, so I knew what a mess it could be. I worried how difficult this routine cholecystectomy might turn out to be. I had seen how briefly Dr. Coulter interacted with his hospitalized patients and wondered if he had taken as much time in his office interviewing this patient as I had. I was concerned he might not be aware of her long and complicated history of previous surgeries.

The next morning on rounds, we were zipping efficiently from room to room, as usual, before heading to the OR for the first case. Dr. Coulter didn't spend any more time with the woman who had the long and complicated history than he did with anyone else. She was the last patient we visited before surgery that morning, and, as we strode quickly down the hall toward the elevator, I decided I had better say something. I was practically trotting, as usual, to keep up with him, and I was hoping he might slow down a little and listen to what I had to say.

"Dr. Coulter, that last patient is really going to be a tough gallbladder to get out. Did you remember that she has had five…FIVE…previous abdominal surgeries?"

He came to a screeching halt in the middle of the corridor, as if he had forgotten something and was going to turn around and go back. I stopped so suddenly with him that I almost tripped and fell on my face. We were both just standing there staring at each other. I'm sure I had a look of shock and surprise on my face, not knowing whether I had totally insulted him or what. He put his hand on my arm and looked straight at me with a little smile on his face as he said, "Listen, Doc, we can do the tough ones too."

The Coulters invited Martha and me over for dinner at their home a couple of times while I was his intern. He scheduled one of these evenings periodically throughout the year and always invited one or two other intern couples along with his assigned intern. Those were fun evenings. Everyone was off call for the night, and, for me, there was no guilt about being absent from the hospital since my preceptor knew where I was. On both occasions, Dr. Coulter got up and disappeared while we all sat around socializing in the living room after dinner. We thought the doctor had just slipped out to go to the bathroom, but he never came back. We finally asked Marilyn, his wife, what had happened to him. She answered, "Oh, he went to bed, dears, and I am going to follow him shortly. You are all welcome to stay, though, for as long as you like. When you are ready to go, just let yourselves out and lock the front door behind you."

I added Dr. Coulter to my expanding mental list of physicians I admired and wanted to emulate. I had no idea what it was like to be in his shoes from day to day and experience the demands and responsibilities of a busy surgical practice or whether I would even like it. He seemed to enjoy his practice of medicine regardless of the obvious stress and demands. If my mother had known Dr. Coulter, she would have described him with reverence as "dedicated." I would have agreed, and I admired that quality too. I looked up to him as another fine example to aspire to. I hoped in the future, when I had a practice of my own, my patients would think of me as a dedicated physician.

Dr. Everett Coulter and I remained friends for many years following my internship. During the summer of 1990, our family rented a cabin on Lake Coeur d'Alene and cruised over to the Coulter cabin in our boat to pay a visit to my old friend and one of my favorite people. He was 80 years old that year, long-retired from his surgical practice, playing golf several times per week in the summer, and still downhill skiing in the winter. He still looked healthy, strong, and fit. I reminded him of the day he said, "Doc, we can do the tough ones too." He stood on the front porch of the cabin with a cigar sticking out one side of his mouth, grinning from ear to ear and chuckling out loud. "David, I don't remember that at all. Did I really say that?" He then laughed some more. He loved that story. Dr. Coulter lived many more years and died when he was in his late 90s, but that visit in 1990 was the last time I ever saw him.

12

I got home from the hospital one evening in April after spending almost all day in the Operating Room with Dr. Coulter. I had been on call the night before and hadn't slept for over 36 hours. I walked in the door, planted a kiss on my pretty young wife, and picked Jill up to cuddle her for a while on the couch. Martha said, "You got something in the mail from the Navy today," and she handed me a large envelope from the coffee table. I passed Jill off to her, and she tucked her under one arm and went into the kitchen. When she returned with a frosted mug of beer for me, the empty envelope was lying on the coffee table and I was looking over a brochure that looked like a thin magazine with a glossy cover.

The booklet was all about the Naval Aerospace Medical Institute in Pensacola, Florida, and described the Navy's Aviation Medicine training program which led to the designation of "flight surgeon." The cover of the brochure hooked me immediately—a full-page photo of a Navy F-4 Phantom supersonic fighter sitting on the ramp. I had always loved the look of the Phantom and thought there had never been a sexier aircraft built. In the photo, a manly looking aviator stood on the left wing of the aircraft in full flight gear, including a flight suit, boots, torso harness, and survival vest. The pilot held a white flight helmet tucked under his left arm against his side. I read the attention-grabbing caption beneath the picture and discovered this stud was actually a doctor—a naval flight surgeon. What could be more cool? I was captivated. The brochure was having its intended effect on me as I opened it and read every word about the program, including the application process.

I was already an officer in the Navy Reserve. The Vietnam War had been raging for several years, and virtually every young male doctor in the country was being drafted into the military, most commonly the U.S. Army. The military, and especially the Army, needed all the doctors it could get. Future physicians could obtain, by application, a student draft deferment—classification 1-S; this allowed them to stay in school throughout college, medical school, internship, and residency. As soon as a young doctor completed his training, his classification changed to 1-A, and he could expect to be drafted immediately. He was then likely to be shipped off in an Army uniform to a MASH (mobile army surgical hospital) unit somewhere in Southeast Asia. Some of these young physicians never came home or were returned in a body bag. This was a sobering thought for me, so I had applied for an officer's commission in the U.S. Navy during my sophomore year of medical school.

On Tuesday, January 21, 1969, I took the oath of office at the Navy Recruiting Center in downtown Kansas City, Missouri, and was designated an ensign. I then joined the small Navy Medical Reserve unit at the University of Kansas Medical Center. I attended monthly "drill" meetings with all the other medical students who had done the same thing. Commander Ralph Robinson, a young assistant professor of radiology at the university hospital, was our commanding officer. We were all in non-pay, volunteer billets, but the commission each of us accepted assured us of meeting our required military obligation by serving in the Navy. Since Navy physicians are also assigned to duty with the U.S. Marines, it wasn't a 100 percent guarantee of avoiding the front lines of battle, but the odds were in my favor that I would have duty at a naval base or on a naval vessel at sea when I finished my medical education and postgraduate training.

As soon as I finished my internship, my status with the Navy would change from "inactive reserve" to "active duty." I would then receive orders to my first duty station—at shore or at sea—as a GMO (general medical officer). The Navy could assign me to any U.S. Navy base in the world or to any type of Navy ship requiring a medical officer. The voluntary flight surgery program, described in the brochure I was poring over, would narrow my assignment to a naval air station ashore or an aircraft carrier at sea. The Navy only stationed flight surgeons where aviators and aircraft were based and operated. If I applied and was accepted to this program, my first duty station would be the Naval Aerospace Medical Institute, known as NAMI, at NAS Pensacola. The six-month training program would not count toward my two-year military service obligation, so it would add an additional six months of active duty. I already had an obligation for a minimum of three years of service. I had "sold my soul" during my senior year of medical school for an additional program that provided officer's pay for that year, while I remained in school, in exchange for an additional year of obligated service. Becoming a flight surgeon would bring my total commitment to three and a half years. I was thinking: this sounds good. What's another six months?

One summer when I was in medical school, our medical reserve unit had gone on temporary active duty for a few days and travelled to Florida to tour the Pensacola Naval Air Station and NAMI. The trip gave us a chance to wear our uniforms and get a little glimpse of military life. I had a brother-in-law in the Navy then, and he had a friend who was a fairly senior flight surgeon stationed at NAMI; I looked him up shortly after we arrived. He was able to arrange for me to go on a training flight in a T-2 Buckeye jet trainer while I was there to give me an idea what duty as a flight surgeon would include.

My demo flight in the T-2 was more exciting than almost anything I had ever done, but it wasn't as simple as just going out to the flight line and climbing into the back seat. I had to receive high-altitude physiology training and be certified in the operation of the Martin-Baker ejection seat first. My brother-in-law's friend arranged all that for me too. I sat in lectures for one full day learning about rapid and explosive decompression, nitrogen narcosis, hypoxia, visual illusions, night blindness, and vertigo. The next day, I experienced some of these things in the altitude chamber, the "human disorientation device," and the visual illusions simulator. I then got a hands-on familiarization with the Martin-Baker ejection seat.

Everyone in the class was required to do a simulated ejection up a vertical track into the air in a functioning ejection seat. It was a real punch! I have a photo of me shooting up the track. In the snapshot, the instructor is standing on a platform above the pit that the seat and I shot out of; he is looking down into the hole and giving me a thumbs up to pull the ejection handle, and, at that moment, I am already well above his head. After our "seat shots" we all went back to the classroom and received our wallet qualification cards.

The following day, I went for my flight in the nifty little T-2. It is not a supersonic jet, but it is fast and maneuverable and looks like a little jet fighter. The two pilot seats are oriented in tandem, with dual controls, under a bubble cockpit canopy. My brother-in-law's buddy found me some flight gear. The only thing he wasn't able to borrow was a pair of flight boots that were the correct size, so I just wore my white uniform shoes. I was self-conscious that my shoes branded me as the non-aviator I was when we walked across the tarmac.

My flight in the T-2 was a formation training flight. I rode in the back seat of the instructor's aircraft and we trailed a flight of four advanced students as they did a section (formation) takeoff. We flew out to military restricted airspace over the Gulf, and the instructor stayed busy critiquing the students over the radio as they practiced various precision maneuvers as a flight of four and accomplished coordinated configuration changes. He maneuvered our aircraft continuously to different vantage points so he could view the formation from behind, above, below, and beside. The training part of the flight was completed after about an hour, and we broke off from the formation so I could get a full demo ride. The students returned to the base.

My pilot for the day gave me one heck of a ride. He was a cocky young lieutenant in his mid- to late 20s. He was average height and build, looked as if he was in perfect physical condition, had blond hair cut in a crew, and, in short, was a cookie-cutter naval aviator. Before the flight, he had given me a barf bag and instructed me to stick it in one of the accessible pockets in my flight suit, to tell him immediately if I was going to get sick, and then quickly get my oxygen mask off. He told me I would be cleaning out the cockpit when we got back if I tossed my lunch. I had no intention of getting airsick.

Once we peeled off from the students, he let me take the controls and get the feel of the jet in straight and level flight. He then talked me through a couple of gentle turns. I couldn't believe I was being allowed to control a military jet. He had set the ICS (the intercom system) so we each had a hot mic and could easily converse through our helmet systems. After a few minutes of letting me play with the aircraft, he said, "I've got it," and gave the control stick a little shake, signaling me to release my grip on the rear-cockpit stick. After that, we were screaming all over the sky. He did loops and barrel rolls, aileron rolls, stalls, and spins. We went straight up and we went straight down. We pulled G's, and I strained and grunted, as they had taught us in class, to stay conscious. I was grinning from ear to ear as he described each maneuver he performed.

The demo flight changed dramatically when, seemingly out of nowhere, another T-2 jumped us from behind and we were suddenly a participant in a dog fight. I had no idea at the time that this was strictly against regulations. It was ACM (air combat maneuvers) that was taught and practiced, but to do it spontaneously like this, without a thorough briefing on the ground, was against the rules for obvious reasons. From that point on, the previous maneuvers we had been doing seemed mild. My pilot was trying to outmaneuver our pursuer to get him off our tail and turn the fight around so that he was our prey, we were on his tail, and we were in kill-shot position had this been real combat. The maneuvers were violent. I kept my knees wide apart to prevent the control stick from bruising my legs as it slammed back and forth to its full limits. My helmet clanked against the left side of the canopy and then the right side. Looking directly ahead out the windshield, I was staring straight up at the sky and the clouds, and the next moment I was looking straight down at the Gulf of Mexico. The horizon and the instruments were spinning around one direction and then the other direction. The altimeter needles were whirling around as the gauge indicated a higher and higher altitude as we climbed, and then indicated a smaller and smaller number as we plummeted toward the water below. I was spatially disoriented much of the time. There were moments when the airplane seemed completely out of control; it probably was. I could hear my pilot breathing heavily in his oxygen mask through his hot mic and cursing the other plane and its pilot. I could only see the other aircraft in a small combat rearview mirror.

The character of the fight suddenly changed as I realized we were looking up our adversary's tailpipe. In fact, it seemed the nose of our jet was almost poking into it. My pilot started laughing and uttering exclamations of glee which included four-letter expletives. The chase was on, and when the other pilot realized what had happened, he dove down into the solid layer of clouds that had formed over the water and disappeared. My pilot was furious and started swearing and yelling, "You #@!*ing chicken." I was the only one who could hear his rant. We pulled up and stayed above the clouds. After that, it was like a smooth ride in a commercial airliner back to the base. The lieutenant hummed a little tune as he shot an instrument approach through the low marine layer of clouds to a landing. He made it seem as easy as riding a bicycle.

One of the plane captains came out to meet us on the flight-line and climbed up to help us both unstrap. I hadn't gotten sick, but, when I got my feet on the ground, my knees were shaking terribly and I wasn't sure I could walk. Both of our flight suits were soaked with sweat.

The lieutenant and I stood next to the airplane for a moment and he said, "How'd you like that, Doc?"

I liked it a lot, and I told him.

Now, three years later, I was sitting in my living room in Spokane and reminiscing about that flight as I perused the materials I had received, which included the necessary applications for the program.

Martha sat down next to me on the couch as she fed Jill a heated bottle of Similac. I explained to her what I was considering and we talked about it. Martha thought it sounded pretty exciting and said, "Go for it!"

As we ate dinner that evening, I couldn't think about anything else. I had completely forgotten about how sleep-deprived and exhausted I was. After we cleared the dining room table, I sat and filled out the application for the Flight Surgery Program and sealed it up in the self-addressed, stamped envelope included in the package. When I mailed that application off the next morning from the hospital, I had set in motion a chain of events that would ultimately redirect my entire future.

"Fam" flight in the Navy T-2 Buckeye
NAS Pensacola - 1970

13

Deaconess gave everyone seven days of vacation during our 12-month internship. We were allowed to split those seven days up any way we wanted, but we had to get approval from the director of the program for each period to assure adequate coverage at the hospital. I allotted my vacation days judiciously throughout the year, utilizing only one or two days at a time, usually in conjunction with a weekend I was not on call. By doing that, I ended up with several three-day or four-day weekends off. This allowed our little family to take an overnight trip out of the area on a couple of occasions.

Early in the spring, we took a long weekend and raced down to the little town of Yachats on the Oregon Coast. Our intern friends, Mike and Janet Thompson, had told us about a little resort called "The Shamrock Lodgettes" where they had spent their honeymoon. We stayed there, and it was during the peak of the storm season. The resort consisted of individual log cabins situated right on the ocean. The quaint cabins had been built in the 1930s. Ours had a rock fireplace, and the lodge owners placed a bundle of firewood on the porch each day with the morning newspaper. The weather was wild, with strong winds and intense rain almost the entire weekend, but we enjoyed sitting by the fire and watching the storm pelt the picture window with salty brine from the tumultuous Pacific. When the weather calmed a bit, we took hikes along a couple of high-bank trails in a nearby waterfront state park with Jill hunkered down on my back in her baby backpack carrier. It was a type of wild and exciting beauty we had never experienced before. When we got back from our long weekend in Oregon, it coincided with the completion of my surgery rotation with Dr. Coulter. I only had one more rotation and my internship would be complete.

On May 1, I began my elective in radiology. I couldn't stand sitting in a dark room looking at x-rays on a backlit screen all day. I successfully negotiated a change, after one week, to orthopedics, which I'd had strong interest for in medical school. For the rest of the month, Dr. Ed Lester was my newly assigned preceptor. I did his admission work-ups during my time with him and scrubbed on all of his surgical cases. I spent one day a week in his private office on a day I was not on call. In the office, I learned how he treated tendonitis, bursitis, arthritis, chronic low back pain, ankle sprains, and common extremity fractures. I also got a chance to improve my technique in applying plaster casts. Dr. Lester was a fine orthopedic surgeon and an excellent teacher. I enjoyed the surgery we did in the OR, which was a lot like carpentry, employing hammers, chisels, saws, nails, drills, and screws.

At the end of May, I still had a few days of vacation left, and I wanted to use them. We planned another long-weekend trip, this time heading north of the border to Banff, Alberta, Canada. On the drive up, we saw a black bear as it ran across the road in front of the car. When we spotted our first elk, we stopped, got out, and took pictures. By the time we drove into Banff, we had seen so many elk at the side of the road we weren't even slowing down as we whizzed past them. We also saw bighorn sheep and moose.

We couldn't afford to stay at the majestic Banff Springs Hotel; it was way out of our price range. We found a relatively inexpensive motel at the edge of town we could almost afford and stayed there two nights. We picnicked and hiked along the beautiful Bow River during the day and rode the gondola to the top of Mount Norquay. The mountain scenery was the most spectacular we had yet seen. Jill began taking her first tentative steps that weekend, but not without a hand to hold. She was proud of herself, and we got a kick out of the big smile on her face as she wobbled along with one of us on each side holding a hand. When we got back to Spokane on Sunday night, I felt refreshed and renewed, ready to get back in the grind with only one more month to go.

My orthopedic preceptor for June, my last month, was Dr. David Grainger, another fine doctor. My most memorable experience of that month was an operation he allowed me to perform myself. I had seen a man in the free downtown clinic who had a strange-looking dark lesion of some sort underneath the nail on the middle finger of his right hand. The fellow was about 40 years old. He had chosen that clinic because he was going through some hard times and didn't have health insurance. I brought him up to the ER at the hospital and biopsied the lesion. The pathology report came back a couple of days later; the diagnosis was malignant melanoma. I showed the report to Dr. Grainger.

We admitted my patient to the hospital and I did a complete work-up to look for any evidence of metastasis to regional lymph nodes or other organs in his body. We didn't find any other lesions, and I hoped the malignant tumor was still localized to only the tip of his finger. Dr. Grainger decided we should amputate that middle finger of his right hand. He told me I could do the entire operation, under his guidance, and he would be my assistant. We put my patient on the OR schedule for a day later in the week.

Dr. Grainger explained that he thought the best result for our patient could be achieved by doing a "ray resection" of the finger, and he told me he wanted me to go to the medical library and study up on the procedure that evening. I learned that a ray resection of a finger meant removing the corresponding metacarpal bone in the palm of the hand, as well as the respective finger. It involved a fairly major reconstruction of the hand. He explained that this procedure was better for two reasons: first, the palm of the hand would function more normally when grasping something or making a fist; second, there would be no gap between the index finger and the fourth digit, where the amputated digit had been, and it would allow the remaining fingers to function better. The operation would also make the hand look more aesthetically normal. I studied the procedure for a ray resection for several hours that night.

I wasn't nervous as I walked up to the surgical scrub sinks the next morning with Dr. Grainger at my side, but I realized this was a pretty major operation for an intern to be performing. I couldn't have had a better teacher. Dr. Grainger had a special interest in hand surgery, and I believe he may have even done a hand fellowship at some point during his training. His calm, confident manner kept me calm and confident. He walked me through the whole operation, and I did all the cutting and suturing. It went well, and my patient recovered without any complications and with a hand that looked as if it would eventually function almost normally. Since my internship was over at the end of the month, my patient became Dr. Grainger's, and he scheduled the subsequent follow-up visits in his office. I'm sure the doctor realized all of this was without any compensation, but all physicians expect to provide a certain percentage of free services; it goes with the job. I never found out whether or not the man had any recurrence of this aggressive type of cancer. I could only hope we had arrested it in time.

My experience with Dr. Lester and Dr. Grainger, and especially the hand operation I performed under Dr. Grainger's supervision, rekindled an interest in orthopedic surgery that started during my senior year of medical school. I was not primarily attracted by the sports medicine aspect; it was the love of mechanics that drew me to the specialty. I experienced simple satisfaction the first time I reduced a fracture of the distal radius of the forearm, feeling immediate gratification from seeing something I had fixed—a bone was crooked, and I made it straight.

During that final year of medical school, I was so sure I was going to specialize in orthopedics that I wrote my required senior medical thesis on the treatment of supracondylar fractures of the elbow in children, a particularly nasty fracture if not treated properly. My thesis was published in *American Family Physician*, and the blurb about the author, which I provided, stated that I planned to specialize in orthopedic surgery after graduation. That early interest had waned somewhat as my experience and training widened to other fields of medicine. Now I was thinking seriously about orthopedics again, but any decision about that would be made several years down the road due to my upcoming military commitment. The Vietnam War had postponed the careers of many young male physicians of my generation. The path for my immediate future was set. It would be another three and a half years before I was released from active duty in the U.S. Navy. I would be 30 years old before I would be free to choose a specialty and apply for a residency training program. I already had a small family to support, and, if I chose that path, it would mean living in relative poverty on meager wages for several more years. I considered that a lot might happen between now and then, and, in fact, a lot more happened than I ever could have imagined.

14

By the beginning of that last month of my internship at Deaconess Hospital, I wondered when I would hear from the Navy regarding my application for the aviation medicine program. Finally, toward the end of the second week of June, I arrived home from the hospital and found another big brown envelope from the Navy waiting for me. I tore it open, expecting to see a letter of congratulations for acceptance into a flight surgery training class. I was disappointed to find no such letter in the package. What I found instead was a formal set of military orders. I quickly read over the official-looking document. It contained long numbers and codes, the meanings of which I could not comprehend, but there was a narrative buried in it that told where and when to report for active duty.

Most of my physician friends who were being assimilated into the armed forces were finishing their training one day and then reporting for active duty within two or three days after that, allowing only for travel time to the first duty station. My orders instructed that I report to the Naval Aerospace Medical Institute for duty during the last week of September. This indicated I *had* been selected for the aviation medicine program, and I was excited about that, but the report date caused a little panic because it meant I would have no income for the months of July, August, and most of September. My monthly stipend for the internship would stop on June 30, and I had a family to support. This gap in employment was unexpected, and I had no idea how I was going to provide for them. Martha had no job outside the home, and we had no savings.

Very few health care providers, other than the military, paid a physician a salary as an employee. The Veterans Administration did that, but it required a long contract. There may have been some early HMOs then that hired physicians but not on a short-term basis such as I needed. I had experience at a variety of jobs when I was a kid and when I was in high school and college. I knew how to do a lot of different things outside of medicine, so I was pretty confident I could get some type of temporary employment. There was another big issue, though—the one-year lease on our home ended on June 30. A new intern and his wife had already signed a lease on our place, and they would be moving in as soon as we moved out. Where would we live between June 30 and the last week of September when I reported for duty in Pensacola? I only had about two weeks to figure something out.

I went to the internship director's office the next day. Dr. Carl Rowe had passed the torch to Dr. John Collins, a young GP, who was now the new director. John wasn't in the office, so I asked his secretary if the hospital ever kept an intern on the payroll to help the new interns get adjusted and trained. I knew that was unlikely, but I had to ask. She told me she wasn't aware of the hospital ever doing that, but she expected Dr. Collins later that morning and said she would have him beep me when he came in.

I got the page at about 10:30 AM as I was finishing a workup on a new orthopedic admission for Dr. Grainger. I immediately went back to the director's office and posed my question to Dr. Collins. He told me it would be impossible to retain me after June 30. The program was not set up like that, and the hospital did not hire physicians as employees. He had another idea for me, though, that might keep food on our table and a roof over our heads for the next two and a half months.

The administrator of Coulee General Hospital in Grand Coulee, Washington, had called the director's office a few days earlier and talked to Dr. Collins. He was attempting to recruit one or two new physicians to come to the Central Washington town, well known for the massive Grand Coulee Dam and Roosevelt Lake behind it. He told Dr. Collins the last physician in practice there had retired, and his hospital was standing idle. He explained the urgent need to get a doctor there as soon as possible. There had been an enormous increase in the population of the city of Grand Coulee in 1967, when hundreds of construction workers arrived with their families to start building the massive, multimillion-dollar Third Power Plant. Construction of the Third Power Plant would continue until 1980. Besides routine medical care for the workers and their families, traumatic injuries at the construction site, major and minor, occurred almost daily. The situation was dire and the community was desperate to entice new physicians.

I slipped out of the hospital early that afternoon, climbed the hill to our home, and made a phone call to Coulee General Hospital with the hope the crisis in Grand Coulee hadn't already been solved.

A woman answered the phone. "Coulee General Hospital," she announced.

"Hi, my name is Dr. David Crawley. I'm calling long distance from Spokane, and I'd like to talk to the hospital administrator." I gave all this information so I wouldn't be put on hold. I couldn't afford a big long-distance bill.

The woman on the phone said, "Mr. Bristor is right here," and it sounded as if she just handed the receiver to him. I thought: "Mister Bristor?" I stifled a chuckle. I also wondered: don't they even have an operator and a switchboard? I found out later it was Mr. Bristor's wife, Rita, who had answered the phone.

Delos Bristor explained the critical need to staff his community hospital and get it operating again. He quickly outlined the details of a proposal. It was a deal that almost knocked my socks off. He said he would provide the facilities for me to practice in the hospital, process all the billing and insurance claims for my services, loan me a car to drive to and from work, supply the gasoline and maintenance for the car, provide free furnished housing for me and my family, pay all our telephone and utility bills, and pay me a weekly salary.

This sounded too good to be true. If the salary was as much as my $300 per month stipend as an intern, I would be way ahead of the game since our living expenses would be negligible. He hadn't said what the salary would be.

I didn't want to appear motivated at all by money, since that certainly was not why I had chosen medicine as a career, but I did have to ask about the salary. I posed my question as politely as possible, "Mr. Bristor, this seems like a very generous offer, but I would like to think about it for a couple of days and will get back to you. By the way, sir, do you happen to have an idea yet what the salary might be?"

"One thousand dollars per week," he said clearly and distinctly.

I obviously had misunderstood him, or maybe he just misspoke. "I'm sorry, sir, I didn't hear you. Could you please say that again?"

"One thousand dollars per week," he repeated.

"Okay, sir, I think I got it that time; it's one thousand dollars per month?"

"Dr. Crawley, your salary will be one thousand dollars per WEEK."

"Okay, Mr. Bristor; I got it that time. What time do you want me to be there on July 1?"

As soon as I hung up the phone, I sprinted back down the hill to the hospital to find Reg.

15

I found Reg in the interns' lounge munching a sandwich. "Are you sure you didn't misunderstand him, David?"

"Reg, I kept asking him to repeat it. He told me three times that the salary was one thousand dollars per week."

"Did you ask him if he needed anyone else—a second doctor, possibly?"

Reg was scheduled to go into the National Health Service Corps on August 15. He had already been assigned to the town of Gold Beach, Oregon, on the southern Oregon coast for the next three years. This program exempted him from the draft and counted as fulfillment of his required military obligation. Reg and Karen also had a baby daughter, and Reg was concerned about finances as much as I was for the period before he started work in August.

"Reg, I didn't ask him if he needed another doctor. You will have to call him yourself."

I told him I thought it would be great fun for both of us to be there and that I was willing to split the salary with him. That would give us each $500 per week, which was still way more money than either of us had ever made in our lives.

Reg came swaggering into the interns' lounge the next morning with a big grin on his face. Not only did Mr. Bristor hire Reg too, but he didn't even suggest the two of us split the salary. Reg and his family would have to share the house and car with us, but he would receive the same salary as I—$1,000 per week.

Once the two of us were over the shock of this incredible deal, we both felt like running out and dancing in the street. I don't think either of us worried much about practicing medicine on our own for the first time, out in the middle of nowhere and with no nearby support. We were fearless, and both of us were confident we could take care of just about anything that came through the doors of Coulee General Hospital. Less than two weeks later all our education, training, and skills would be tested to the limits.

One possible fly in the ointment was the fact that neither of us was licensed to practice in the state of Washington. We both sent applications to the Board of Medicine, but they would not be complete until we had submitted our certificates of internship. Both of us had taken and passed all three parts of the National Board Exam, so we did not have to take the

Washington written exam, but it seemed there was no way we could get our licenses in time.

Mr. Bristor made a couple of calls to the Washington State Department of Medical Licensing in Olympia and pulled some strings. Reg and I were both issued temporary licenses to practice medicine and surgery in the state of Washington, effective July 1. We each would receive our permanent certificates several weeks later. Apparently our dilemma was common and occurred every year around July 1, and the folks in Olympia were experienced with accelerating the process.

During the last week of June, packers from Beacon Van Lines came out to our house and packed our household goods for moving. A couple of days later a big green and white moving van pulled up to the curb and loaded the packed cartons and our furniture to transport to Pensacola, courtesy of the U.S. Navy. We wouldn't be in Pensacola when our shipment arrived there, so it would all be stored on pallets in a warehouse until we got there and found housing.

It was still dark on the morning of July 1, 1972, when a 1971 Oldsmobile station wagon, following a 1971 Toyota Land Cruiser, headed out of Spokane on U.S. Highway 2 for Grand Coulee, Washington. The little Crawley family and the little Williams family were off on a new adventure. Over the next few weeks, I would find out what it was like to be a country doctor in a small western town.

✈ 16 ✈

As we approached the town of Grand Coulee, we all noticed how bleak the landscape looked. The essentially barren terrain was all the same color—light brown—with no trees and only sparse desert-like vegetation. We drove past the shore of the enormous Lake Roosevelt, above the dam. The lake was nice, but the shoreline was featureless and was as I imagined the Persian Gulf might look. The whole area appeared truly godforsaken. We were excited about our adventure though, and we all kept those observations to ourselves. When we pulled into the little town itself, we saw green lawns and mature shade trees, a result of irrigation from the massive reservoir. The town was like a small oasis in the middle of the Sahara Desert. Some nice, neat little well-kept clapboard houses looked as though they might have belonged in any small town in America. We all wondered which one of these cute places we would be living in.

Our little caravan arrived at Coulee General Hospital at about 8:30 AM. The hospital was quiet; there didn't seem to be much going on. Delos Bristor and his wife Rita were there waiting for us. After we introduced ourselves, Mr. Bristor suggested the first order of business be settling our two families in the house he was providing for us. Our convoy then continued, with the administrator now in the lead, driving west to the separate community of Electric City, just a short distance away. Martha and Karen looked back longingly at the little oasis of lawns, trees, and cute houses as he led us back out into the barren desert. Leading the way in a relatively new Cadillac sedan, he took us into a rather permanent-looking trailer park located on the shores of Banks Lake. He stopped in front of a double-wide modular home—a trailer really, without wheels. It looked pretty nice for a trailer, and it had a small lawn and a concrete patio in front furnished with a charcoal barbecue and a couple of folding chairs.

We all traipsed through the front door and did a walk-through. It had a nice-sized living room area with a couch and a black and white television, and there was a small folding dining table with four chairs between the kitchen and the living room. We proceeded down a narrow hallway and found three bedrooms, and we were surprised to find two full bathrooms. That was a nice feature and would provide our two families some degree of privacy. All in all, it didn't seem too bad considering the fact it was free and we were each going to be paid $1,000 per week.

Mr. Bristor told Reg and me to take our time unloading and moving in and to let him know if we needed anything. He asked us to come back down to the hospital as soon as we got settled so he could outline our duties and then take us out for lunch in town. Before he left, he warned us that the rattlesnake population of the area probably outnumbered the human population, so we should all be careful whenever we stepped outside the house. For $1,000 per week, we were all inclined to accept the risk. He then left and headed back to his office.

It didn't take us long to unload both vehicles. We left our wives to organize the house and settle in, and we drove back to town. We were sitting in the administrator's office by 11:00 AM, anxious to get to work.

Delos Bristor was an intense little man. He was probably in his mid 50s, balding, short in stature, and a little overweight. He emitted an aura of self-importance, and he reminded me of a little Napoleon, with this small hospital, and even the town itself, as his kingdom. His manner was friendly but serious, and he looked like someone who was wound up pretty tight. We soon learned the cause of his stress.

Before Mr. Bristor began outlining our clinical responsibilities, he laid a Grand Coulee marketing pitch on us. It was clear he wanted us to be looking at Grand Coulee as a fabulous place to practice medicine for the rest of our lives and as a wonderful location to establish a home and raise our families. We had both informed him during our initial telephone conversations of our upcoming commitments—for me, to the U.S. Navy, and for Reg, to the National Health Service Corps. Reg and I both reiterated these obligations and reminded him I would be leaving for Pensacola in two months, and Reg would be departing for Gold Beach, Oregon, in only six weeks. Delos seemed to have a bit of an inflated impression of his power and influence, and, just as he had expedited the issuing of our licenses, he proclaimed he could easily get each of us out of these commitments. This was, of course, ridiculous, but he seemed to believe, now that we were both there, that he had full control over us. He was not about to let the U.S. government take his boys away from him now that he had them in his clutches. He would just make a couple of phone calls, and, once the government realized whom they were talking to, both of our service obligations would be dissolved. Neither of us would then have any excuse not to stay in Grand Coulee for the rest of our days on Earth.

Reg and I listened to all this and then respectfully told him we didn't doubt his influence, but each of us had our plans made. We assured him that we both found his town and the surrounding area to be charming, beautiful, and an attractive place to live and practice. We both said we would seriously consider coming back after our respective service commitments to Uncle Sam were completed. We weren't exactly lying, since we were both excited to be in Grand Coulee, and I even thought it was possible I might find some things I liked about the place once I had been there for a while. I couldn't quite picture Martha ever getting enthused about it, though.

Reg and I steered Mr. Bristor away from his visions of us as his dream team for the next 20 years and asked about his plans for establishing a practice for us for the next few weeks so we could earn our generous salaries. He began by giving us a little background information about the hospital, and we immediately understood why he looked like someone whose head was about to explode.

Mr. Bristor explained that he was not just the administrator of the hospital. Coulee General Hospital was not a public institution—it was private. Mr. Bristor and a partner, who was a Los Angeles physician, actually owned the hospital. The Los Angeles partner had paid for the building, and Delos Bristor had bought the hospital's furnishings and equipment. He didn't tell us how much of this was financed, but I suspected these two guys were servicing a pretty large debt. When the last physician had retired and left, they had converted the inpatient wing of the hospital into a nursing home, and all but a few beds were occupied by elderly residents requiring skilled nursing care. This provided some income, but not enough to cover expenses. They needed to get some real patient care going again to stay in business. The Emergency Room, the Operating Room, the clinical laboratory, the physical therapy department, and the remaining inpatient beds were standing idle. This had to change if the facility was going to survive. Reg and I now understood why our new boss was so stressed out.

Mr. Bristor suddenly stood up. "If I didn't already mention it, my wife Rita is an RN and the director of nursing. She is also a certified nurse anesthetist. Let's go find her and we will give you boys the tour."

When we had briefly met Rita Bristor earlier that morning, she was wearing regular civilian clothes. We found her at the nursing station desk in the inpatient wing of the hospital, and she was now dressed in a white uniform, complete with a white nurse's cap. She appeared also to be in her late 40s or early 50s in age, was of average height, and sturdily built. She had short, black hair and a nice face. Rita had a much warmer and quieter personality than Delos. She seemed serious but didn't, however, show any of the signs of stress I had noticed in her husband. She had a calm, deliberate, and self-assured aura about her that I had seen before in highly competent nurses. When Reg and I talked later, he told me he had formed the same opinion. Over the next few weeks, we found our initial impressions were correct. She was like a wise mother hen, tactfully offering advice at times to these two young physicians who were well trained but had rather limited experience in the art and science of medical practice. Rita was a fine nurse with many years of experience, and it was reassuring to have her working alongside us over the next few weeks.

We strolled past the open doors to the rooms at the end of the wing where the nursing home patients resided. We didn't go into any of the rooms, but, from what we could see, everything looked clean and neat. As we walked past one of the rooms, an LPN in a white uniform came out carrying a patient's lunch tray, and Rita introduced her. She was the only staff member or employee, besides Rita, whom we saw on our tour. It appeared they were operating the place with a skeleton crew, but it looked as if the patients were getting good care as far as we could tell.

The hospital had a total of 25 beds for inpatients. Most of the rooms were doubles with two beds; only four of the rooms were unoccupied. Our guides took us into one of those rooms so we could see what a typical patient room was like. We then proceeded through double doors at the end of the hall and back into the main core of the hospital. Delos and Rita showed us the Operating Room, which also served as a delivery room, the Emergency Room, the x-ray room, the clinical laboratory, and a small room set up for physical therapy. Everything looked well organized. The whole tour lasted about 15 minutes, and we finished outside the door to the administrator's office.

Mr. Bristor said, "Let's go to lunch," and we walked out the back door and climbed into his Cadillac. Rita stayed at the hospital; Delos hadn't invited her, and she was the one we really wanted to talk to. He drove us into town and stopped his car at a spot where we could see the downstream side of the massive dam. Dump trucks, earthmoving machines, giant cranes, and other equipment operated near one end of the structure. Hundreds of workers in yellow hardhats scurried all around, and some of them dangled from rope harnesses, several hundred feet in the air, on the side of an adjacent cliff face. A thick haze of rock dust mushroomed up into the atmosphere above.

We then drove a few more blocks and parked in front of a place with a sign that said: "Flo's Cafe." It looked like an old house that had been converted into a restaurant. While we waited for our food, Mr. Bristor began outlining what he expected of the two us. He explained that we would have to do a little marketing for the hospital, since it was going to require some effort to get the word out that the facility was finally staffed and operating again. He had already placed an announcement in the local paper but thought it would take at least a few days before word spread. He told us folks had gotten used to going 50 miles downstream along the Columbia to the town of Brewster or 80 miles east to Spokane for medical care. There was an independent ambulance company in town, which had been transporting all the major trauma and serious medical cases to one of those two cities. Mr. Bristor had contacted them and requested they now bring patients directly to Coulee General. We would have to win patients back and then earn their trust, and he expected it to take at least a few days before Reg and I would have much of a patient load.

On the ride back to the hospital after lunch, we told Delos we wanted to spend the afternoon conducting an inventory of the equipment in the Emergency Room and Operating Room so we would know the tools and supplies we would have to work with. We hoped Rita would be free to assist us.

When we stepped out of the Cadillac back at the hospital, Mr. Bristor pointed to a small, one-story house across the parking lot and said that was their home. It was a plain looking house made of concrete blocks with a flat roof. It looked clean and neat but had no landscaping. It seemed to fit in with the featureless landscape of the surrounding area. An antique car with dents, scratches, and faded beige paint was parked in front of the house. It looked like a collector's item. I wondered how long it had been sitting in that same spot. I had always loved old cars and started to ask him about it.

"I promised you boys a car as part of the deal, and there it is. The keys are in it and the tank is full, so when you leave today, one of you can drive it back to your house. Bring me the receipts for any gas you buy for it." He told us it was a 1941 Chevrolet five-passenger coupe. He never said where he got it or how long he had owned it. Years later, I wished I had asked those questions.

We spent the afternoon, with Rita assisting, looking over the medical equipment and supplies. We discussed with her where we would see patients. The hospital was not set up to see outpatient clinic patients, but there was one small examination room across the hall from the Emergency Room. One of us could examine patients there, while the other used the Emergency Room for exams. There was no waiting room or reception desk, but the hall was furnished with a few chairs where patients could sit while waiting to be seen. It wasn't a traditional clinic set-up, but we could make it work.

When we finished checking out the equipment, Reg and I went back to the inpatient area and reviewed the charts of the nursing home patients. Rita then accompanied us as we made rounds, and she related a bit of information about each of the residents.

Not a single patient presented for treatment that first day. It was 6:00 PM and the sun was still fairly high in the sky when we left the hospital, but the shadows in the canyon below the dam were starting to lengthen, and the desert landscape hinted of a beauty I hadn't appreciated before.

Reg and I walked out to the old Chevy in the parking lot. I raised the hood and checked the oil and water, walked around it and made a visual inspection of the tires, and then slipped into the driver's seat and rolled down the window. Reg stood next to the car with a doubtful look on his face. I turned the key and pressed the starter button. The old Chevy fired right up, purring as smoothly as a little sewing machine. We exchanged smiles and gave each other a thumbs-up. I was grinning from ear to ear as I drove back out to our trailer-home with Reg following in his Land Cruiser. I hadn't driven an old car since I had sold my 1929 Model A Ford seven years earlier. I was enjoying the experience of running through the gears on the three-speed transmission and gripping the seemingly oversized steering wheel. I stopped in front of our new home and tooted the horn a couple of times so Martha and Karen could come out and take a look at our stylish "company" car.

The doctors' car – a 1941 Chevrolet

First day of medical practice for Reg and me
Grand Coulee, Washington

July 2, 1972

17

A few patients dribbled in over the next couple of days. We treated a toddler with an ear infection, splinted a fractured finger for one of the construction workers, and sewed up a couple of minor lacerations. Reg and I sat in the hall with a stack of medical journals to study while we waited between patients. Whenever a patient came through the front door, we almost pounced on him or her. We alternated caring for each case in turn and didn't find a need for two examining rooms yet, since we never had more than one patient at a time. We were both a little embarrassed whenever Mr. Bristor wandered by and we were just sitting there. We knew he was worried.

Reg and I had no reason to worry about the slow pace of our practice during those first few days, though. The community was a cluster of three small towns near the dam: Grand Coulee, Coulee Dam, and Electric City. A fourth little town, known as Coulee City, was located about 28 miles to the southwest, at the other end of Banks Lake. The total population of the four towns that summer was about eight thousand. The patient base was definitely there for us if we could get folks trained to come to Coulee General for their medical care.

Those four little towns we hoped to serve were originally boom towns that had arisen as a result of the construction of the massive dam and the largest hydroelectric power plant in the United States. Construction started in 1933 and became part of FDR's New Deal program to create jobs and pull the country out of the Great Depression. It employed an estimated 11,000 construction workers at an average wage of 75 cents per hour. The dam was completed in 1942, but in 1967, the four little towns became boom towns again as the population of the area soared with the arrival of thousands of construction workers. The addition of the massive Third Power Plant commenced that year, and the new construction was still going strong that summer of 1972. The project wasn't completed until 1980. The dam today is 550 feet tall, 5,223 feet long, and is the largest concrete structure ever built in the entire world.

Reg and I and our small staff at the hospital were all aware of the potential for serious construction accidents with all that was going on. During the initial construction in the 1930s and early 1940s, there had been 77 traumatic deaths, most of them resulting from falls from extreme heights. The new addition for the Third Power Plant involved demolishing the northeast side of the dam and building a new fore-bay section. It was a giant project and involved dangerous work; the potential for accidents was high. Reg and I hoped we would only have to tend to minor injuries during our tenure, but we knew that was highly unlikely.

There was no method of paging us when we were needed at the hospital. This was many years before the invention of cellphones, and Grand Coulee didn't have any kind of a wireless paging system or even a physicians' answering service. This was generally true for physicians everywhere in 1972, but the larger cities at least had answering services for doctors to check in with periodically and retrieve messages. So, anytime Reg and I were away from the hospital and an emergency arose that summer, a nurse would call our home phone. If we were out somewhere, such as at a restaurant, we would call the nursing station at the hospital from the restaurant and provide the telephone number of the establishment to the nurse on duty, who, more often than not, was Rita Bristor. During our first three days in Grand Coulee, we didn't get any emergency calls from the hospital. That changed on the Fourth of July.

18

On Tuesday, July 4, a community picnic was held in a park a few miles east of town on the southern shore of Lake Roosevelt. It was one of the biggest celebrations of the year, and our boss told us to forget about coming to the hospital that day. He invited both of us and our families to join him and Rita at the annual Grand Coulee picnic. He assured us the entire population of the area would be there, so if any medical emergencies arose, we would know about it. In any case, there was a payphone at the park, so we could check in with the duty nurse at the hospital periodically.

Reg and I decided to drive the '41 Chevy and have Martha and Karen follow along in our Olds with Baby Jill and Baby Heather. This provided our two families with a way to get home in the seemingly unlikely event the two of us got called away to the hospital. It was 86 degrees when we arrived at the park just before noon, and I didn't see a single cloud in the deep-blue sky above us. The park was like another little green oasis of grass and trees that was landscaped, obviously irrigated, and well maintained. As Mr. Bristor expected, mobs of people were there to enjoy and celebrate the holiday. There was a sandy beach and a roped off area for swimming. Sunbathers were sprawled on beach towels in the sand and kids were playing in the water, splashing and throwing beachballs. Other folks had claimed spots on the lush grass where they had thrown down blankets, set up folding chairs, and positioned picnic baskets and coolers. The water beyond the swimming beach was crowded with boats—ski boats, fishing boats, houseboats, and sailboats.

We found Delos Bristor sitting under the roof of a picnic shelter out of the intense July sun. He was "holding court" with the mayor of Grand Coulee and several other city officials. As soon as Reg and I walked up, he ceremoniously introduced us, with great flourish, to the dignitaries. Neither of us had to say much; Mr. Bristor did all the talking. He embellished our credentials, training, and experience so heavily that it was downright embarrassing. I suspected he had been bragging about us well before we got there and had probably told them we had been doing heart transplants and brain surgery for years before deciding to come to Grand Coulee to practice. His audience was looking at us now and likely wondering how these two kids in front of them could possibly be old enough to be licensed physicians. As I looked around at the faces studying us, I detected a little skepticism in their expressions.

Reg and I broke free of the politicians after a few minutes and joined our families on a blanket in the grass. I had just taken my second bite of a ham sandwich when I heard the wail of a siren. Everyone looked toward the highway just south of the park, and we saw an ambulance speeding east out of town with red lights flashing. A couple of minutes later Rita Bristor walked up to our little camp. She pointed up the lake shore to the east where, about three quarters of a mile away, a small crowd had gathered around a beached speedboat. We could see the ambulance turn in on a dirt road above the gathering. It kicked up a cloud of dust as it headed down toward the water's edge.

Rita said calmly, "I'll meet you two at the hospital."

Reg and I ran to the parking lot, jumped into our jalopy, and headed west on the highway into town. It was showtime!

19

The three of us beat the ambulance to the hospital. We stood in the Emergency Room and peered out through the double glass doors, not knowing what to expect, but waited with eager anticipation. Reg and I had no fear that it might be something we couldn't handle; we were both supremely confident. Rita Bristor was going to witness first-hand whether or not our confidence was justified.

The ambulance made a sweeping arc in the parking lot and then backed up to the entrance. We propped the double doors open as the attendants pulled our patient out of the vehicle on a stretcher. He was a stoutly built middle-aged man who was clutching his chest, writhing around, and moaning. His wife got out of the right front seat of the ambulance and rushed into the Emergency Room alongside him. We transferred our patient to a gurney in the center of the room and asked his wife to step into the hall and have a seat. We told her one of us would be out to talk to her. She disappeared quietly into the hallway.

We didn't need to ask a single question to know this fellow was experiencing severe chest pain, and that was all we needed to know for the moment. The presumed diagnosis was "myocardial infarction" until proven otherwise. We would obtain a complete medical history after we got him stabilized and admitted. Our first priority was to start monitoring his heart rhythm, get some diagnostic lab work ordered, and begin treatment.

All three of us went to work. Rita administered oxygen, then quickly got a blood pressure cuff on his arm and reported his pressure was a little on the low side at 85/50. Reg popped a nitroglycerin tab under his tongue to see if it would alleviate his pain; it did not. He initiated a physical exam, listening to his heart and lungs. His pulse was weak and rapid at 120 beats per minute. His skin was cold and clammy, and he had beads of sweat on his forehead. I was attaching leads to his chest for the cardiac monitor when he turned his head to the side and vomited. I turned the monitor on and announced that the rhythm was sinus tachycardia—nothing too ominous yet. Rita started an IV without either of us having to ask. She ignored the mess on the sheets and concentrated on what was important. Reg and I had been right about Rita. She was just the kind of nurse you wanted by your side when you were dealing with a major medical emergency.

Now that we had an IV route established, we started pushing morphine in 2mg increments. Morphine is an amazing drug and does more than just relieve pain. It has sedative effects and reduces anxiety, and it has a vasodilating effect, potentially relieving some of the coronary artery spasm during a heart attack. Morphine is also thought to improve the congestion and difficulty breathing associated with pulmonary edema through a number of mechanisms. For this reason, it is a first-line drug for a patient experiencing a myocardial infarction.

I had never seen morphine be as ineffective as it was in this case. We pushed it in and pushed it in until we had reached doses higher than any of us had ever administered before. He finally seemed to be relaxing a bit but was still complaining of severe chest pain. We had to stop. His blood pressure was already a little low, and morphine could exacerbate that problem.

We hooked up a 12-lead EKG and ran a full tracing. The EKG was not recorded with all the various leads printed on a single page as it is today on the more modern machines; back then the tracing came out in a long linear strip that curled onto the floor as it was generated. I ripped it off and took it to the counter along the wall where I could lay it out and look at the full strip.

There was not a course in medical school that taught interpretation of electrocardiograms. The only way for a student or an intern to learn to read them was to take the initiative to study it on his/her own. I had completed a cardiology clerkship during medical school at the Texas Medical Center in Houston. The prestigious center then included several hospitals and medical schools and was known worldwide because of its two bold, innovative, and famous heart surgeons, Dr. Michael DeBakey and Dr. Denton Cooley. The Texas Medical Center remains today the largest medical complex in the world, and patients travel from all points on the planet for treatments they could not receive anywhere else. When I got back to Kansas after my training, I didn't lie to anyone and tell them I had worked with Michael DeBakey and Denton Cooley but didn't try too hard to correct them if they had that misconception. My preceptor was a brilliant and energetic young cardiologist named Faber McMullen, Jr. As far as I know, he was never on the DeBakey-Cooley team, but the two of us did attend a cardiology conference each week in a small auditorium, and the two giants of cardiac surgery were reportedly in the room with us. I had no idea what the famous doctors even looked like, but I found myself looking around the room each week and trying to guess which of the faces belonged to these legendary surgeons. In any case, I studied books on interpretation of EKGs at night and interpreted all the hospital tracings with Dr. McMullen each morning. After I started understanding what I was doing, he tested me by letting me read all of them myself early each morning, and then he checked my work after morning rounds. By the time I finished my clerkship, he was making very few corrections or additions to my interpretations.

There are two ways to read EKGs: by memorizing common patterns and recognizing them or by doing an electrical vector analysis derived from the recording. Dr. McMullen had insisted I understand and learn to draw the electrical vectors that caused the normal and abnormal squiggles on the tracings. He made me draw the vectors on a piece of scratch paper and attach it to every EKG I read so he could check my understanding. Most physicians learn to recognize abnormal patterns without ever learning the underlying physics. After I had read several hundred cardiograms in Texas, though, I had started recognizing pathological patterns and rarely had to draw out the electrical vectors anymore to establish an interpretation. I only had to glance at our patient's EKG that day at Coulee General to identify the pattern of an acute anterior myocardial infarction.

Reg had spent two months on cardiology at Deaconess and was also well versed in the interpretation of EKGs. He came over to the counter and studied the strip with me; he agreed with my diagnosis. It was bad news. This type of infarction has a high mortality rate, and our patient was not looking good.

Our patient, Jim Peterson, was 51 years old. He was from Toppenish, Washington, about 125 miles to the south of us. He and his wife had, along with several other boating friends, trailered their boat up to Lake Roosevelt for the four-day holiday weekend. Jim had been drinking beer all morning and was water skiing behind his own boat, with a friend driving, when he developed severe chest pain. They hauled him back into the boat and headed for the boat ramp. They called the ambulance from there on a payphone.

After talking with Jim's wife for a little while, I had painted a picture in my mind of the type of person we were dealing with. Jim Peterson was a highly competitive fellow who considered any obstacles he faced in life as challenges. He worked hard, played hard, and never stopped; he thrived on stress. He was a heavy smoker, and he enjoyed alcoholic beverages outside of work. He'd known he had high blood pressure for a number of years but he couldn't be bothered with taking medication for it. He had the perfect recipe for a coronary occlusion, and now it was "cooked."

We admitted him to a private room directly across from the nursing station and converted the room into a makeshift critical care unit. The alarm on the cardiac monitor could be heard at the nursing station if it sounded, but our patient would need to be under direct observation at all times until he was out of danger. Reg and I planned to alternate 12-hour shifts for the next few days so that one of us was with Jim Peterson continuously, day and night.

Reg stayed in the room with our patient all afternoon. I took care of a few minor Fourth of July injuries in the ER—a kid with a burned finger from a firecracker, a young woman with a sprained ankle from a beach volleyball game, and a couple of patients with superficial lacerations requiring sutures.

It was 8:30 PM when I ducked back into Mr. Peterson's room. He seemed to have settled down and was not nearly as agitated. The large doses of IV morphine were finally having an effect. He told me he still had a lot of chest pain, though. Reg showed me the results of the blood tests we had ordered in the Emergency Room; the reports were back from the lab and recorded in the chart. All three cardiac enzymes—CPK, SGOT, and LDH—were through the roof. These enzymes are found in cardiac muscle cells and are released into the bloodstream when the heart tissue is damaged from lack of oxygenated blood. The extremely high enzyme levels in the blood confirmed the diagnosis of a massive myocardial infarction.

I ran a rhythm strip off of the monitor and studied it with Reg.

"Well, he's still in sinus tach, but the rate has slowed down a bit," Reg said.

"That's good, but look at the P-R interval. It looks a little prolonged. Let's measure it out," I said, and we did.

The P-R interval is the distance between two of the squiggles on the monitor tracing. It indicates the transmission time for the heart's internal pacemaker signal to reach the ventricles and initiate a contraction of the cardiac muscle to produce a heartbeat. The normal interval is less than 0.20 seconds. Our patient's P-R interval was 0.24 seconds.

"David, this meets the criteria for first-degree heart block."

This meant there was a conduction defect developing in the heart which was delaying the electrical impulses from the internal pacemaker in the right atrium as they were being transmitted to the ventricles to stimulate contraction. So, the coronary occlusion had not only injured the heart muscle, but it was now also damaging the electrical conduction pathways that initiated the rhythmic beating of the heart.

"I agree. At least he's not dropping any beats. I think we'll just have to keep a close eye on it for now," I replied, and then added, "I'm going home, Reg. I'll ask Karen to bring you some leftovers from dinner and I'll see you in the morning. Call me if you need me during the night." I left.

I didn't get called. When I came back in at 6:00 AM, I found Reg asleep in a chair next to the bed. Rita was at the nursing desk, and I went out to talk to her; I asked her how the night had gone. Mr. Peterson still had low blood pressure but had otherwise remained fairly stable throughout the night. I woke Reg and told him to go home and get some rest.

Reg couldn't stay away for long. He looked really tired when he shuffled back into the room shortly after noon. "How's he doing?" he asked. We stepped out into the hall.

"He's dropping some beats. He's in second-degree heart block at times. Not only that, but he's now getting short of breath and I can hear some crepitant rales in both lungs. He's got a little pulmonary edema. I just pushed 80mg of Lasix IV; we'll see what that does."

The "crepitant rales" (crackling, rattling sounds) meant fluid was backing up in the lungs. Our patient was showing signs of right heart failure caused by the damaged heart muscle from a blockage in his right anterior descending coronary artery. Lasix is a powerful diuretic drug that would hopefully lower our patient's total body fluid volume by accelerated excretion through the kidneys. If it worked, it would reduce the workload of the damaged heart and ease the shortness of breath. We had to be careful with the Lasix though, since it could lower the blood pressure further; it could also cause electrolyte (body salts) abnormalities that could induce heart rhythm problems. We were monitoring his electrolytes through the lab, but it was a delicate balance.

Reg looked more worried than I had ever seen him. "David, this is not good. If the heart block gets worse, he's going to need a pacemaker."

21

Nothing changed much during the afternoon and evening. Our plan to alternate 12-hour shifts was falling apart, though, because neither of us wanted to leave our patient's bedside. Rita was putting in some long hours too, but she had started alternating shifts with another nurse whom we had not previously met. We knew Rita could be back in the hospital in a matter of minutes if we needed her.

At 10:00 PM, I finally talked Reg into going home to get a full night's sleep. He looked as if he was about to fall over. Before he left, we talked Mrs. Peterson into going to a nearby motel for the night. She had been sitting at her husband's bedside all day and holding his hand. She and Reg walked down the hall together, and I could hear him trying to comfort her with some reassuring words. I was glad he was doing that; I wouldn't have been able to think of anything encouraging to say to her.

I dozed fitfully in the big easy chair at the bedside until sometime after midnight when the beeping on the cardiac monitor woke me. It was detecting irregular heartbeats. I was instantly wide awake. I printed out a strip and studied it.

Our patient was now continuously in second-degree heart block. The irregular beats were "escape beats" generated by the ventricles themselves when they had not received a normal electrical signal from the heart's pacemaker after a period of time. There are times when suppression of these extra beats with an anti-arrhythmic drug might be advised—but not in this case. With the heart block, these escape beats were keeping Mr. Peterson alive.

I listened to his chest and found there was more fluid in the lungs and his breathing was labored. I studied the record of intake and output in the chart and noted he had only excreted a few cc's of urine since admission. I inserted a urinary catheter so I could better monitor his output and determine whether the Lasix was having any effect at all.

When Reg got back to the hospital at 5:30 AM, he looked well rested for a change, but our patient, Jim Peterson, was going down the tubes. I feared that July 6, 1972, might be this poor fellow's last day on Earth. We both knew if he had a cardiac arrest and we had to perform CPR on him, he wouldn't survive.

Reg took a quick glance at our dozing patient, and then we both stepped out to the nurses' station.

"He is really deteriorating, Reg. He's becoming lethargic, and I can barely get him to respond to me. I catheterized his bladder at about 1:00 AM, and there's just a dribble of urine in the collection bag. The pulmonary edema is worse; he's having considerable difficulty breathing and coughing up pink, frothy sputum. I can no longer get a diastolic blood pressure; I'm getting a systolic of 60. So, his BP is 60/0, as best as I can determine."

"David, it appears he's going into cardiogenic shock. The low blood pressure, the lethargy, the pulmonary edema, and now, what appears to be impending renal failure, all indicate that. He needs an artificial pacemaker."

"Let's call one of the cardiologists in Spokane and see if we can transfer him there ASAP," I suggested.

Reg made the call. He knew all those guys better than I did, since he had done his two-month elective at Deaconess on the cardiology service. The cardiology group at Deaconess was comprised of Doctors Shields, Sutherland, Burroughs, and Judge. Those guys were all great, and it didn't matter which one Reg talked to. Terry Judge was the cardiologist on call for the group that morning. I listened as Reg presented our case to him, but then, as Dr. Judge spoke, I could only hear one side of the conversation as Reg said, "Yes…no…I think so… we could probably do that," and, finally, "we'll call you later and let you know how it went."

Dr. Judge told Reg it would be dangerous to try to transport a patient in such an unstable condition. He said he would most likely die en route. He agreed with our assessment that the only thing that was going to save our patient now was the insertion of an artificial, temporary, electronic pacemaker. Reg then told me what Terry Judge was arranging for us.

"David, a U.S. Army National Guard helicopter will be landing in the parking lot behind the hospital sometime in the next two hours with a pacemaker, an electrode, and all the supplies we need to insert it into a central vein and into the right lower chamber of the heart. You and I are going to insert the pacemaker."

22

The old "see one, do one, teach one" phrase from our training days was coming up again. Reg had seen a pacemaker put in; now he would do one, and, at the same time, teach me how to do it. This was crazy. Neither of us were cardiologists, and this was a procedure only cardiologists normally performed. In fact, we had only been licensed to practice medicine for five days, but we didn't have a choice about this if we were going to save Jim Peterson's life.

While waiting for the arrival of the helicopter, we had Mrs. Peterson sign the operative consent form as her husband's representative. She was shaking so severely she could hardly hold the pen as she signed. I wondered what she thought when these two young doctors who looked like a couple of teenagers explained what they planned to do to her husband.

Rita brought to the room sterile surgical packs containing instruments, gowns, gloves and everything else we anticipated we might need. Reg and I suited up in surgical scrubs.

We heard the pulsating beat of the rotor blades as the helicopter approached. It touched down at about 10:15 AM. All the ambulatory nursing home patients were out of bed and pressing their faces to the windows. It was the most exciting day any of them had experienced in a long time.

Delos Bristor met the flight crew and delivered the package to us in the inpatient wing. He strutted in with long, confident strides and dramatic flourish. Delos was enjoying his important role in all this.

The pacemaker had barely arrived in time. Mr. Peterson had deteriorated into third-degree heart block with complete atrio-ventricular dissociation. This meant the atria, the two upper chambers of the heart, were beating completely out of synch with the two ventricles, the two lower chambers. His pulse rate had dropped below 50 beats per minute. His condition had become as dire as it could be.

When we opened the package containing the pacemaker and electrode, we found Dr. Judge had supplied us with two of everything. This was great forethought. He had done this in case one of the two pacemakers happened to fail, and also so we would have a spare electrode in the event we dropped the long, sterile conductor onto the floor or otherwise inadvertently contaminated it.

We put on surgical caps and masks, scrubbed, and got gowned and gloved. We prepped the skin in the area of the right collarbone, and placed sterile surgical drapes over our entire patient except for the small area where we would be inserting the electrode. Rita carefully opened the long plastic packaging containing the pacemaker electrode cable and, without touching it, dropped it onto the sterile drapes covering our patient's chest and abdomen.

Reg infiltrated the skin with Xylocaine, then inserted a large-bore needle through the skin of the upper anterior chest wall and got right into the large subclavian vein. He knew he was in when he pulled back on the plunger of the syringe attached to the needle and saw dark venous blood. Reg then picked up the electrode and curved it over the draped chest wall from the needle insertion point to the heart. He made a mental note of the point on the marked cable that would indicate the appropriate length to feed in. He removed the syringe from the needle hub and I handed him the end of the electrode cable and he began sliding it through the needle into the vein. I assisted by holding the advancing cable and keeping it over the sterile field.

If the electrode cable followed the path of least resistance as we advanced it, it should drop from the subclavian vein into the superior vena cava, then into the right atrium, through the heart's tricuspid valve, and into the right ventricle. That is where we wanted it to end up, with the metal tip lodged against the inner wall of the right ventricle. We prayed the cable wouldn't kink or twist and curve up the jugular vein into the neck or take a turn up the left brachiocephalic vein toward the left side of the body.

Reg had described the whole procedure to me as he had remembered it. He wanted me to be completely briefed. I asked him how we would know when the electrode was properly positioned in the right ventricle, since I knew this procedure was normally done with the aid of a fluoroscopy machine. The hospital didn't have a fluoroscope, which would have allowed us to see the electrode's path through the vessels and pull it back or give it a twist if it took the wrong route. He explained that it would indeed be a blind insertion but that we would see a rapid series of premature contractions on the heart monitor as soon as the metal tip of the cable touched and irritated the ventricular wall.

Reg carefully fed the cable through the needle hub. Just as he reached the roughly measured point on the electrode cable, I announced, "You're in," as a whole series of premature contractions danced across the monitor and the alarm started sounding continuously. Reg had told me the

94

irritation from the electrode could set off a fatal rhythm known as ventricular fibrillation and had emphasized that I would need to get the pacemaker hooked up to the other end of the cable and turned on as quickly as possible.

Reg slipped the large needle out and off of the end of the cable. "Get the pacemaker hooked up, David—quickly, quickly!" The panic in Reg's voice unnerved me a bit—I had never heard that before. I was praying we wouldn't have to rip the drapes off of Mr. Peterson's chest and start doing CPR.

I tore my gloves off; the sterile part of the procedure was over for me. I attached the two leads of the electrode cable to the compact temporary pacemaker box and turned on the switch. We had pre-set the rate on the device to 72 beats per minute. I looked at the monitor. The alarm had stopped and it showed a nice regular pattern with an indicated rate of exactly 72 beats per minute. I couldn't believe my eyes. We had done it! To be perfectly honest, Reg had done it.

Reg put a couple of anchoring sutures through the skin and around the electrode cable to hold it in place. I assisted him as he fashioned a sterile dressing around and over the insertion point

Over the next few hours, Jim Peterson's blood pressure came up to an amazingly normal reading of 105/75. His lungs started clearing and his labored breathing subsided quickly. By evening, his urine collection bag had a couple hundred cc's of urine in it, and our patient was starting to talk to us again.

Mr. Peterson wasn't out of the woods yet and had a long way to go to full recovery, but it was a happy day at Coulee General Hospital.

Reg made a phone call that evening to Terry Judge in Spokane to report our success. He suggested we both consider applying for residencies in cardiology, since we were both obviously "born" cardiologists.

Maybe Dr. Judge's compliment applied to Reg, but he shouldn't have included me. I had been willing to take on the risky pacemaker insertion, but only because I was emboldened by Reg's cool self-confidence. My relatively short career in medicine so far had been characterized by safe and conservative decisions. I had strayed way out of my comfort zone only because Reg was there.

23

During that first two weeks of July, we got progressively busier at the hospital. Reg and I both suspected Delos was strutting around town like a banty rooster and bragging about his boys after our practically miraculous insertion of the cardiac pacemaker. The approach and landing of the National Guard helicopter was a great advertisement too, and I don't think many residents of town missed its arrival. For folks who hadn't witnessed it swooping in over the hills, they had at least heard about it fairly quickly through the grapevine. We were both spending a lot of time at the hospital now, well beyond a normal workday. We treated more folks in the ER at all hours of the day and night while continuing to keep a close eye on our cardiac patient.

We finally weaned Jim Peterson off the electronic pacemaker after six days. We had the mode on the unit set for "demand," so it only kicked in if his heart rate dropped below the rate we had entered. We gradually turned the rate knob down lower and lower, and, by Day Five, we found he was pacing on his own and his vital signs were all within normal range. We were worried about infection and wanted to pull the electrode out as soon as possible, but we left it in another 24 hours to be sure he would continue pacing normally on his own. We removed it on Day Six.

Once we got Mr. Peterson disconnected from his tethers—the IV line, the heart monitor leads, the pacemaker electrode cable, and the urinary catheter - we initiated a protocol intended to carefully and gradually begin some physical activity. We started by having him sit on the edge of the bed and dangle his feet over the side. He was extremely weak, and we proceeded slowly. The day after disconnecting everything, we sat him up in a chair twice for a few minutes—once in the morning and once in the afternoon.

As soon as his strength began to return and he started feeling better, we had trouble holding him back. Reg and I had some serious talks with him about the importance of following our regimen of carefully supervised and gradually increasing activity. We practically had to tie him to his bed. I suspected from the beginning that, if he survived, he would become a difficult patient during the recovery phase. Reg and I could no longer be with him every minute, so the nurses and Jim's wife had their hands full over the days that followed.

Our cardiac patient was doing well after two full weeks in the hospital. His electrocardiogram still showed the pattern of an anterior MI, but the acute changes were resolving, and he remained in a normal sinus rhythm with only an occasional premature ventricular contraction. His cardiac enzyme levels were not normal yet, but they were all decreasing, and that was the right direction to be going. He was definitely improving and stabilizing.

Dr. Judge in Spokane recommended a cardiologist in Yakima, Washington, for follow-up care after we released our patient from the hospital in Grand Coulee. Yakima is about 20 miles from Toppenish, where the Petersons lived. Reg talked by phone to the Yakima doctor and presented the case and outlined the treatment we had provided. The cardiologist was amazed to hear we had put in a pacemaker at Coulee General; he was just as surprised to find out our patient had survived for two weeks and was continuing to improve after being in profound cardiogenic shock. We all agreed, if his remarkable progress continued, it would probably be safe in another couple of weeks to transfer him by ambulance to the hospital in Yakima for the rest of his recovery and cardiac rehabilitation. The facilities there could provide more advanced care; Mr. Peterson would then be under the direct care of a board-certified cardiologist, and he would be much closer to his home. So, assuming no further complications arose, we planned to shoot for discharge and transport toward the end of the first week in August.

On Saturday, July 22, Reg and I both slept in and didn't leave for the hospital until around 8:30 AM. As we drove up the hospital drive toward the parking lot, I said, "Reg, stop the car right here."

Reg stopped the car in the middle of the drive and I pointed toward the front entrance of the hospital. Mr. Peterson was sitting on the steps of the building, fully dressed and smoking a cigarette, and he had a suitcase sitting on the step next to him.

Both of us sat on the steps for the next 30 minutes begging and pleading with him to put down his cigarette, go back to his room, put his gown back on, and get into bed. Our words fell on deaf ears. Jim told us he'd had enough of doctors, hospitals, and being told what he could and couldn't do. He was going home.

His wife pulled up at 9:30 AM and I loaded his suitcase into the trunk. She had been living with him for a long time and knew it wouldn't do any good for anyone to argue with him. Mrs. Peterson thanked us both for all we had done. Jim didn't even say goodbye. Reg and I stood on the front walk for several minutes trying to make sense of a kaleidoscope of thoughts running through our heads.

Finally, I turned to Reg and said, "Our life here is going to be easier now; let's go make rounds, and see what's waiting for us in the ER."

24

W hile Reg and I were busy at the hospital during those first few weeks, Martha and Karen kept up the house, took care of the two baby girls, shopped for groceries and household supplies, and entertained themselves as best they could. They took Jill and Heather for stroller rides around the trailer park, which involved some fancy maneuvering to evade the ubiquitous rattlesnakes. They also spent a few hours at the beach on Lake Roosevelt almost every day.

Our wives didn't do much cooking for us. Reg and I were hardly ever home, so it was difficult for them to plan meals. We ate a lot of evening meals out, and Martha and Karen frequently drove into town and met us at one of the restaurants in Grand Coulee. Reg and I almost always went right back to the hospital after dinner, and when we finally got home, everyone was asleep.

Our wives had more money than they knew what to do with, and there was nothing to spend it on, since essentially all of our living expenses were being paid by Mr. Bristor. Going out to restaurants for almost every meal didn't seem to put a dent in either of our family budgets. I had paid off the balance on our Oldsmobile loan with the second paycheck, and we still had "money to burn."

Our first weekly paychecks did not come without a small confrontation with Delos Bristor, though, at the end of our first week as contract physicians. Mr. Bristor had not told us how and when he would pay us for our services, and when we asked him about it, he said he planned to issue our paychecks at the end of each month. I think he believed this would give him more control over us and keep one or both of us from running out on him. He likely was confident neither of us would quit in the middle of a month and leave money on the table. We explained during our meeting with him that we both expected to receive our checks weekly, and we firmly stated that was the way it had to be. He argued a little bit with us, so I was glad we had broached this topic early in our employment. I think he was afraid we didn't completely trust him at that point, and he finally saw the light to "show us the money" in order to cement our relationship with him. Reg and I stayed seated in his office until he had written out two checks for $1,000 each. After that, we stopped by his office each week at about the same time. He paid us without argument, if somewhat grudgingly, from that point on.

101

We didn't have any other medical emergencies quite as dramatic as the Peterson case during our time in Grand Coulee, but we did stay busy. There was the usual wide array of minor illnesses and trauma to attend to. We took care of everything from sore throats to sprained ankles, and occasionally something slightly more serious.

One of those "slightly more-serious" things was a 12-year-old boy who was brought to the ER one afternoon after he had been bitten on his right index finger by a rattlesnake. The kid was from some other town in Eastern Washington, and he was visiting a friend in Grand Coulee who was his same age and owned a pet rattlesnake he kept in a cage in his room. The guest of honor had stuck his right hand into the cage to feed the snake its daily ration of dead mouse when it made a lightning-fast strike at him after only a brief warning with its tail rattle. The visitor had come from a town where most of the kids' pets were dogs or cats and probably wasn't aware that precautions were necessary with some of the household pets in Grand Coulee. I'm not sure we ever got the whole truth about how this incident evolved, but, thinking back on my own childhood and the things I did at the same age, I suspected there might have been some kind of dare involved.

The father of the friend of our patient brought him to the hospital, and they arrived about 15 minutes after the snake had bitten him. His index finger was already swollen to about twice normal size, the skin was tense and pale, and he couldn't bend it at the joints. Reg started checking him over, got vital signs, and started an IV. I placed a call to the Poison Control Center in Salt Lake City.

When I got off the phone, Reg reported that our patient was stable, with normal vital signs, and all of the symptoms were related to local soft tissue swelling. I told him we needed to start administering antivenin and we needed to give a lot of it. The Poison Control Center recommended at least 10 to 12 vials for a patient of his size and weight.

Reg said, "David, it's called antivenom, not antivenin."

"That's what I thought too, but the toxicologist called it antivenin," I replied. "He even spelled it for me."

"Well, the toxicologist is wrong, David."

Reg was starting an argument, and I didn't think we had time for that. We needed to start treating this kid.

While we bickered about what the antidote was called, Rita appeared in the doorway with two large vials in her hands. "We only have two doses," she announced, "but I'll get on the phone with Brewster and Spokane and find more and get it on the way."

102

We took the vials from Rita and saw that the labels read, "Rattlesnake Antivenin." Reg looked them over and said, "Why do they call it that?"

We filled a large syringe and administered both vials via IV according to the instructions in the package insert. Simultaneously, we placed cool packs on the boy's hand to slow the systemic absorption of the poison.

I stayed at the hospital all that night. Making our rounds the following morning, we checked our patient's status again. His entire hand was so swollen that it looked like a rubber glove someone had blown up like a balloon; the swelling extended all the way up to his elbow. His pulse was rapid, his blood pressure had dropped to 80/50, and he was sick to his stomach.

We put his arm in a stockinette—the type used for lining plaster casts—and hung his right arm up by an IV pole in an attempt to reduce the swelling. Our concern was that he would get what is called a "compartment syndrome" from the swelling, which could cause serious soft-tissue injury and even result in an amputation.

The vials of antivenin kept arriving all day, by ambulance and by Washington State Patrol, from surrounding cities and towns, and we administered them as soon as we received them. By the end of the second day, "The Rattlesnake Kid" had received 12 vials. We made several more calls to the Poison Control Center, but they remained vague about how many vials of antivenin should be given, and the package insert didn't give us any guidance either.

Over the next couple of days, the swelling had crept all the way up to his shoulder and into his chest wall, but, by the third day, it had started to go down a little bit and improve. We kept his blood pressure from falling further with IV fluids, compensating for the fluid loss into his soft tissues. We gauged the amount of fluids to give by monitoring his blood pressure closely and his urine output.

By the fourth day, it seemed our patient had turned the corner and would survive, but his index finger had turned completely black and looked gangrenous. I again called the Poison Control Center and told them I thought the finger would have to be amputated. The toxicologist I spoke to said I needed to talk to a physician who was the world's foremost authority on rattlesnake bites before making a final decision. He gave me a number to call. Reg was already agitating to take the little guy to the OR, but I thought we should consult this expert first.

A gravelly voice answered the phone with a distinctly Texas accent. I assumed this "world expert" would probably be a Harvard professor at Mass General, but he sure didn't sound like anyone from New England. I asked him where he was located and he told me he was in practice in a little town in East Texas. I didn't catch the name of the town.

"Don't y'all amputate that finger," he drawled. "They always turn black like that and look terrible, but it'll survive. Keep it protected and clean and just be patient and wait. I've treated lots of these, and chances are it's gonna be fine."

He asked me a few more questions about our patient and wanted to know how many vials of antivenin we had administered. He was just as vague as everyone else, though, about what the proper dosage should be. He said to call back if we had any other concerns or questions; I thanked him for his advice, and we hung up.

A week later, all the swelling in the boy's finger, hand, and arm was gone; the finger was pink, and he could move the joints. I wouldn't have believed it if I hadn't witnessed it firsthand. We discharged the little guy after a 10-day stay at Coulee General. We didn't need to tell him to never play with rattlesnakes again.

I read a newspaper article in 2014 about a fellow who was bitten by a rattlesnake on the tip of his index finger. The article said the finger turned completely black and had to be amputated. I suspect the expert snake doctor in Texas is no longer alive. If those doctors had known to call me or Reg, their patient might still have his index finger.

25

One Sunday morning in early August, Dr. Fred Viren, an internist and endocrinologist from Spokane, stopped by to see us. He had been one of our preceptors during our internship at Deaconess and was vacationing in the area with his family in their motor home. Fred was a fine physician, whom we both thought highly of, and we invited him to make Sunday morning rounds with us. As it happened, every bed in the hospital was occupied that day. Reg and I took him into each room, introduced him to the patient, and then went out in the hall and gave a little presentation of the case, just as we had done in training. Jim Peterson, our cardiac pacemaker patient, had already broken out of the hospital by then and was on the lam back in Toppenish. We described his case in detail to Fred, even though he had heard all about it already in Spokane. The two of us were probably doing some major showing off. I'm sure Dr. Viren recognized that, but I think he was, nevertheless, impressed that we were both out in the middle of nowhere doing what we were doing. He had a hard time believing we had put in a cardiac pacemaker at Coulee General Hospital.

The following week, Reg and I kept referring to Dr. Viren's visit to the hospital as "Grand Rounds." That was the term used in medical school for a formal weekly conference at which students presented patients before a panel of professors and the entire student body. We had gotten a lot of mileage and enjoyment out of Dr. Viren's visit, and I suspect he enjoyed it as much as we had.

Dr. Viren was a brilliant physician whom Reg and I both admired, but that didn't entice either of us to the field of internal medicine. It is a specialty that is a little too cerebral for me, and both of us were more attracted to the surgical aspects of medicine, where problems are fixed with tools rather than just pills. An opportunity for some hands-on medicine, just the thing we both liked, came our way the weekend after Dr. Viren's visit.

It was the second weekend in August, and Reg had just a few days left before he and his family would pack up and head for Gold Beach, Oregon. On that last Sunday for him in Grand Coulee, we had another one of those "slightly more-serious" emergencies. We were making early-morning rounds when a fellow in blue jeans and a colorful plaid shirt came walking up the hall of the inpatient wing looking for us. He had a red bandana tied around his forehead and his black hair sported two long braids that hung down his back. He told us he was the ambulance driver for the

Colville Indian Reservation and that he had three patients for us from a late-night/early-morning highway accident. We walked back to the ER with him.

The "ambulance" was backed up to the door of the Emergency Room and was a beat-up, gray 1956 Chevy station wagon. Reg and I walked out through the double doors and peered through the open tailgate.

The vehicle was not equipped with patient stretchers. The three seats in the back of the station wagon were folded flat, and three adult males lay, stacked like logs, with two lying on the flat surface and the third piled on top of them. The two underneath had their heads forward in the car, just behind the front seat. The one on top had his head toward the back with his boots in the faces of the other two. They were all three covered with dirt and grass, and there was a fair amount of dried blood on their clothes. We saw no signs of movement and couldn't tell if any of them were even breathing.

I usually had some adrenaline flowing through me when I faced any medical emergency, but, as the three of us stood outside the ambulance that morning, I had a strange sense of calm. It was a beautiful morning, the sun was just coming over the ridge to the east of the hospital, and the air was still and quiet. It was going to be another warm, clear day in Grand Coulee. You could have heard a pin drop in the parking lot. This general atmosphere may have contributed to my tranquility, but I think I was mainly feeling so serene because I thought there probably was no emergency. When Reg and I talked about this scene later, we both admitted that we assumed we had three DOAs and our only duty would be to call the morgue.

Finally, Reg broke the silence. "Are any of them alive?" he asked.

"I have no idea," answered the driver. "A witness said he thought they were going over 100 miles per hour when their car left the road and rolled several times down a steep embankment. All three of them were thrown from the car."

Reg reached through the rear tailgate and put his hand on the side of one victim's neck to feel for a carotid pulse. "This one is alive," he reported.

I walked up to the left rear passenger door and checked the victim on that side. He was alive too, as was the third one.

"Let's bring them in," I said.

We spent the whole day working up our three accident victims. They were all unconscious, but breathing, and had reasonable blood pressures. There was no sign of any major hemorrhage—at least externally. They all reeked of alcohol, so we didn't know whether they were unconscious because of head injuries or alcohol intoxication, but none of them had any asymmetrical neurological findings that might indicate an intracranial hemorrhage.

Reg and I first got IV lines started on all of them and inserted Foley urinary catheters. We then obtained lateral x-ray views of the cervical spine on each of them with the portable x-ray machine and put cervical collars on all three men. The x-rays looked okay, but we were still careful not to move them much and paid particular attention to their necks when we did have to move any of them.

Some of their injuries were immediately obvious. Each had a few superficial lacerations that would require sutures, one had a deformity of his right forearm just above the wrist, and another had a probable fracture of his left lower leg above the ankle. All of these could wait, though, until we determined whether or not any not-so-obvious life-threatening injuries existed. This assessment was difficult, since none of the three were awake to tell us where they felt pain. We noted in their charts that they were all in profound levels of coma without even any response to deep painful stimulation. We determined this by the classic method of pressing a knuckle firmly into the sternum.

One of our main concerns was internal bleeding, which could be caused by a ruptured spleen, ruptured liver, or other internal injury. After we cut off all their clothing, we tapped each of their bellies by inserting a plastic catheter through a large needle into the peritoneal space. We then ran two liters of saline into each of them. When the IV bottles were empty, we took them down from the IV poles, setting them on the floor next to each patient. We then massaged the patients' abdomens and watched the saline flowing back down into the bottles to see if any of the fluid appeared to be blood-tinged. They all passed that test, which indicated none of them had any sign of internal abdominal hemorrhage. With all this critical preliminary work done, Reg wheeled them, one at a time, to the x-ray room, while I stayed in the ER and monitored the other two. We got skull x-rays, full spine x-rays, chest x-rays, and pelvic x-rays on all of them. For the two with obvious extremity deformities, we took x-rays of those specific areas.

The patient with the right forearm deformity near the wrist had a displaced fracture of the radius, and the other patient, with the swollen left lower leg near the ankle, had a fracture of the fibula. We reduced and casted both of these. The reduction procedure was simplified by the fact that no anesthesia was needed. We sutured all the lacerations. By the time we had finished and had moved them into hospital inpatient rooms, it was 9:30 in the evening. The ambulance driver had stayed with us all day and helped us move the patients around when needed. We finally thanked him for his help, and he left the hospital to head back to the reservation. The x-ray tech had been on duty with us all day too, and we were all exhausted. Our patients were now all tucked in and seemed stable, so we went home for the night.

The sun was just coming up as Reg and I left for the hospital early the following morning. We were both hoping our three accident victims would be awake and responsive by now. We would then be able to re-examine them, ask them questions, and possibly discover some other injuries that hadn't been obvious the day before. We might have to order a few more x-rays or other tests after poking around on them a little more and interviewing them. We talked about the fact that the fractures would require careful follow-up and need to be re-x-rayed over the next few weeks. I would have to do all the follow-up since Reg would be gone. I would make sure the fellow with the fibula fracture was supplied with crutches and instructed on their use, and I would need to replace his cast with a walking cast in a couple of weeks. I would also schedule return visits for removal of their sutures.

When we arrived at the hospital that Monday morning, no patients were in the hall waiting to see us, so we headed back to the inpatient area to make rounds. We decided we should check on our car-accident victims before we made rounds on everyone else. We had admitted them all to one room with three beds, so when they eventually woke up they would be together. We walked into the room and they were all gone. The room was empty.

The IV bottles were all still hanging up, but the IV tubing dangled down to the floor where puddles had formed at the end of each plastic cannula. The Foley catheters were all lying on the sheets in the middle of each bed with the balloons still inflated. Those balloons were supposed to prevent them from being inadvertently pulled out of the urinary bladder. I didn't want to think about how it must have felt when they all three yanked them out.

The nurse on duty for the night told us they were all in bed when she last checked their vital signs at 4:00 AM and that she didn't see them making their escape.

We put the word out around town for folks to call the hospital if they saw three males with long black braided hair wandering around town, clothed only in white hospital gowns which were open at the back and wearing cowboy boots. We explained that they were most likely to be seen hitchhiking along the highway and heading north. We were confident of our descriptions and how they were dressed, since we had cut up all of their torn and blood-stained clothes in the process of removing them, and we had deposited them in the trash in the ER.

Apparently no one in town spotted our three escapees, and we never saw any of them again.

26

R eg had been dying to do some surgery, and, on his second-to-the-last day at the hospital, a fellow showed up and asked him if he could remove a lump from his back. This was another "minor" case Reg and I managed in Grand Coulee. We took the patient to the OR the following morning and excised a soft-tissue tumor the size of a baseball from the center of his back. Delos was happy because we performed the surgery in the Operating Room and therefore he could charge a nice fee for the use of the room and equipment. Rita was happy since she finally got to utilize her skills as an anesthetist. The patient and I were relieved when the pathologist's diagnosis indicated it was a benign tumor. Reg was gone by the time I received the report, but I called him later in Gold Beach to relay the good news.

When Reg and his family drove out of the trailer park on the 15th of August, my confidence in my own competence and abilities dropped a couple of notches. I no longer had another physician there to confirm a diagnosis, assist me with procedures, share call, and, most important of all, provide moral support. I was now completely on my own. Two days after Reg left, it was my turn to put the Operating Room to use for a second time.

Rita called me at home after I had just fallen asleep for the night. An ambulance had arrived with a young man in his early 20s who had been the driver in a one-car highway accident. His little sports car had left the road at high speed and he had been thrown violently through the windshield. I groggily got up from our bed and pulled on my clothes.

By the time I got to the ER, Rita had already carefully examined the patient and started an IV. The only significant injury she found was a major facial laceration extending far back into his scalp. I had never seen such a severe laceration, and the young man was bleeding profusely from it. The wound was several inches long and extended up and back from the bridge of his nose to just above and slightly behind his ears on each side of his scalp, forming a giant "V" shape. It created a large flap of skin and subcutaneous tissue that could be pulled up and back to expose the surface of his skull from his nose to the top of his head.

Scalp and facial wounds always bleed profusely, but most of them aren't large enough to result in significant blood loss, and they often look worse than they actually are. Treatment usually just amounts to closing the

111

wound with a few sutures under local anesthesia. This case was different. The patient had an enormous, gaping wound and had lost a lot of blood.

I did a quick exam. Our patient was conscious and responsive and told me about the accident. I couldn't find any injuries other than the enormous laceration. His clothes were completely soaked with blood, and it was probably the most blood I had ever seen. His blood pressure was 90/60 and his pulse rate was 110 beats per minute. I needed to get the hemorrhaging under control as quickly as possible. There was no blood bank in Grand Coulee, but we did have two fresh units of Type "O" negative blood—considered the "universal donor"—in the refrigerator. I didn't want to transfuse him with blood that hadn't been typed and cross-matched with his, though, and take a chance on a fatal transfusion reaction. I hoped we could get by without a transfusion, but, to do that, I needed to control the bleeding quickly.

I injected Xylocaine around the edges of the wound in the areas where little arterioles were spurting jets of blood into the air, and I started clamping and tying as fast as I could go. I told Rita we would have to take him to the OR to repair the wound, because there was no way I could do it under local anesthesia; the amount of Xylocaine needed would likely exceed toxic levels. I would have to accomplish the repair under general anesthesia, but I at least wanted to stem as much of the hemorrhage as possible right there in the ER.

Administering general anesthesia to a patient who had been eating and drinking over the past several hours was risky. Rita and I both knew that, but we didn't have the luxury of waiting. I had to control the bleeding, and the only way to do it was to close the wound.

It took another half hour for Rita to set up the Operating Room with the required trays and instruments. Rita gave our patient an IV dose of a sedative, and then she smoothly passed an endotracheal tube and inflated the balloon on the end of it. This protected his airway from any regurgitation of stomach contents. She then continued with the anesthesia, and I went to work right away.

I had no assistant, no scrub nurse, and not even an OR circulating nurse; it was just Rita and me in the room. I was used to a full crew, but Rita had thought of everything and had laid out all the required tools and suturing materials neatly on the surgical trays.

The first thing I had to do was clean out all the little shards of glass that were scattered throughout the wound. I laid the big flap, which included his whole forehead, back over the top of his skull while I did this.

Rita had a Polaroid camera and took several pictures of the gory scene. A few particles of glass were embedded in the bone, and I picked out each shard carefully, one at a time, and then irrigated the wound copiously with sterile saline. I had learned in training the importance of thorough cleansing of a contaminated wound and remembered the adage, "The solution to pollution is dilution." I used a lot of saline that night, shooting it forcefully into the wound with a large (50cc) syringe.

I finally pulled the forehead flap back down over the bone and put in some subcutaneous absorbable sutures. I started by attaching the pointed tip of the "V" where it belonged on the bridge of his nose and worked my way back from there on each side. I then started on the skin using thin 6-0 nylon, approximating the edges of the wound with closely spaced interrupted sutures. I tried to keep a count of the number of sutures I placed, but I eventually lost track after the number grew to well over 100.

I finally finished, and Rita and I wheeled him to an inpatient room that served as a makeshift recovery room. The whole operation lasted a little over five hours. The first morning light was breaking when I walked out to the parking lot. It had been a long night.

27

I went back to the hospital early that afternoon, after getting a few hours of rest at home. My patient was sitting up in bed with a meal tray in front of him and was eating some Jell-O. He looked like a mummy, with only his eyes and mouth visible through the gauze dressing I had applied that morning. I talked to him a little about the accident and explained what I had done. He seemed like a nice young man.

His blood pressure was back in the normal range, but his nailbeds were pale and I knew he was anemic from blood loss. I ordered a hemoglobin and hematocrit to serve as a baseline for monitoring the replenishment of his red blood cells over the next few days and weeks. I was glad I hadn't had to transfuse him.

I left his compression dressings in place for three days before taking a peek. When I checked the wound, it was starting to heal nicely. I took another couple of pictures with Rita's Polaroid camera and added them to the chart. I discharged him the following day and scheduled him to return a few days later for suture removal. It took me almost an hour to pull all the sutures out. I then took more "after" pictures and added them to his record.

The young fellow didn't seem too unhappy with his appearance when he looked in the mirror. I explained that the scar would fade and be less noticeable after a few weeks but also warned him he would always have that large "V" on his forehead. I had done a meticulous plastic closure, but it was impossible to eliminate the scar completely. He understood that and told me he was just happy to be alive.

This case had pulled me out of my comfort zone, but I felt pretty good about it. I was forced into doing what needed to be done by the nature of the emergency and was satisfied with the result.

One other significant trauma case confronted me shortly after Reg departed. A construction worker was operating a jackhammer from a boson's chair several hundred feet up on the face of the dam and was controlling the height of his seat with a rope that looped up and over a pulley at the top. He had not secured this hoisting line properly, lost control of it, and started plummeting downward. He never let go of the rope and kept his right hand tightly around it, with his left hand squeezing over the top of his right. He was able to slow his descent enough to prevent what could have been a fatal plunge, but the rope caused some serious damage to his right hand as it smoked through his leather gloves and then his fingers.

The middle finger of his right hand was the most severely injured. The skin and subcutaneous tissue on the flexor surface, between the second and third joints, was completely gone, and the flexor tendon was exposed. This would require a skin graft. The fingers on either side of the middle finger had small areas of skin loss as well, but they were all less than one-half centimeter in diameter, and those would probably heal on their own by what is referred to as "granulating in" and then reepithelialization.

I called Dr. Grainger in Spokane and asked him if I could send this patient to him, knowing his interest and expertise in hand surgery. He said he would be happy to perform the required grafting and, after I described the wounds in detail, explained how he would perform the surgery. He agreed with my planned treatment of the two fingers that were less severely injured, and thought they could just be cleaned up and dressed. He said the large loss of tissue on the middle finger would require a full-thickness graft. He pointed out that the skin on the palmar surface of the hand and fingers is thick and tough, and there is no donor site elsewhere on the body that is entirely suitable for grafting onto fingers with that necessary quality of toughness. The skin for the graft would have to be harvested from the man's palm.

He then described in detail how he would flex the finger down into the palm and create a full thickness flap on a pedicle from the skin at the base of the thumb. He would sew this in place over the exposed tendon on the middle finger, but he'd leave the pedicle attached to the palm to retain the original blood supply until the tissue firmly established itself on the finger with a new blood supply of its own. After a couple of weeks, he would sever the pedicle and then close any defect at the donor site.

I was fascinated by his description and asked a lot of questions until I had a clear picture of the entire procedure in my mind. I had drawn a hand on a piece of scratch paper as I listened and made a rough pencil sketch of the operation as I envisioned it. I told Dr. Grainger I was sorry I couldn't break away for a day and come with my patient to Spokane to watch him do the surgery.

Dr. Grainger then said, "David, I think I've explained how to do this flap graft well enough that you can probably just do it yourself out there in Grand Coulee." I started to think about it.

"Dr. Grainger, we always said 'see one, do one, teach one' during our training. I haven't even seen one of these surgeries."

Our conversation went on for another few minutes and he somehow talked me into doing the flap graft myself. He pointed out that my patient would need close follow-up and frequent dressing changes and that it would be much more convenient and cost-effective if I just did his surgery and took care of him locally. I got off the phone and asked Rita to prepare the OR.

My first solo hand surgery went well. The graft "took" and I completed the final follow-up exam a couple of days before my scheduled departure from Grand Coulee for Pensacola. Ideally, I would have liked to have followed his healing progress for a few more weeks, but Rita could monitor his progress, perform dressing changes, and send him to Dr. Grainger in Spokane if any problems arose.

The decision to take on this grafting procedure was out of character for me. Why had I done it? The injury was not an emergency requiring immediate action, and I could have easily sent the patient to Spokane for the repair of his mangled hand. I had strayed from my straight and narrow conservative path when Reg was no longer by my side for moral support. I had made a push to be bolder and was starting to take on risks with the possibility of failure. Maybe the rewards of doing so would outweigh the possible risks involved and the end result would make it all well worth it. I was happy, in this case, that my decision hadn't backfired on me.

28

I was confronted with two other major surgical emergencies during the last half of August at Coulee General. One of these was a young woman with a ruptured ectopic (tubal) pregnancy; the other was a middle-aged man with acute appendicitis. I shipped both of these cases out, and Delos Bristor was a bit unhappy with me for doing that. He thought I should have operated on both of them, but his wife Rita had a lot more medical knowledge and experience than Delos, and she stuck up for me. She thought I had made a wise decision in both cases.

Reg and I might have tackled the appendectomy if he had still been there, but I wasn't going to do major abdominal surgery by myself. An appendectomy can range from a fairly straightforward procedure to a complicated operation that has the potential to turn into a real mess. It can even end up being something other than appendicitis causing the abdominal pain and other symptoms, which might require surgical skills, knowledge, and experience I did not possess. I sent the man to Brewster, where a general practitioner with lots of surgical experience operated on him. It did turn out to be acute appendicitis, his appendix was removed, and the patient recovered without any complications.

The case of the ectopic pregnancy almost ended in disaster because the woman's inexperienced young doctor (me) didn't figure out what was going on in her pelvis for almost 24 hours—until it became apparent she was lapsing into hypovolemic shock from blood loss. I wasted most of that time conducting a workup for gallbladder disease while she was slowly bleeding to death.

The young woman presented late in the afternoon complaining of pain in the right upper quadrant of her abdomen, the anatomical location of the gallbladder. Inflammation of the gallbladder, known as cholecystitis, is usually caused by stones in the organ, and the term for that is cholelithiasis. I ordered a cholecystogram, a contrast study to visualize her gallbladder, to be performed the following morning.

When I made morning rounds the next day, my patient had just returned to her room from x-ray, and I noticed for the first time that she appeared a little pale. She hadn't looked that way when I had admitted her the day before. I had been taught whenever a woman of child-bearing age presents with abdominal pain, the cause should be attributed to an ectopic pregnancy until proven otherwise. This was a good rule to keep in mind, since a patient can go downhill rapidly when a tubal pregnancy ruptures, as it always does.

Rita Bristor was accompanying me on morning rounds, as always, and commented on our patient's pale skin color. I checked her pulse and blood pressure and both were well within normal range. I poked around on her abdomen and found that she had some generalized tenderness. Everywhere I pressed, it seemed a little sore. Her pain was fairly mild, but we had been giving her morphine for suspected gallstones, and I knew the narcotic was masking some of her symptoms.

"Dr. Crawley, what would you think about doing a culdocentesis?" Rita suggested.

A culdocentesis is a procedure in which the physician inserts a needle into the cul-de-sac of Douglas, a pouch between the uterus and rectum, to check for blood. Since this space is the lowest point in the pelvis, blood from a ruptured ectopic pregnancy can be expected to collect there. Even though I still didn't think that was what was causing my patient's pain, I thought Rita had made a good suggestion. The only problem was: I had never done a culdocentesis, nor had I ever seen one done.

"That's a good suggestion, Rita. We should probably do one just to rule out an ectopic. Go ahead and set up a culdocentesis tray in the exam room, move her in there, and get the permit signed. I'll be back in a few minutes. I want to go look at her cholecystogram x-rays."

I didn't actually go to X-ray; I raced to the small medical library and found a surgical text that outlined the procedure for performing a culdocentesis. I studied it for a few minutes and then headed back to the treatment room on the ward.

I did the culdocentesis, as I understood the procedure, inserting a long needle through a vaginal speculum. It was obviously painful for my patient, but she didn't complain much. I had no idea whether or not I had gotten the needle into the cul-de-sac of Douglas since I didn't aspirate any blood into the attached syringe. The absence of blood in the space should have reassured me she didn't have a ruptured ectopic pregnancy, but it didn't, since I harbored serious doubts of whether I had performed the test with any degree of competence.

I didn't learn anything from the cholecystogram since the gallbladder failed to visualize, making it an inconclusive study. So, when I left my patient that morning, my working diagnosis was still suspected gallbladder disease. The young woman's condition didn't change, and she remained stable until that evening when everything suddenly went to hell.

Rita called to tell me our patient's blood pressure had dropped out the bottom and she was going into shock.

Rita started an IV with a large bore needle and began pouring Ringer's Lactate solution into her while I raced back to the hospital. I rode with the young woman in the ambulance to Spokane's Deaconess Hospital, my alma mater. I told the crew that time was of the essence in this case, and we covered the 80 miles in record time. It was a wild ride, with lights flashing and the siren blaring all the way.

We called ahead, and one of my favorite general surgeons, Dr. George Girvin, was at the hospital waiting for us at my request. He trusted my diagnosis, so we bypassed the Emergency Room and took the patient straight to the Operating Room and opened her up. We found an ectopic pregnancy that had ruptured through the right fallopian tube. A lot of blood had migrated up under the right rib cage, high in the abdomen. The blood had irritated the peritoneum in that area, and that explained the confusing and misleading location of most of her pain. We removed the tube and the ovary on that side and suctioned almost two units of blood from her abdomen. She was left with a normal fallopian tube and ovary on the opposite side, so she would still be able to have future pregnancies.

The ambulance crew from Grand Coulee waited for me until the operation was over and my patient was in the recovery room, and they then drove me back to Grand Coulee—a little slower this time. It was after midnight when I got home. As I lay in bed trying to get to sleep and thinking about what had transpired, I vowed I would never again miss the diagnosis of an ectopic pregnancy.

29

As the last day of August approached, I reminded Mr. Bristor I was going to be hitting the road on September 1. He told me he had another young physician lined up to arrive on my scheduled departure day. He was happy that coverage would not be interrupted now that patients had gotten used to coming back to Coulee General for care, but he complained that the doctor would only be temporary as well, since he too had orders for active duty in the military.

I suspected Mr. Bristor had been making covert phone calls to the state's congressional offices in Washington, D.C., the whole time I had been in Grand Coulee. I don't think he ever gave up the belief that I would be thrilled to stay in Grand Coulee if only he could get me released from my military obligation. His thinking in both respects had been a pipe dream.

I came home early on the afternoon of August 30 to start the process of loading up the car for our departure. When I drove up in front of the trailer, I saw Martha and Jill on the front patio; Martha was sitting in one of the chairs and Jill was perched on her little scooter car. As I trudged up the walk, Martha said, "Jill has a big surprise for you today."

She walked over and picked Jill up, set her back down on her feet in the grass, and then let go. Jill started tentatively stepping toward me with a big, proud smile on her face. That was her first day to take a step on her own without a supporting hand. She was lurching around like a drunken sailor, but, whenever she toppled over in the grass, she got right back up and took off again. Once she realized she could walk, she never got down on her hands and knees to crawl again. Her dogged determination that day was a harbinger of her future approach to every challenge she later faced in life, and it was our clue that this kid was headed for success in reaching any goal she set for herself.

I still to this day recall in every detail that moment in Grand Coulee when I watched Jill take her first steps. I can remember the exact little sunsuit she wore and the look on her face that reflected her excitement and pride. That moment was the highlight of my time in Grand Coulee.

I had packed almost everything into the car that evening and was getting ready to go to bed for the night when the phone rang. I thought: Oh no. What do I have to go in for now?

It turned out the call wasn't from the hospital; it was from the physician who was going to be relieving me and whom I was expecting to arrive the following morning. His name was Vince Stevens. He explained that he had orders to report for active duty in the military soon, and he needed a job in the meantime—just as I had. He had a few questions for me about what it had been like practicing in Grand Coulee, and, in particular, he wanted to know how it had been working for Delos Bristor. I answered all his questions. He then explained that he would be a few days late in arriving due to a family emergency. He had already notified Mr. Bristor, who had asked Vince to call me and request that I remain on duty at the hospital until he was able to get there. This development did not fit into my plans.

I went into Mr. Bristor's office the next morning and told him my departure date was firm, our car was packed, and I would be leaving Grand Coulee the next morning as planned. I was not going to stay and wait for the arrival of Dr. Stevens. I even had some concern he might not show up at all.

Mr. Bristor was upset, to say the least. He threatened not to pay me for the last week. He asked me what they would do with the medical emergencies that showed up at the door. I told him they would just have to do what they had done before Reg and I arrived—ship them off to Brewster or Spokane.

When Martha and I drove out of the trailer park the next morning and headed south out of Grand Coulee, I couldn't help but feel guilty for leaving the hospital in the lurch. I had plenty of time to get to Pensacola, and I could have easily stayed a few more days, but I had made my plans and was anxious to put Grand Coulee behind us. In retrospect, the right thing to do would have been to alter my plans and stay until Dr. Stevens arrived to relieve me. I think a big factor in my decision to leave as planned was a fear, somewhere in the back of my mind, that a big emergency might present that was way beyond my abilities to take care of. I am sure, on some level, I realized this "fear of failure" might have been the main reason I refused to postpone my departure. I knew I hadn't done the right thing, though, and it haunted my conscience for a long time.

As we drove along the rural Washington highways that day, ticking off the miles and putting Grand Coulee behind us, I wondered for the first time if I was tough enough for this business. I enjoyed the challenges presented every day in a medical practice, but I didn't like the ever-present anxiety lurking in the back of my mind that I might encounter something beyond my abilities. Was it there only because I was still young and relatively inexperienced, or would it continue to haunt me throughout my entire career in medicine? I don't think my friend Reg ever experienced that type of uncertainty. I wondered why I couldn't be more like Reg.

W e spent 10 days on the road, driving diagonally across the United States from northwest to southeast. We stopped for two days in Gold Beach, Oregon, to visit Reg and Karen Williams. They had rented a cute little house in the country situated on several acres next to a rushing stream and nestled in a secluded glen. It was surrounded by Douglas-fir, alder, and Ponderosa pine, with willows bordering the stream. It was an idyllic setting, and we envied them. I would have seriously considered staying in Gold Beach and going into practice with Reg if I hadn't had a commitment to Uncle Sam. It would be several years before we could make any such decisions.

Reg took me into town and gave me a tour of his office and Curry County Hospital. While we were in the hospital, the operator paged Reg to the delivery room for a patient who was in labor and crowning. I scrubbed, gowned, and gloved with him, and then he insisted I sit on the stool and perform the delivery. That was a skill we hoped to exercise in Grand Coulee, but it didn't happen. All the pregnant women were receiving prenatal care out of town, and neither of us was in practice there long enough to establish an OB following. So, this delivery in Gold Beach was my first opportunity to do one since completing my internship at Deaconess. It was a routine delivery with no complications, but that didn't make it seem "ho-hum" to me. I have always enjoyed being present and assisting in the miracle of childbirth.

Reg was busy with his practice, and I didn't want to just follow him around the hospital and clinic for two days, so Martha and I toured the area with Karen and the two toddlers and took a jet boat ride up the Rogue River on the mail delivery boat. Our time in Gold Beach quickly came to an end, and, on September 4, we continued our transcontinental journey.

We had driven over 3000 miles when we pulled into Pensacola five days later. We were tired of being on the road and anxious to get settled again, but we expected we'd have to spend at least a few more nights in a motel while hunting for a place to live. As we cruised down Pensacola Boulevard toward the center of town, we passed dozens of motels along both sides of the road. We spotted a big blue and orange sign ahead that said "Howard Johnson," and it seemed to be beckoning us. We had plenty of money from the job in Grand Coulee, and we thought, "Why not go first class and stay at Howard's?"

That Howard Johnson motel became our home for the next few weeks, but it didn't seem so first class after a few days. We had gotten used to our relatively spacious accommodations in the Grand Coulee trailer home, and the motel room seemed a bit confining in comparison.

I went to the Navy Housing Office the morning after we arrived in Pensacola to explore our options for living accommodations. No junior officers' quarters were vacant on base, so we'd have to find a place in town. The yeoman supplied me with a list of known rentals which were currently or soon to be available. I left Martha and Jill to enjoy the pool at the Howard Johnson while I cruised all over the city finding addresses on the list.

It didn't take me long that first day to find the perfect place—a cute little three-bedroom brick house—which was clean and neat, in a suburb to the northwest of town. The house and the neighborhood appeared to be of relatively new construction. The home was owned by a young military family who had received orders to a new duty station. They had decided to keep the house and rent it out, but they weren't moving out until the end of September. The rent was $130 per month. I signed a six-month lease, and we were all set. For the next few weeks, until the house was vacated and we could move in, we were on "vacation" at the motel, just lying around the pool every day and going to the beautiful snow-white beach on Santa Rosa Island.

By the end of the month, Martha and I had the blue and orange menu in the blue and orange Howard Johnson restaurant memorized. The food wasn't all that bad and was relatively cheap, but, after a while, we longed for a home-cooked meal. We enjoyed taking trips to the beach and long drives to explore the area almost every day. That helped break the monotony of seeing Howard's two favorite colors every direction we looked—the outside of the building was blue and orange, the tables in the restaurant were blue and orange, the carpet and bedspread in our room were blue and orange, the curtains were blue and orange, and the bathroom had a blue counter with an orange sink.

We splurged and went out to dinner a few times at one of the all-you-can-eat shrimp restaurants. The shrimp were boiled, and we peeled them at the table. The price was $3 per adult, and children ate for free. I couldn't imagine the restaurant was making a profit on me. Each time we did this, I felt as if shrimp were coming out of my ears by the time we left. One night Martha counted each shrimp I put in my mouth and came up with a total of 75. I definitely got my $3 worth that evening.

That month of September, 1972, was a nice, long, relaxing vacation for me. As for Martha, she received some overdue assistance with childcare as I got to know my baby daughter. The three of us played together in the pool at the motel and in the warm, emerald-green water at the beach on the Gulf of Mexico. We bought Jill a few little beach toys, including a plastic bucket and shovel, and we built a number of elaborate sand castles. Martha and I enjoyed watching Jill toddling along Santa Rosa Beach, with the gentle waves lapping at her bare feet, and squatting down to carefully examine every seashell she found before dropping the treasure into her bucket.

By the last week of September, we all had deep, dark suntans from our many long days under the intense Florida sun. It was probably one of the most relaxing and care-free times of my life. When I reported for class at the Naval Aerospace Medical Institute on Monday, September 25, I felt well rested and ready to find out what this upcoming flight surgeon training was all about.

My orders to NAMI required me to formally check in by midnight on Sunday, September 24, 1972. I made a special trip to the air station that evening to report to the duty officer and sign the official log. The officer of the day (OOD) entered his endorsement on my orders and I was officially on active duty in the United States Navy. The Vietnam War wasn't over yet, but it was starting to wind down; nevertheless, the military was still snatching up every male doctor in the country as soon as he finished training.

The next morning, after my previous evening check-in, our class of new medical officers assembled in a classroom for initial indoctrination. There were 41 doctors from medical schools all over the U.S., and we would all be in training together for the next six months. At the end of that time, assuming we all successfully passed, we would receive our wings of gold, be designated naval flight surgeons, and receive our individual assignments to the fleet. Our class was the third of three classes of prospective flight surgeons for the year, and we overlapped with the second class, which had started a few months earlier and was convened in an adjacent classroom that morning. Those new medical officers were in their final academic sessions and would soon be heading to NAS Saufley Field for flight training, just as we would in about three months.

Almost everyone in the room wore the Service Khaki work uniform, but a few of the new officers were decked out in Summer Whites or the Service Dress Blue uniform. We would all learn shortly to consult the POD (plan of the day) and check the prescribed "uniform of the day," but this was our first day and none of us knew what we were doing.

Two docs in our class stood out right away. One was a fellow who appeared much older than the rest of us and had a silver oak leaf insignia on his right collar, indicating the rank of commander. His Service Khaki uniform was old and faded, and he looked comfortable wearing it. Another classmate wore silver lieutenant bars on his right collar and the medical corps insignia on the left collar, as did everyone else in the room, but he also had naval aviator wings pinned above an impressive, colorful array of campaign ribbons over the left breast pocket flap.

With the exception of those two officers, everyone else in the room wore nice, fresh, new uniforms. For many of these young, new medical corps officers, it was the first time they had worn a uniform. A few had their collar devices on the wrong side or upside down. Since I had been in the Navy Reserve, I knew the medical corps insignia went on the left collar point, and the rank device went on the right collar point of the Service Khaki uniform.

The commander in the faded uniform, as the senior-ranking officer among us, was designated our class leader. His name was Don Huber. He had been a general surgeon with a busy private practice in a little town somewhere in the Midwest. Don had served as a medical officer in the Navy many years before any of us. He had gotten tired of the demands of his busy surgical practice and decided coming back on duty as a flight surgeon would bring an exciting change to his life—a change he felt he needed at that point in his career. I think he had missed some aspects of his previous life on duty with the Navy and wanted to relive those experiences. He looked at it as a new adventure.

Don's main duties as class leader were to call us to muster every day, make announcements regarding our schedules as needed, bring us to attention when a senior officer entered the classroom, and make sure the class members were in the right place at the right time for the various scheduled training events. This probably shouldn't have been as difficult as it turned out to be, but in fact, we were a bunch of unruly, cocky, irreverent young physicians who didn't seem to realize or even care that we were now *military* physicians.

Whenever Commander Huber tried to bring us to attention or form us into ranks and columns during that first week, his commands were often completely ignored. We called him "Barney" because he had an uncanny resemblance to Barney Fife, the lovable but bungling sheriff's deputy (a character played by Don Knotts) on *The Andy Griffith Show* on television. He even had a squeaky, high-pitched voice that sounded exactly like Don Knotts when he got excited. He would command: "Class, atten…hut," in the most authoritative voice he could muster up. When that didn't have the desired effect, he would go from his stance at attention himself, to placing his feet apart and hands on his hips while yelling, in a shrill voice, "Come on guys, I said 'attention,'….please."

To picture what our class was like, imagine the two main characters from the television series, *M*A*S*H*, Hawkeye Pierce and B.J. Hunnicutt, and put them in a classroom with 38 other irreverent, disrespectful practical jokers exactly like them.

So that is the sorry lot poor Commander Don Huber had to deal with. I believe the main reason for this complete lack of military discipline and demeanor was the fact that none of these young doctors wanted to be there at all. A war was going on, though, and all of us had either been drafted into the Navy or volunteered for a naval officer's commission to avoid being drafted into the Army. I suspected every single one of us—with the exception of Commander Huber and possibly the fellow with the wings and all the ribbons on his chest—would have preferred, if given a choice, to be starting a civilian practice of medicine. So, order and discipline were big problems for that first week. No one was taking any of this "officer" stuff seriously.

.....but that was before we met our Marine drill sergeant.

32

That first week at NAMI primarily involved accomplishing necessary administrative tasks. We filled out dozens of forms to establish our permanent individual service records and pay accounts and to provide information required for issuance of military ID cards. Everyone completed a medical history questionnaire and received a thorough aviation physical exam. We filled out emergency "next-of-kin notification" forms and were issued metal dog tags attached to a chain to be worn around the neck. Legal officers assisted each of us in drafting a last will and testament and power of attorney.

It was Friday afternoon when we finally completed the seemingly endless sea of paperwork. The commanding officer of the flight surgery training program then came in and gave us an outline of the entire six-month course. For the first three months—October, November, and December—we would spend every morning in the classroom receiving lectures from various medical specialists on topics related to aviation medicine. Afternoons, those same three months, would be spent at the pool for swimming lessons, in order that each of us could successfully pass the Navy's rigorous and demanding flight crew swim test. The final three months—January, February, and March—were operational in focus, with training that included land and sea survival, high-altitude physiology, ejection seat training, and basic pilot flight training in the T-34 Mentor aircraft at NAS Saufley Field.

Classes commenced at 0800 every weekday, with a one-hour lunch break at 1200, followed by a three-hour swimming workout from 1300 to 1600. No weekend classes were scheduled, but each of us would be added to the on-call schedule at Pensacola Naval Hospital to serve as medical officer of the day in the Emergency Room. With our class overlapping the other class in session, almost 100 student flight surgeons shared that call schedule; this meant each of us would pull night duty only once or twice during our six-month training course. All in all, our schedule sounded pretty cushy compared to the grueling schedule we had all been used to as medical students and interns.

Then, right before we were released that Friday afternoon, the CO added one more instruction. "Gentlemen, you are dismissed for the weekend, but you are all to report to the parade grounds at 0600 sharp on Monday morning where you will meet your Marine drill instructor who will

135

begin training you to march in formation. Don't be late. Class dismissed."
He then walked out of the room.

Some of the docs just sat there with shocked looks on their faces, as others made various comments.

"What did he say?"

"Did he say 'march?' That can't be right."

"Don't these guys know we are doctors?"

"This is ridiculous; I'm not a soldier."

These are just a few of the disgruntled comments flying around that afternoon, accompanied by a lot of grumbling and a few sarcastic laughs. We all then slowly stood up and filed out of the room.

33

If anyone had been watching us marching on the parade grounds on Monday morning, they would have thought we were a group of professional circus clowns from Barnum and Bailey practicing antics for *The Greatest Show on Earth*. Our Marine drill sergeant was the most professional looking soldier I have ever seen. His uniform was so perfectly pressed and starched that he looked like one of those full-size cardboard Marines propped up in the window of the Marine Corps Recruiting Centers.

Our instructor was African-American but wasn't the least bit intimidated by this unruly and disrespectful group of white guys. He was accustomed to training officer candidates who had no official rank, but instructing a class of commissioned officers who all out-ranked him didn't seem to soften his techniques. He was extremely serious and barked out all of his commands, which got the attention of even the most disruptive members of our group. He knew we were all officers on paper and that his job was to make us start looking and acting like officers.

Our drill sergeant taught us how to stand at attention in formation and then walked through the ranks and inspected every one of us, making comments about haircuts, uniforms, shoes, and belt buckles. He taught us how, when, and whom to salute. We learned that prior to every command there was always a preparatory command, followed by the actual command itself: "Forward, MARCH." "Dress right, DRESS." "About, FACE."

Over the next few days, we learned these commands and many more, what they all meant, and how to respond to them. We marched and marched and marched. These first few days were pretty comical, and a few guys couldn't seem to remember which foot was right and which was left; they would left-face instead of right-face and crash head-on into the person next to them. At times like this, even our disciplined drill instructor had a hard time keeping a smile off his face.

Toward the end of that week, one brave fellow mustered up the nerve to ask our instructor how long we were going to be doing this. He answered politely, but firmly, that we would be marching every day until we all did it perfectly. After that, we all took the marching and drilling much more seriously.

By the end of the second week, these drills seemed to be having a noticeable effect on almost everyone in the class. Our drill sergeant started allowing Commander Huber to call out the commands for at least part of our drilling session each morning. It wasn't long until everyone started treating Commander Don "Barney" Huber with much more respect throughout the rest of the day, when our drill instructor was not with us. Don still chirped his commands in his high-pitched Don Knott's voice, but when he called "atten…hut," we now all jumped to attention in unison. He was getting a grip on this disorderly bunch. It even seemed possible that a few of us might eventually turn out to be good officers.

We continued to march every morning for several weeks, but, right when we all seemed to have gotten the hang of it, the marching was replaced by physical fitness training to prepare for the Navy's basic physical readiness test (PRT), which would be given just before Christmas. Our perfectly fit and toned Marine drill sergeant led us in daily runs and calisthenics, and our leader never seemed to break a sweat. Despite the fact most of us had been sedentary bookworms for the past few years, some of the docs in the class were in top-notch physical shape. The rest of us struggled through this torture, but we got stronger each week. The poor guys who were in the worst shape had to put in some extra sessions, but no one died from the training, and everyone qualified in the end.

34

Each day, after completing the early-morning drill on the parade grounds, we reported to the classroom at 0800 for the academic portion of the training. This included courses in cardiology, otorhinolaryngology (ENT), ophthalmology, psychiatry, and aviation physiology. The scope of each specialty lecture was narrowed to aspects related specifically to aviators.

Over the course of three months, we learned all of the exacting physical requirements for qualifying and remaining qualified as a naval aviator, naval flight officer (bombardier-navigator), and enlisted air crewman. The standards were a little different for each position, with the highest degree of fitness required for naval aviators—in particular the standards for visual acuity. We were taught how to fill out the physical examination forms that went into an aviator's medical record. We learned the procedures for grounding an aviator from flight, either temporarily due to a minor illness or permanently because of something more serious. We learned how to return an aviator to duty after being temporarily grounded.

Our class learned the mechanics of the Field Naval Aviator Evaluation Board (FNAEB) and the flight surgeon's role on that board as well as on other types of boards—the Medical Board, the Pilot's Disposition Board, and the Human Factors Board. These various boards were usually convened as a result of an aircraft accident, an aircraft incident, or when some question arose regarding a member's fitness for aviation duty or for any and all duty. A considerable portion of our classes was devoted to teaching us these administrative duties.

We also took a course in basic aircraft accident investigation. This was one course we all hoped we would never have to use.

After our lunch break on the afternoon of that first Monday of class, we all mustered at the side of the Olympic-size indoor pool in our swimming trunks. An instructor explained that the training we would receive in the pool over the next three months would prepare us to pass the aviation swim qualification test. He told us it was a difficult test and no one was likely to pass it without this preparatory training. He asked if there was anyone in the class who didn't know how to swim. Our class leader, Commander Don Huber, slowly raised his hand.

"Do you not know how to swim at all, Commander?" asked the incredulous chief petty officer.

"Not at all, Chief. I've always had a fear of the water," Don answered.

"Commander, we can teach you to swim—I guarantee you that, sir, but in all honesty, it is unlikely you will be able to pass the required test. I'm not saying you are old, sir, but this test was designed for much younger service members."

"I am going to try, Chief," he squeaked out in his warbling, high-pitched voice, and then he added, "I'm just going to do it; that's all there is to it."

At that point, cheers erupted from the rest of the class, and a couple of guys hollered out, "You can do it, Don," and, "We'll help you, Commander." Several guys walked over and gave him an encouraging slap on the back.

The chief then announced that any of us who were particularly strong swimmers and thought we could pass the test right now were welcome to try. He explained that, in the unlikely event any of us passed, we would be excused completely from the afternoon training and have every afternoon off for the next three months.

With this information, it seemed to me it would certainly be worth a try. There was nothing to lose other than getting wet, and I had always considered myself a good swimmer. The chief asked for a show of hands of those interested in attempting it, and apparently almost everyone was just as attracted as I was to the idea of being released from training every afternoon. Commander Don "Barney" Huber was the only one in the class who didn't raise his hand.

35

The first phase of the test was a 50-yard screening swim to the other end of the pool. We were told we could swim any stroke we wanted. The pool was divided into lanes for lap swimming, and we formed lines behind each lane at the deep end.

Several instructors were stationed on each side of the pool watching and evaluating us. They held long, orange fiberglass poles, and we were told if any of us was poked with a pole, we should swim to the side, move to a ladder, and climb out.

The first students in line were commanded to enter the water and start swimming in their designated lanes. After that, the next swimmer in each line was ordered into the pool every 15 or 20 seconds. The lines moved up quickly, and within a few minutes everyone in the class was in the water and heading toward the other end of the pool, exhibiting a variety of swimming styles. Three or four guys were ahead of me in my lane, and in the short time it took me to move up to the edge and launch, I saw several swimmers get poked with a pole. Some of these were dog-paddling while holding their heads out of the water, and it didn't surprise me when the instructors immediately disqualified them. I saw a couple of others who appeared to be doing okay but were ejected, and I wasn't sure why they had failed.

I did the American crawl stroke and concentrated on style. I reached the other end without getting poked, but we had already lost several members of the class when we finished this simple first test. Some of those eliminated guys stuck around to see what was coming up next, but a couple of them just headed dejectedly to the locker room. Most of the class was still in the game, and we were all counting on passing each phase and having every afternoon off.

The advanced screening swim was next. This exercise went a little slower. We had to climb up, one at a time, to a platform on top of a 12-foot tower that was positioned halfway down the pool on one side, 25 yards from each end. Students were told to jump off the tower and then swim four different strokes, 25 yards each, for a total of 100 yards.

One of the instructors gave us precise instructions as to what was required and then climbed to the top of the tower and demonstrated. He did the 12-foot jump into the water, swam the crawl stroke to the shallow end, turned without touching the end of the pool, and swam back to the center of the pool doing the sidestroke. He then continued to the deep end doing the elementary backstroke, turned, and swam the breaststroke back to the center of the pool, finishing at his starting point in front of the tower. He swam every stroke exactly as I had been taught, and his form was perfect.

There were many ways to fail this part of the test. Some of the guys didn't know how to swim one or all of the four strokes correctly. Several of them did them in the wrong order—different than what had been instructed and demonstrated. A few of them touched or grabbed the rim of the pool when reversing course, and a couple of them turned left and went to the deep end first after entering the water instead of turning right toward the shallow end. These students all got poked with a pole. When we finished, only 18 of us were left from the original 40 that had started. I thought to myself—so far…so good. What's next?

We each climbed back up the tower for the underwater swim test to simulate abandoning a ship and swimming out from under a burning oil slick. We had to jump off the tower again, but this time we couldn't come to the surface; we had to stay underwater and swim the 25 yards to the shallow end and touch the wall before surfacing.

Next, we had to repeat the same four strokes we swam in the advanced screening phase for 25 yards each, but this time performing in full flight gear: Nomex flight suit, leather flight boots, Nomex gloves, and flight helmet. When that phase was completed, those of us remaining in the game, and still in full flight gear, jumped back in and were timed for 30 minutes of treading water. A couple of guys had to reach out and grab the poking pole and be dragged to the side.

Our group got a little smaller as we finished each phase, and I could feel a sense of camaraderie developing; we were the survivors. I wondered what was coming next.

The final phase of testing was a one-mile swim in full flight gear. Again, there could be no touching of the sides, ends, or bottom of the pool. Any stroke was permitted, and you were allowed to change strokes at any time, but the mile had to be completed in less than 80 minutes. I realized the key to passing this endurance swim was to stay relaxed in the water and just plod steadily along. The wet flight suit and boots created considerable drag and slowed everyone down, but I continually reminded myself that this wasn't a race. I kept a close eye on the clock and could see, at the rate I was going, I should be able to finish in 80 minutes.

I did the breaststroke almost the entire time and finished the one-mile swim in just under an hour. Only six of us passed all phases of the test and, as promised, we would be completely free every afternoon for the next three months. We were six happy guys.

We hung up our flight gear, went to the locker room and showered, put on our khaki uniforms, and headed for the Officers' Club for a little celebration.

Our leader, Commander Huber, and several other classmates who hadn't passed the swim test accompanied our group of six celebrators to the club. Those guys had hung around to see if anyone in the class would actually pass. I don't think any of them felt too dejected about their failure, since it was a hard test and the instructors had told us they didn't really expect anyone to pass the first time. So the "flunkies" just wanted to join in the festivities with us, and they accepted the success of the six of us in good spirit.

The O' Club at NAS Pensacola was a popular hangout every afternoon. The bar was a noisy place, and the air was thick with cigarette smoke. Almost all the patrons were naval aviators or naval flight officers (NFOs). We found an empty table and ordered a couple of pitchers of beer. Our little group of new medical officers occupied the only table in the room at which everyone wore a uniform instead of a flight suit.

Although the bar was dark and smoky, it was a nicely appointed room, and the rest of the club was classy. The building was situated right on Pensacola Bay, with a beautiful view of the water from the dining room windows.

I had gotten the opportunity to chat with a few of the guys in our class over the previous week, and now I had the chance to socialize with a few more and get to know them a bit better. I was especially interested in talking to Chuck Woodworth. We had all heard his story by then. He was the fellow with aviator wings and campaign ribbons on his uniform. He had been a Marine aviator before attending medical school and was a fighter pilot in Vietnam early in the war. I was dying to hear some of his air combat stories. When we selected a table, I tried to maneuver myself so my chair would be next to Chuck's, but another of my classmates wormed his way between us.

I was a little irritated with the guy who'd wedged his way in between us but decided, since he was now sitting right next to me, I would have to talk to him instead. When I turned and introduced myself, I noticed he was looking at me with a strange smile on his face.

He replied with, "I already know who you are, Dave. How was Grand Coulee?"

This took me by surprise. I didn't remember telling anyone about my experience in Grand Coulee since I had arrived at NAMI. He saw my confusion.

"I'm Vince Stevens. I'm the guy who replaced you at Coulee General." He stuck out his hand.

I couldn't believe the coincidence. Since Vince arrived there after my departure, I had never met him. I had known the physician replacing me was going into the military after he left Grand Coulee but had no idea there would be this intersection of our paths.

I couldn't speak for a minute or two and just mechanically shook his hand while staring at him with what must have been a look of shock and surprise.

Vince was one of the successful six in the swim test, and I had been sloshing around in the water next to him all afternoon without knowing who he was. I forgot all about talking to Chuck Woodworth for the moment as Vince and I became acquainted and compared notes on our experiences practicing rural medicine in Central Washington.

Vince and I quickly became good friends. He was from New York and had the characteristic accent. He was average size, with dark hair and a neatly trimmed mustache, and he had a friendly, easy-going manner that made him immediately likeable. We traded stories about our experiences in Grand Coulee, and I discovered the interesting fact that Vince had been in the seminary to become a Catholic priest before leaving and deciding to go into medicine. We enjoyed that evening in the O' Club, both celebrating our success in the pool, and Vince and I stayed buddies throughout our course of training.

Chuck didn't tell any air combat stories that night, even after we tried to loosen him up with a few beers. He was a quiet, humble fellow who didn't want or need that kind of attention. I made an effort to connect with him over the next few weeks, though, and was able to pull a few stories out of him. He related several aviation incidents that made me think it was amazing he had made it back alive from Vietnam.

Chuck was returning from a mission over North Vietnam in an A-4 Skyhawk fighter when an electrical fire erupted and the cockpit filled with smoke. He got off a mayday call on the radio but stayed with the plane and ran the appropriate emergency checklists until the hydraulics failed and he started losing control of the aircraft. The fighter went into an uncontrollable roll to one side, and, when it was going through 45 degrees of bank, relative to the horizon, he reached up and pulled the overhead ejection handle. He

146

was, thankfully, out over the Tonkin Gulf and not far from a Navy aircraft carrier when he got into trouble. His wingman watched helplessly from his cockpit as Chuck floated down in his parachute. The pilotless airplane was in a steep bank and, for a few moments, Chuck thought it might circle back and hit him. It was, fortunately, below him when it got close, and he watched it from above as it smacked into the water. As he floated down, he inflated his life vest and dropped the one-man rubber raft from the seat pan attached behind him as he had been trained to do. The rubber raft inflated as it hit the end of the attached lanyard and dangled below him until it touched the water. His feet hit the water next, and he disconnected the Koch fittings to free himself from the parachute. He had just climbed into the raft when he heard the whop-whop-whop of a Navy H-1 rescue helicopter. He was back on board the carrier in less than 30 minutes from the time he had ejected. Chuck joked that he got to practice five minutes of sea survival that day.

He cheated death another time when he was launching off a temporary runway made of pierced-steel planking at Chu Lai Marine Air Base, South Vietnam, for a night mission. The runway was very short—only 3,500 feet long—and his aircraft had to be fitted with external JATO rockets in order to get airborne with the heavy ordnance he was carrying. JATO is an acronym for "jet-assisted takeoff." One rocket is attached to each side of the fuselage at the tail and, when lit, they burn until the solid fuel is expended, making them only good for one shot. Chuck set the brakes at the downwind end of the runway, applied max power, and lit off both JATO rockets. He then released the brakes and started hurtling down the short runway. Almost immediately, he noticed a strong asymmetrical pull to one side and knew one of the JATO rockets had failed to light. He quickly aborted the takeoff by pulling the throttle to idle, deploying the speed brakes, and applying maximum braking. Almost as soon as he had initiated this sequence, he felt a surge of power and the aircraft was suddenly tracking straight down the runway. He realized the "failed" JATO rocket had belatedly ignited and, despite full braking, he was accelerating. He was still well below safe ejection speed, so punching out was not an option.

Fortunately for Chuck, the runway at Chu Lai was equipped with arresting cables, just as on an aircraft carrier's flight deck. This was necessary to keep the A-4s from running off the end of the runway when landing. So, Chuck just kept maximum pressure on the brakes and dropped the tailhook. The aircraft was "squatting" on the nose gear with the full braking, though, and, with the tail high in the air, he was afraid the hook was going to pass over the arresting cable and miss it. Just before reaching the cable, he thought to release the brakes and pull all the way back on the control stick allowing the nose to come up and the tail to drop. This quick thinking resulted in the tailhook successfully catching the arresting cable. He slammed into his harness as the little fighter hooked the cable and came to a violent stop. This sequence of events all happened in less than five seconds, and Chuck made all the correct decisions in that brief time, but he had one more important action to take.

Those solid-fuel JATO rockets were both mounted close to a full load of jet fuel and explosive ordnance and were not meant to burn on an aircraft sitting still on the ground. Both JATOs spewed out their skyrocket trails into the dark night. Chuck didn't just sit there. He pulled the handle that blew off the canopy, released the Koch fittings that attached him to the ejection seat, jumped over the side, and ran like a jackrabbit into the black night.

Meeting Chuck and hearing of some of his experiences made an impression on me. My life in medicine up to that point had seemed pretty challenging and exciting, but in comparison to his life, it almost seemed dull. My medical career was likely more interesting than that of a public accountant, but it certainly didn't compare with Chuck's exciting life. I envied his experience as a military pilot and couldn't imagine why he had given it up to become a doctor. For the first time, I was troubled with the thought I might have chosen the wrong career path. I tried to put such thoughts out of my mind whenever they popped up.

✈ **37** ✈

That night at the club, the six of us who were champions of the swimming pool talked about what we planned to do with our time off each afternoon. I mostly listened, already knowing what I was going to do, but the other five decided to meet for a golf game every day on the Navy course on base. I had a good excuse to opt out of this activity—I didn't know how to play golf. The few times I had tried playing the game, I was horrible and considered a menace and a hazard to everyone around me. When I explained this, none of the other five pushed it much further, and I was comfortably excused.

I didn't tell those guys what I intended to do with my free time because I was actually planning to study for several hours each day. We were being presented with a mountain of material to digest in our classes each morning, and I had been taking copious notes. I wanted to keep up with it all and know the material well because we were told we would have only one final written exam at the end of the academic portion of the class. A score of only 70 percent was required to pass, but we were also advised we would be ranked in the class according to our test scores, and each of us would then have our choice of operational assignments to the fleet in that order. The number one student in the class would get his first choice, the number two would then choose from what was left, and so on. This was a strong motivation to study hard and do well on the final exam.

The doctors in the class who were married, like me, seemed to be more interested in doing well on the final exam to provide a chance to be awarded a shore-based assignment where they could be home with their families. A lot of the single doctors either didn't care where they were assigned or actually wanted an assignment aboard a carrier or with a squadron that would deploy overseas. A few of the guys in the class didn't even care whether or not they passed the final exam. With the war going on and the shortage of military doctors, those guys thought: "What are they going to do if I flunk the test—fire me?"

I wanted to get back to the Pacific Northwest that I loved, and I had my eye on NAS Whidbey Island in Washington. I hoped there would be a billet available there when we finished the course. My goal was to be number one in this class of 41 doctors and be guaranteed of getting my first choice. Every day I headed straight home after morning classes and spent the afternoon studying my notes and manuals. I went over all the material

149

from the morning and then reviewed everything that had been covered to date. I was motivated.

Martha and Jill went out for walks, took trips to the beach, or just planned household errands to the Navy commissary and exchange to coincide with my study time so I could concentrate. I studied on the weekends too, but made a point to spend a few hours on Saturday and Sunday with my family.

I met another fellow whom I connected with during those first few days. His name was Paul Broadbent, one of three U.S. Army physicians the Navy was training to serve as Army flight surgeons. The Army didn't have a need for a large number of flight surgeons and, therefore, the Navy trained all the Army's flight surgeons at NAMI in Pensacola.

Paul had done his medical internship at Madigan Army Hospital near Tacoma, Washington. The thing that made him immediately interesting to me was how he had traveled from Tacoma to Pensacola. While he was an intern, he got interested in sailing and had learned how to sail on Puget Sound. He bought a used Cal-20 and starting honing his sailing skills in his 20-foot sailboat on the Sound on days when he had a little time off. The weekend before finishing his internship, he borrowed a boat trailer and towed his boat to Omaha, Nebraska. He launched it into the Missouri River, tied it up to a tree, and hurried back to Tacoma to return the borrowed trailer and finish the last week of his internship.

On July 1, 1972, Paul and his girlfriend, Marilynn, flew to Omaha. The boat was right where he had left it, tied to the tree. They stocked it up with supplies and started sailing down the Missouri River. At St. Louis, they joined the Mississippi and continued to New Orleans. From there, they crossed the Gulf of Mexico, cruising along the northern shore to Pensacola Bay. The journey took one month. Paul and Marilynn rented a little beach cottage with a dock and enjoyed the rest of the summer while waiting for our class to start on October 1.

I had done some sailing myself around Kansas City when I was a medical student. Dr. Harvey Fisher, a professor of biochemistry at the medical center, raced a Thistle (an Olympic-class boat) every weekend during the spring, summer, and fall. Harvey was a serious racer and he taught me to be a good crewman. We did well, and I learned the rules of racing and lots of good tactical strategies from this enthusiastic teacher.

I told Paul I had done some sailing myself and would like to go out with him on his boat sometime. He didn't even laugh when I said my sailing experience was all in Kansas and Missouri. We went sailing in the Gulf on the Cal-20 several times after that.

Paul told me he had big sailing plans. When he got released from active duty with the Army in a couple of years, he planned to buy a bigger boat and sail the Caribbean and possibly sail around the world. He was reading lots of books on long-range sailing and methods of navigation. He had bought a sextant, and he was out on the beach after dark every night teaching himself celestial navigation.

Paul had a book titled *Heavy Weather Sailing*, written by an English racer named Adlard Coles. Paul read the book and then loaned it to me. He said he wanted to take his Cal-20 out on the Gulf during a storm and apply the techniques that Coles used for sailing in heavy weather in the stormy North Atlantic. He wanted the practice for his future ocean cruise. I was curious and also read the book.

Paul called me one evening just before dark and told me there was a gale blowing along his beach and asked if I was ready to go try some heavy-weather sailing. It was dark when I got to his house, and we estimated the wind was blowing 35 to 40 knots by then. We turned on the boat's navigation lights, put on life jackets, attached ourselves to the boat with safety lines, and sailed out of Pensacola Bay into the Gulf. The waves were eight- to ten-foot rollers and they crashed over the bow at times and into the cockpit. Whenever a particularly strong gust hit us, it set up vibrations and we could hear the wind singing through the rigging. It was apparent that the Cal-20 was a strong little boat.

We tried all points of sailing and experimented with different sail configurations that night. The little boat handled well in the strong winds and rough seas. As we headed back to the mouth of the bay, we trailed warps and sea anchors, practicing what we had read in the book, and sailed downwind with the curling rollers towering ominously just behind the stern. We got back to the dock in front of his beach house several hours later; it was a little after midnight. We were soaked to the bone, and I was glad the water of the Gulf was so warm.

Paul was happy with our little excursion because it gave him a chance to put theory into practice. I was happy because we had made it back alive. Paul was a risk-taker, and I found myself admiring his adventurous nature. I had always avoided unnecessary risk and wondered if I was changing.

Paul started hanging out at the Pensacola Yacht Club on weekends to see if he could get on a racing crew. He was asked to join the crew of an

Islander-37. It was a beautiful 37-foot boat owned by a member of the club who raced it every weekend. It wasn't long before I was a regular crew member too. Frank, the owner, wasn't a real good sailor and we never won a race, but he was a true southern gentleman, and we all had a wonderful time sharing his fun with him.

I felt I was meeting some of the most interesting people I would ever encounter in my life. There were some real adventurers in our flight surgery class, and Paul Broadbent was certainly near the top in that category. I made a point to keep track of Paul and Marilynn after Pensacola. They never sailed around the world, but, a few years after leaving Pensacola, they sailed the Caribbean for two years. After that, he got a job as a physician for the U.S. State Department and they lived in American embassies in several foreign countries. I suspected he was also working for the Central Intelligence Agency as well during those years, but he neither confirmed nor denied my suspicion.

Paul seemed to know how to get the most out of life. I admired that. I didn't know at the time that his influence would help me, years later, to make some critical decisions and drastically change my own life's path and find the same kind of fulfillment he enjoyed. He became, in that respect, another mentor.

The aviation medical program was made up entirely of volunteers who signed up for it, and almost every one of those volunteers in my class had an interesting story to tell. I wondered if maybe the flight surgery class itself might be a magnet for such seekers of adventure.

Our last day of class for the academic portion of the course was Friday, December 15. We had the weekend to study up for the final written exam. When I walked into the classroom on Monday, the 18th, I was confident I would do well. The test consisted of 100 questions; all were either multiple-choice or true-false. I was so over-prepared that I thought it was pretty easy, and there was only one question I was unsure how to answer. I thought the question was unfair because it was confusing and poorly worded. I was confident that, if I guessed the correct answer for that one troublesome question, I'd likely have a perfect score. We wouldn't know the test results, though, until the first week of January.

That same afternoon, the guys who had been taking swimming lessons took the swim test. Everyone passed this time, including our class leader. I went to the pool to watch and cheer them on. Commander Huber struggled through the one-mile swim in full flight gear and went a little over the maximum time allowed, but they passed him. We were all happy about that and congratulated him profusely.

On Tuesday, December 19, everyone in the class felt like little kids on Christmas morning. We went to a warehouse-like building, which was probably an old aircraft hangar, where we were issued our personal flight gear. The equipment included two olive-green fire-resistant Nomex flight suits, a pair of Nomex flight gloves, a brown leather flight jacket with a fur collar, a pair of black leather flight boots, a flight helmet, and a survival vest incorporated in an LPU flotation vest. We also received a big canvas parachute bag to carry it all in.

The petty officers outfitting us were all rated parachute riggers. These sailors not only rigged and packed parachutes, they were also responsible for acquiring, storing, maintaining, and issuing flight gear to pilots and air crewmen. They seemed to know what they were doing and made sure each item fit properly. Issuing our helmets took the most time, since they had to custom fit them by gluing in foam shims of various shapes and thicknesses. A properly fitted flight helmet is critical, and I was impressed with the skills these guys demonstrated.

I learned later that it is wise to get to know the parachute riggers in your unit and maintain a good relationship with them. If any of your gear needed repair or if you lost a piece of your equipment, the rigger would fix you up. If you needed a length of parachute cord, the rigger would fix you up. If you needed a few leather name tags with your name and rank engraved on them for your flight suit and jacket, the rigger would fix you up. Once I figured this out, I always made a point to buddy up to the parachute riggers whenever I checked in at a new duty station. I couldn't wait to get home that day and suit up in my new gear to show Martha.

I made Martha and Jill stay in the living room while I suited up in our bedroom. I came out with everything on, including the flight helmet. I swaggered around like a fighter pilot and practiced a few poses as Martha took some pictures. I then took off my survival vest and put it down on the floor so I could check out all the items in it. The vest had several pouches, and I explored them all. I found a large survival knife in a leather shcath, a sharpening stone, a parachute shroud cutter, a compass, a whistle, a signaling mirror, a pack of waterproof matches, a flint and steel kit for starting a campfire, a pack of high-energy emergency rations, a flare gun, two hand-held flares (one for day and one for night), a first aid kit, a container of shark repellent, a water flask, a flashlight, insect repellent, sunscreen, lip balm, and water purification tablets.

When I opened up one pocket that had a holster for a sidearm, I felt a little disappointed we hadn't been issued a service pistol. A couple of years later, I qualified at the shooting range with both the 38 caliber and 45 caliber service pistols, and they still didn't issue me a sidearm, but I did receive a colorful "pistol qualification" ribbon to wear on my uniform. In any case, I thought this gear was cool stuff, and the Navy had given us all of this completely free of charge. For someone who had spent most of his life in a classroom, this was an exciting time!

While I was busy inspecting my new toys, Martha slipped on my flight helmet and started striking poses too.

✈   ✈   ✈

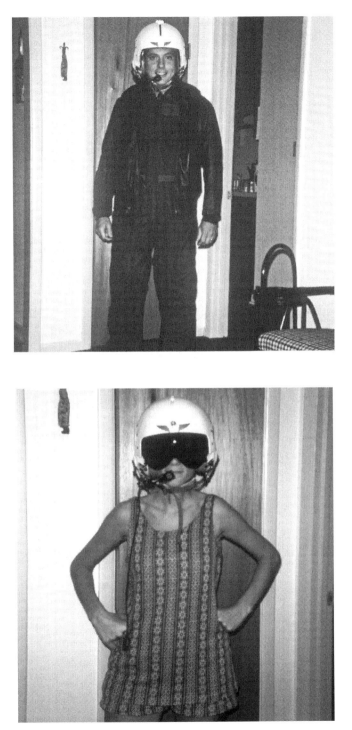

We spent the rest of that week in aviation physiology training. We learned about hypoxia, hyperventilation, and visual illusions, and were taught the difference between vertigo and spatial disorientation. We all experienced hypoxia and an explosive decompression in the altitude chamber. We saw visual illusions in the night-vision chamber and each took a whirl in what was referred to as the "human disorientation device."

On Friday, December 22, we spent the morning learning all about the Martin-Baker ejection seat. We learned how to pull out the safety pins to arm the seat before flight and how to re-insert them to "safe" the seat when we returned to the ramp and secured the aircraft. We were taught the importance of the correct posture and head position before punching out, how to get out using the overhead primary handle, and how to eject using the alternate handle between the knees. We learned the normal automatic sequence of events triggered when either handle was pulled and what could be done manually if something in the sequence failed to happen as advertised.

That afternoon we experienced an ejection up the same vertical track I had been fired up a few years earlier when our medical reserve unit had come to Pensacola. Back in the classroom, we each received our wallet qualification cards, which were our tickets for flight on any Navy jet with a Martin-Baker seat.

No more classes were scheduled until January 2, allowing us a vacation for the week between Christmas and New Year's. A lot of the guys in the class travelled back to their hometowns to visit their families for Christmas. We stayed in Pensacola, and Martha's mom and dad flew down from Kansas City and spent the holidays with us. I enjoyed giving my father-in-law, Bill Scherman, a tour of the air station and describing my training to him. Bill and Martha's mother, Teresa, both enjoyed seeing the area and spending time with their daughter and granddaughter.

The first week of the new year, 1973, brought the next phase of training—land and sea survival. Before getting into that, our flight surgery class assembled in the classroom, on January 2, to hear the results of our final exam and submit our list of top choices for duty stations.

I had gotten the wrong answer on the one test question I had been unsure of. That put my score as fourth from the top of the class. We were each given a list of 41 available billets. NAS Whidbey Island was on the list with one available slot. We each filled out a form with our requests. I only had to select four choices, with Whidbey listed as my number one choice, and then three others in order of preference. All four of my choices were for shore duty.

Frank Kilpatrick aced the test, scoring 100 percent, which made him number one in the class. He was very smart, but I don't think he could have studied for the test nearly as hard as I had because he had been going to swimming lessons every afternoon like most of the rest of the guys in the class. He only had to write down one choice on his form. His first choice of duty was the billet at NAS Whidbey I wanted. It really didn't make much sense to me. Frank had grown up in a big city somewhere back East and didn't seem like much of an outdoorsman. Whidbey Island is in a remote part of the country, far from any large city, and the weather is wet and rainy most of the time. I couldn't imagine he would like it, but it had been my fault it came to his attention since I had been shooting my mouth off right and left about the wonderful Pacific Northwest. I tried to talk him out of it, but it seemed the more I tried, the more set he became in his choice.

The other two guys ahead of me, ranked second and third in the class, both wanted sea duty on carriers. So, I got my second choice, which was air station flight surgeon for NAS North Island in San Diego. I sure could have done worse than that!

The rest of that first week in January, we trained for sea survival. It started in the pool with the Dilbert Dunker.

39

We had all heard about the Dilbert Dunker, and I don't think there was anyone in our class who didn't have a few jitters about climbing into that scary-looking training apparatus. It was designed and put to use during World War II in an attempt to reduce the significant number of pilot drownings after ditching damaged aircraft at sea. The device simulates a water crash landing in which the aircraft somersaults and sinks, requiring the pilot to free himself in the most expedient manner. In operation, the trainee straps in to a seat within a steel framework that simulates an aircraft cockpit. For our training in 1973, we wore full flight gear, and each of us had a parachute strapped on his back. The Dilbert Dunker rolled down a track at a 45-degree angle, reaching a speed of 25 miles per hour when it hit the water and overturned, coming to rest inverted in about 12 feet of water near the bottom of the pool. To successfully pass the test, you had to unstrap yourself from the seat and do a proper exit, which required swimming downward and away from the cockpit at a 45-degree angle before finally coming to the surface.

I wasn't nervous about this since I was comfortable in the water, and I had, after all, aced the Navy's aviation swim test a couple of months before. This confidence started to melt away as I stood in line and watched as my classmates ahead of me hurtled into the water and flipped over. Everyone made nice escapes and got a thumbs-up signal from the evaluator as they exited the pool. I was a little shaky when I climbed the ladder and strapped in but figured I would pass the test as everyone before me had. I was thinking it likely looks worse than it really is.

On my dunking, I was surprised how fast the steel cage zoomed down the track, slammed into the water, flipped over, and continued down the track to the bottom of the pool. The flip to upside-down was so fast that it left me disoriented. My head was surrounded by swarms of bubbles and I couldn't see much. I was underwater for a long time and got my parachute straps mixed up with the seatbelt and shoulder harness release. By the time I got out of the cage, a diver had arrived to assist me, but I had already freed myself. At that point, I had run out of air and inhaled a mouthful of water. When I surfaced, my parachute was half-on and half-off with one leg strap dangling, and I was choking and coughing. The instructor told me to sit on the side of the pool until I recovered and then get back in line.

I didn't see why I had to go through this exercise again. I had gotten out on my own without assistance from the diver but was informed it was not a "clean" exit. I knew there was no point in arguing about it and was wondering how many young doctors the Navy was going to drown that day. I thought: If they need military physicians so badly, why are they trying to kill us?

The first time, I'd had some jitters about the whole thing, but for my second go-around, watching the dunker plunge into the water again and again, I became almost paralyzed with fright. Climbing the ladder to get into the cage, I could feel my knees shaking. I somehow organized my thoughts and rallied, making a nice clean exit on my re-test. When I surfaced, my parachute on my back this time, I was relieved to see the instructor giving me a thumbs-up. If I'd had to repeat the dunk a third time, I wouldn't have had to go to the end of the line; there was no line and no one left to test.

At that point, I had no desire to get back into the Dilbert Dunker ever again, and it would have been a real test of my courage if required to repeat the test a third time that day. Even today, over 40 years later, it spooks me to even look at a picture of the contraption.

40

While still suited up in flight gear, we accomplished the last of our pool training. This evolution utilized the same tall tower we had leaped from for our underwater swim test. It was fitted with a hoist similar to those found on all Navy helicopters, and it swung out over the pool and was used to simulate being cabled up into a helo. Several lifting devices could be attached to the hook at the end of the cable, each having a different purpose; these included the horse collar, the two-person basket, the jungle penetrator, and the Stokes litter. We learned what each apparatus was used for and watched a demonstration on how to properly connect each one to the hoist cable. Then we got in the water and were lifted with each device, one at a time, up to the platform. The purpose of this exercise was to simulate being rescued at sea. I didn't like to think too much about why I might someday need rescuing from the ocean, since it would most likely involve a sinking ship or a crashing airplane.

The next event of the day was a simulated parachute drag. For this, we started out at the deep end of the pool wearing a parachute harness. A cable was attached to the harness with standard Koch fittings, which, on a real parachute, provide a method of disconnecting your harness from the risers when you hit the ground or water. The fittings are cleverly designed to prevent them from being accidently disconnected—as when you are still hanging 5,000 feet in the air. They have a protective, spring-loaded cover over the actual release tab; you have to lift that cover before you can release yourself.

For the simulated drag, we started out face-down in the water. The other end of the cable was attached to a winch with a fast motor at the far end of the pool that dragged us through the water at a rapid clip. The first proper action was to reach up, grab the risers, and twist yourself onto your back. Once you were cruising along on your back, you needed to find the Koch fittings, raise the spring-loaded covers with your fingers, and pull down on the release tabs. I assumed the winch operator would, if I failed to reach my Koch fittings in time, bring it to a stop to prevent my head from slamming into the wall at the other end of the pool and fracturing my skull. Unlike my Dilbert Dunker fiasco, I was golden—out of the harness by mid-pool.

That was the last event scheduled in the pool. The rest of our sea survival training would be accomplished in nearby Pensacola Bay and the Gulf of Mexico.

The next day started with parachute training, but we didn't actually jump from an airplane. Instead, we were each dropped in a parachute harness from a tall tower and the plunge was arrested by a cable, to simulate the jolt of the canopy opening. The device then lowered us quickly to the ground at a speed equivalent to a descent under a full canopy. We were instructed on how to absorb the shock of landing by keeping our knees bent and then rolling to the side onto the ground. I thought the tower jump was a much better idea than jumping out of an airplane. I wanted to save that drill for a day that had turned sour and I really needed to jump out of an airplane.

The next event was intended to give us the experience of a parachute landing on water in a strong wind. For this simulation, the training device consisted of a small trolley that shuttled down a cable that was strung from a tower on a pier and ran at an angle down into the water. Students were suspended, in turn, by parachute risers below the trolley and landed in the water with a resulting horizontal and vertical motion. We were expected to release ourselves from the risers by opening the Koch fittings as soon as our feet touched water. The instructors emphasized how important it was to get free of the parachute as soon as we hit the water, since a parachute sinks quickly and will take you down with it. This was kind of fun and similar to the zip-line rides people today pay to experience.

After completing these two exercises, the whole class, outfitted in full fight gear, boarded a boat with a tall tower at the stern and proceeded out of the bay into the Gulf.

We were suspended individually from two rails that projected out behind the boat at the top of the tower. We each had a seat pan attached when we released ourselves and dropped into the water behind the boat, again by opening two Koch fittings. The seat pan was the only component of the ejection seat that didn't automatically separate from the pilot in a real-life ejection sequence; it contained a one-man life raft and would remain attached as the airman floated down over the ocean. For this training module, we had been instructed to inflate our LPUs (flotation vests) before releasing ourselves from the tower. Once in the water, we were expected to inflate the life raft, climb into it, and then begin our survival at sea.

We looked like little duckies lined up behind the boat, with a new ducky hitting the water every few seconds, until 41 of us bobbed along in an almost perfectly straight line in the wake of the craft.

I climbed into my raft and immediately dispersed the shark repellent into the water all around me. The movie *Jaws* didn't come out until 1975, two years later, and that was a good thing. If I had seen that movie, my heart would likely have beaten a little faster. I shot my flare gun into the air and then lit one of my handheld signaling flares as we had been instructed to do.

Once in the water, we all had a chance to play with our emergency incendiary devices and other new toys, and it wasn't long until we heard the whop-whop-whop of a Navy H-1 helicopter approaching. When all of us had been successfully "rescued" by helicopter, our sea survival training was complete. Land survival was next on the agenda.

For the Navy's Land Survival Course, our class was bused 50 miles to Eglin Air Force Base, the East Coast location for the Air Force SERE School (Survival-Evasion-Resistance-Escape). The Navy survival instructors would be training us in the wilderness area at Eglin, with its sprawling areas of forested land, which included creeks, swamps, and a variety of wildlife.

The course was scheduled for three days and two nights. We were expected to survive in the wild during those three days. I wondered how some of my classmates might handle this, since I suspected a few of the physicians from back East had probably never even slept outside in their own backyards. Most of them seemed to consider it just another exciting new adventure, though. As it turned out, the event wasn't too different from the Boy Scout campouts I had participated in back in Kansas, with one exception: we didn't have any tents, sleeping bags, or food this time. Other than those minor details, it was just another campout for me.

Our land survival training was the first training session I suspected had been watered down a bit to accommodate a bunch of wimpy doctors. I say "wimpy" but soon found out some of these dandies were tougher than they appeared. I knew the SERE School course for aviation candidates was a full two weeks, and it included some realistic physical and psychological hazing to simulate torture in a POW camp. That phase was not on the agenda for us. I decided it was probably best not to complain about that, though.

We were instructed to show up in our flight suits and flight jackets with our survival vests. The idea was that we had each punched out of an aircraft and just happened to have landed in the wilds of Eglin Air Force Base. The only survival gear we would have would be our parachute canopies and what we normally carried in our survival vests and the pockets of our flight suits.

We were all warned the air temperatures in January could be quite low in northern Florida. I dressed for winter flying and put on a set of long underwear and a wool sweater beneath my flight suit. The naval flight suits have lots of pockets, and I stuffed mine with a little extra "survival food"— several candy bars and a couple of granola bars. I hoped the instructors wouldn't search us at the start of the course, but I didn't consider this cheating. I rationalized that I might normally have a few snacks like this with me on a real flight. In any case, after talking to my fellow classmates, I found I wasn't the only one who had such foresight.

When we got to Eglin, we boarded two deuce-and-a-half (2½-ton) troop trucks that transported us out into the wilds. During the morning, we watched field demonstrations of shelter construction, fire building, and first aid. That afternoon, we were taught methods of finding water and sources of food, and we learned camouflage techniques, land navigation, and evasion tactics. The instructors then seemed to suddenly vanish, leaving us to prepare our camp for a long, cold night.

Several of us rigged up a couple of large tents out of old parachute canopies we had been kindly provided. A couple of guys appointed themselves as the group's hunters. They whittled a long spear out of a green tree branch and, using materials from one of the parachutes, fashioned a hurling sling. The hunters then headed out in search of prey, while others started collecting firewood and building a fire ring with rocks from the creek.

The hunters came back to camp about an hour later with a snake, a frog, and a robin. The robin was the most impressive kill. Phil Ceriani had knocked the bird off a tree branch, from a distance of about 20 yards, using his handmade sling and a small stone from the creek. The stone struck the robin in the head, killing it instantly. Phil was proud of his marksmanship but readily admitted he probably would never be able to repeat the feat, even if he tried every day for the rest of his life.

The three successful hunters became the designated cooks, preparing the meat then roasting it on skewers made from green sticks. The meal itself was a festive affair that night, but the portions were somewhat meager. Everyone participated in the meal, if only to humor the hunters, with each of us getting just one miniscule bite.

The emergency rations soon started coming out of pockets. A couple of the survivalists objected to this and suggested munching on a candy bar might detract from the experience and dilute the training. We weren't too far into a discussion about this when I silenced one of the objectors by offering to share with him. He grudgingly accepted, but then voraciously ate the candy bar I'd given him. The other zealot soon came on board with the rest of us when one of my compatriots offered him a granola bar.

No one slept in the parachute tents; it was too cold. We spent the entire night crouched around the campfire. It was a long night, and we all stayed awake by swapping stories and engaging in lively conversation. By dawn, we all knew each other pretty well.

The second day of survival training was spent practicing compass navigation, refining our campsite, foraging for food, and collecting firewood in preparation for another long night.

The third and last day was our "evasion" day. We divided into four-man teams to proceed along a planned course through the woods to a finish line. Each group was given a map and compass. Instructors, posing as enemy combatants, hid all along the course—some of them positioned up in trees. The idea was to reach the finish line without being seen and tagged by any of these "enemy soldiers."

My team consisted of Vince Stevens, Phil Ceriani, Rich Imes, and myself. We elected Phil, aka the robin killer, as our team leader. He devised a plan to make it past the enemy to the finish line without being detected. He looked over the course on the map and noticed that we all had to pass through a narrow section of high ground between two swamps. The high ground was forested, but it was an obvious corridor for the instructors to trap and capture us. Phil's idea was to wade into the swamp on one side of this choke area and bypass the bottleneck where we were vulnerable to being captured. He thought we could come out of the swamp behind the finish line and then sneak up on it from the opposite side—a direction the instructors would unlikely anticipate.

When Phil told us his plan, we all looked at him as if he were nuts. He was taking this training all too seriously. The rest of us figured the sooner we got captured, the quicker we would be finished and get to go home for a meal and a hot shower. Somehow, though, Phil's enthusiasm seemed to rub off on me, and I started feeling the power of my competitive spirit taking control of me. I thought how cool it would be if we were the only team to evade capture. We would surely be celebrated heroes in the eyes of our colleagues.

With Phil and me now both on board with his idea, it didn't take much to coerce Vince and Rich. Phil made the final push by giving a heartfelt speech in which he reminded us that the Vietnam War was still going strong, that any one of us might be in a situation someday in which this training could save our lives, and so we had better take it seriously. That speech sealed the deal. We were in it together as one unit now. Phil gave the orders, and the rest of us followed those orders. To this day, I don't know how he talked the three of us into following him through freezing cold swamp water in the middle of winter. He did it though, and I suspect it may have something to do with being a strong leader.

The swamp water was a mucky green color and chest-deep in places. Almost all I could think about was confronting a 300-pound alligator lurking in those waters, something we had been warned about. When I wasn't thinking about the gators, I found myself scanning the tree limbs above me, which were draped with Spanish moss, and expecting a water moccasin to drop down on me from above.

By the time Phil estimated we had circumnavigated the narrow enemy trap point, we were all shivering violently, and I could no longer feel my toes. When we finally crawled out of the swamp, I estimated we had probably walked a mile in the water and been immersed for close to an hour. I had almost completely forgotten we were in a military training exercise and was in full survival mode. The enemy seemed real; I felt our very survival depended upon outwitting them, and pushing ourselves to the physical limit was required to do that.

The plan worked. We sneaked across the finish line, coming from a direction none of the instructors expected. Our team, Phil's team, was the only squad that didn't get captured.

The rest of the guys in the class thought we were completely out of our minds to do what we did. The instructors were furious. They had warned us of the dangers of the swamps and had a hard time believing the four of us had taken such risk. Now they had to drive us back to the base facilities and get us some dry clothes, which the Air Force would need to provide—an embarrassment for the Navy.

In spite of the instructors' reprimand, the four of us remained smug and proud of our accomplishment.

Learning to fly was next on our agenda, and I could hardly wait.

42

Basic flight training was conducted at NAS Saufley Field, located about ten miles north of NAS Pensacola and only five miles from our rental house. We started the third week in January. It was a crisp and clear Monday morning in the Florida Panhandle as I approached the entrance to the base for that first day of flight training. I picked up my khaki fore-and-aft cap (commonly called the "piss cutter") from the seat next to me and placed it squarely on my head, with my lieutenant's bars on the left and the Navy anchor insignia on the right. I steered the car with my knees as I ran my fingers down the front and back creases, made sure the fore and aft corners were up, and then pulled down the bottom front corner to center it smartly just above the bridge of my nose.

I was pumped up with excitement as I eased to a stop at the guard post for the main entrance to the airfield. The Marine guard on duty snapped to attention when he checked the blue officer's sticker on my windshield, clicked his heals, gave a crisp salute, and said, "Good morning, sir." I returned his greeting and proceeded onto the base, following my printed directions to the training building. I drove past rows of World War II-era buildings, each identified with a large painted number. These included administrative buildings, aircraft hangers, the mess hall, the enlisted barracks, the bachelor officers' quarters (BOQ), and the Officers' Club. I peeked between the buildings and got glimpses of rows and rows of little orange and white aircraft parked on the tarmac, a few of their bubble canopies throwing out blinding reflections from the early morning sun.

I could hardly contain my exuberance as I parked my car in a lot designated "VT-1 Student Parking." I caught a glimpse of myself in the rearview mirror and saw I was smiling from ear to ear. I had a view from the parking lot of row after row of T-34 Mentor training aircraft—several hundred of them. It was a beautiful clear morning, still early, and there was no activity on the airfield. I stepped out of the car and just stood there gazing at the sight and inhaled a deep breath of cool, fresh air. I was glad I had come early and could enjoy this moment of quiet reflection before lines of cars started streaming into the base and aircraft engines began charging the morning air with their cacophony of guttural sounds.

My moment of reverie was broken by another car pulling into the lot and parking next to me. My friend Paul Broadbent got out, glanced over at me, and followed my gaze toward the tarmac. "Wow" was all he could say. He released a long sigh as he took it all in for a moment, then we walked together quietly toward the door to the training building.

Our class convened in a large room where, for the first time, our group of student flight surgeons was integrated with student naval aviators. The first two weeks of training was all classroom work, and, during this initial ground school, there was no distinction made between the doctors and the future naval aviators; we were all held to the same standard. Our group stuck out like a sore thumb though, since the student aviators were all ensigns, with one gold bar on their collars, whereas we all had the double silver bars of full lieutenants on ours. At the first classroom break of the morning, we all fielded questions as to "who the hell" we were.

At exactly 0800, the ensign in the first desk in the first row of the classroom called out loudly, "Attention on deck," as the commanding officer of VT-1 entered the door at the front of the room. We all jumped out of our seats and snapped to attention. He gave us the "duty, honor, country" speech, and, after a couple of minutes, I doubt if anyone in the room was absorbing much of what he was saying.

I thought the CO's "welcome aboard" speech was about over when he suddenly got the attention of every officer in the room. He described a training accident that had occurred just a few weeks prior to our arrival involving the mid-air collision of two T-34s. The accident had resulted in four fatalities, which included an instructor and student in each airplane. One of the two students killed happened to be a student flight surgeon and was slated to be one of the first female naval flight surgeons to receive her wings. The CO had everyone's rapt attention at that point, and he went on to say he was not telling us this to incite fear and anxiety regarding our training; he explained he just wanted to be sure we all took the training very seriously. He made it clear he did not want to have another accident on his watch.

When the commanding officer walked out of the room, a strange hush descended upon the group. No one moved or said a single word for a full minute. This was serious business and we all got that message loud and clear.

43

Flight training began with ground school. The classroom was large and well-lit but had no windows, so we could not be distracted by the flight operations going on almost continuously just outside the building. That was a good thing.

An instructor issued each of us a stack of training materials that included the NATOPS manual (Naval Air Training and Operating Procedures Standardization) for the T-34B aircraft, which we would all be learning to pilot over the coming weeks. The NATOPS manual had a green cardboard cover with a picture of a T-34 soaring through the air. A spiral-bound checklist contained normal and emergency procedures, and several other study guides and workbooks were provided. These covered aircraft systems, federal air regulations, aviation meteorology, and basic air navigation; an additional pamphlet described airspace designations and the U.S. airway system. We were also given a large paper mockup of the T-34 cockpit depicting its controls, switches, and instrumentation.

The lieutenant in charge of the ground school outlined the course and gave a brief introduction to the study materials. He told us to expect a written test every day, covering the material presented on the previous day, and a written and oral final exam upon completion of the course. The officer informed us that no one would be advanced to flight training who had not passed all the ground school exams with a minimum score of 70 percent.

I was shocked to learn the minimum score for passing was as low as that. After hearing the sobering description of the recent fatal accident, I had immediately decided my goal would be to get 100 percent on all exams. I wanted to know this stuff and know it well. I later learned everyone else in the room was taking it just as seriously. I doubt there was a score on a test below 95 during the entire course. I'd never before been in a classroom filled with more self-disciplined and focused individuals.

The lieutenant handed us off to one of his ground school instructors, a first class petty officer whose specialty was aircraft systems. He delved right into it, and we began learning how to take a T-34 completely apart and put it back together again. This last statement is, honestly, somewhat of an exaggeration, but, by the end of the first day, we knew almost everything there was to know about the Continental E-185 piston aircraft engine and what made it hum.

Over the next few days, our instructors also covered the mechanics of the McCauley variable-pitch propeller, the flight controls, the fuel system, the electrical and hydraulics systems, the landing gear, cockpit instrumentation, and the radios and communications system.

The instructor advised us to start memorizing the normal and emergency checklist items and the response to each. He explained that the oral test at the end of the course would include reciting each item and the corresponding response verbatim. This was one test to which a minimum score of 70 percent did not apply; it had to be done perfectly, without a single error. He recommended we practice this litany several times each day and that we pair off and practice together, both between classes and at home. He suggested each of us tape the paper mockup of the T-34 cockpit to a wall at home or in our living quarters, sit in a chair in front of it, and touch each control as we read the items on the checklist.

We learned, later that day, there was a room on the first floor of the classroom building that housed a real T-34B cockpit to use as a procedures trainer. It was an actual airplane with wings and tail removed. This modified T-34B was a much better hands-on tool than the paper mockup poster I had put up on the wall of our bedroom, but it was in high demand. The only time I was able to grab any time in it was late in the evenings and on weekends.

Arriving home from that first day of ground school, I felt as if I had been drinking from a fire hose all day. I was almost overwhelmed by the thought that learning the aircraft systems and all the associated procedures was just one facet of this intense training. In the days that followed, the instructors continued to hurl a barrage of information at us. The ground school was very compressed, and I found myself studying furiously for several hours each evening. The only time I could spend with Martha was when she was quizzing me on the material I was expected to know, and Baby Jill was not happy I was paying less attention to her.

The days and weeks flew by quickly, and, by the time we took our final exam—both oral and written—we all felt as though we had completed a six-month course in three weeks. I must say it was very efficient, and I had to presume the training squadron must have been under a mandate to turn out the greatest number of pilots and flight surgeons in the shortest amount of time. The end of the Vietnam War seemed to be nearing, but no one could be sure what would happen; the number of new naval aviators and naval flight officers completing training needed to approximate the rate of those being killed or captured in Southeast Asia. We were told one in every four naval aviators coming out of training died in air combat or an air training accident. The numbers were staggering, and the training numbers had to match or exceed those grim statistics. I don't think they could have pumped us out any faster, though.

With ground school over, we continued to study and review the material presented to reinforce all we had learned in such a short timeframe. We were all aware our survival in the skies might one day depend on how well we had prepared ourselves in the classroom phase.

Our class did well on the exams and all of us were advanced to the next stage—learning to fly a military aircraft.

44

It was the first week in February when ground school was over and we finally took to the air. We quickly found we were spending a lot more hours sitting in the Ready Room waiting to fly than actually flying. The Ready Room was on the first floor of the classroom building and was arranged like another classroom, but, instead of desks with writing surfaces, it was furnished with comfortable leather chairs, which almost resembled Barcaloungers, arranged in orderly rows.

The flight scheduling officer sat at a desk at the front of the room facing a sea of student faces. A large erasable white board, with the day's flight schedule roughed in, covered the wall behind his desk. Next to each time period were rows of student names and their assigned instructors; next to each pair of names was an assigned aircraft number for that flight. On the far right of each row was a box for notes and comments, and this area usually specified the lesson number, from the flight syllabus, to be completed that day. "PS-1" was in the box next to my name, indicating pre-solo lesson number one. The configuration of the Ready Room was a standard layout, as I would learn later, in every squadron space in the U.S. Navy—whether aboard an aircraft carrier or ashore at a naval air station.

Each of us was issued a printed copy of the week's tentative flight schedule on the last day of ground school, but we were instructed to check the scheduling board frequently for changes and updates. We were expected to be suited up and ready to go each day, regardless of whether we were on the schedule or not. Some members of my class were not scheduled to fly at all until later in the week, but all were there in their flight suits standing by. Practically everyone had brought study materials to review, which gave us something to do while we waited. I had my T-34 NATOPS manual with me as well as the normal and emergency checklist.

My first flight was scheduled at 1100 hours on Tuesday, February 6. The instructor's name, next to mine on the white board, was LTJG Paul Bradney. I came to know LTJG Bradney well over the next few weeks, but, on that morning, I couldn't help but wonder what he looked like, whether or not he was a good flight instructor, and what kind of a military officer and person he was. I had heard stories about some of the instructors and wondered whether he was a hard-ass or a softie. I could see from the scheduling board that Bradney had been on the 0900 launch and I would be his second student of the day. I didn't know the student naval aviator he was instructing, and, even if I had known him, there wouldn't be time to ask him what Bradney was like before my flight.

By the time the hands on the clock at the front of the room indicated 1100 hours that Tuesday morning, I had been checking it several times per minute. It was 11:17 when LTJG Bradney walked into the Ready Room. I watched him as he studied the scheduling board and then turned, called out "LT Crawley," and scanned the room with a serious expression on his face. His eyes met mine with a piercing gaze as he saw me pick up my helmet bag from the floor and pull myself out of my chair. I gave him a weak smile and then walked to the front of the room, ready to shake his hand and introduce myself; when I got to him, he turned his back to me, headed for the door, and said, "Let's go, sir." I followed him out the door and down the hall to the parachute loft. There was no introduction and no handshake.

We picked up our parachutes, and I followed his lead by throwing one shoulder strap over my shoulder to carry it to the aircraft. He said, "We'll wriggle into these things when we get to the airplane. I have to be in one of these all day long, and I don't want to be in it any longer than I have to."

He was a little guy with blond hair. Now, I'm not a big person at 5 feet 9 inches tall—but I stood two or three inches taller than Bradney, and I guessed he didn't weigh more than 125 pounds. He was all business as we walked across the tarmac toward aircraft number 140092.

By the time we found our assigned plane on the flight line, I was beginning to think LTJG Bradney had a bit of an attitude. I was getting the impression he was looking at me as a waste of his time and instructor skills and wondered if he thought his role would be that of a glorified babysitter over the coming weeks. When he asked me if I planned to solo, I answered that I hadn't yet decided, an honest answer that seemed to generate a subtle smirk from him.

A couple of the student naval aviators in our ground school class had spread the word that some of the instructors didn't like the idea of giving flight lessons to student flight surgeons. They knew we weren't required to continue past the pre-solo phase of basic training and solo flight was optional for the doctors. So, when I reached the point in training where my next flight would be solo, I would have the choice of doing it or not, depending on my confidence level at that point. In order to reach a decision, I would try to assess the level of fear factor within me and balance it against the instinct for self-preservation. None of the student naval aviators were given this luxury, and the first solo flight for each of them

176

was just another requirement on the long road to receiving their wings of gold.

LTJG Bradney's coolness to me that morning and the little smirk he gave planted a seed within me, and I challenged myself to turn his attitude around 180 degrees. I began pumping up my confidence and developed a hardened resolve. By the time we reached the aircraft for my first flight, I believed I would show Bradney not only was I a serious student, but I'd possibly prove to be the best student aviator he had ever instructed.

45

The traffic pattern and operational flight procedures at NAS Saufley were designed to get the most airplanes, instructors, and students into the air in the shortest possible time. On a nice, clear day—an optimum day for flight training—it wasn't uncommon for 250 Saufley aircraft to be aloft at the same time. That was impressive, but even more amazing was the fact that those 250 aircraft could all be airborne in about one hour—a launch rate of four planes per minute. I wondered how in the world that was possible.

The active runway on a given day depended on the wind direction, as is the case with any airport. All the runways at Saufley were 4,000 feet in length and 200 feet in width. On the first morning launch, aircraft taxied to an entry to the active runway that was at the midpoint of the length of pavement. The two planes at the front of the line taxied onto the runway facing into the wind and lined up, side by side, to take off in the 2,000 feet between this midpoint position and the end of the runway. The 2,000 feet of runway behind those two departing aircraft was reserved for landing aircraft. This arrangement enabled landings and takeoffs to be done simultaneously on the same active runway.

In order to make this system work even more efficiently, no radio clearance was required to initiate a takeoff or landing. There was an operational control tower on the field, but the tower controller didn't issue any instructions or even say a word over the tower frequency unless there was an emergency or he observed a maneuver that caused a safety concern. Once the two aircraft were positioned on the runway and ready to go, the aircraft on the left would initiate a takeoff roll, and then the next aircraft in line would taxi onto the runway, circle behind the aircraft still in position on the right side, and take the spot on the left that was just vacated. As soon as the first aircraft's wheels lifted off the runway, the pilot on the right started his roll, and the next aircraft in line would take its place, so that each launch occurred sequentially in a continuous stream as long as aircraft were in line on the taxiway.

As the day progressed and aircraft began returning to the field, landings would be made behind the aircraft lining up for the takeoff sequence. The pilots landing were all acutely aware that, even though the runway was 4,000 feet long, they only had 2,000 feet to get on the deck and stop. The dire consequences of landing long were obvious to instructors and students. After a pilot touched down, he watched the tails of the two aircraft stopped in front of him on the same runway appear to get bigger and bigger in his windscreen as he braked his aircraft and decelerated.

The traffic pattern was another well thought-out design. It was a left-hand pattern with two levels—at 800 feet and at 1,200 feet AGL (above ground level). An aircraft departing the pattern would climb to 800 feet and then level off until clear of the airport traffic area. This procedure was to avoid arriving aircraft entering the traffic pattern above at 1,200 feet. The arriving aircraft completed one circuit at 1,200 feet and, after making a thorough scan for traffic, dropped down to 800 feet for the downwind leg, continuing the descent to land after reaching a point abeam the touchdown point. Our instructors taught us to have our heads on a swivel whenever we were approaching or departing the traffic pattern. It was a busy block of airspace and no place to be daydreaming or sightseeing. Each pilot was responsible for his own spacing and sequencing, and, again, there was no clearance to land issued from the tower, and the tower controller was quiet unless he saw a problem.

When we arrived at our aircraft that morning for my first lesson, Instructor Bradney slid the plexiglass canopy of the airplane open and propped his parachute up in the rear seat. I copied this action and dropped mine into the front seat. We performed our walk-around inspection, and I thought I'd impressed him with quick answers to his questions about the function of each component and my explanation of the purpose of each check we were doing. He nodded appreciatively several times as he saw I was well prepared.

With the walk-around complete, we wriggled into our parachutes, cinched up the straps, and climbed into the cockpit and strapped in, with me positioned in the front and Bradney in the rear. He read the "before start checklist" to me as I completed each action and called out the memorized response. He had to shout each item, and I had to holler back the response, until we got to the point of powering up the electrical system. We could then talk in normal tones through our helmet ICS (internal communication system).

My goal of impressing my instructor started falling apart with the checklist. I knew all the responses perfectly, but, for some reason, I started adding unnecessary words. When he called "trim tabs," I checked the settings and responded, "Set at zero."

He corrected me immediately and mercilessly: "What is this 'Set at zero,' sir? The response is 'Zero,' sir."

"I'm sorry, sir. I meant zero, sir," I respectfully responded.

His voice got louder. "And.....don't call me sir, sir. You are the sir. I am a lieutenant junior grade; you are a full lieutenant. I call you sir, sir; you don't call me sir. You need to learn what these rank insignias on our collars mean, sir."

I was getting a little rattled and responded, "I'm very sorry, sir....I mean I am sorry, Mr. Bradney."

The next item called out was "throttle." My response was "It is closed."

He now sounded as if he was speaking through clenched teeth. "The response, sir, is 'closed,' not 'IT IS CLOSED.' Please give me the correct response and possibly we may be able to go flying sometime today."

My goal of changing LTJG Bradney's attitude about instructing a flight surgeon was quickly crumbling. I wanted to tell him I was sure I would astound him with a dazzling performance of natural aeronautical ability once we got in the air, but I was starting to feel pretty humble, and I managed to keep that pipe dream to myself for the moment.

46

I had an absolutely wonderful time on that first flight (Lesson PS-1), despite the fact I felt my performance had been dismal. The lesson involved some very elementary maneuvers. Instructor Bradney made the takeoff from the rear cockpit with me following along in front with my hand on the stick. When we got to the practice area, he introduced straight and level flight, shallow angle bank turns, and then constant-airspeed climbs and descents. He demonstrated each maneuver and then let me try each one.

I couldn't imagine having a better instructor than Paul Bradney. He seemed like God's gift to aviation. When he demonstrated a maneuver, he performed it with perfect precision. It all appeared completely natural to him, as if the plane was an extension of his body. It seemed almost as though he was "wearing" the aircraft.

His seemingly magical performance certainly impressed me, but it also intimidated me. I felt I couldn't have been in better hands and, if any emergency arose, he would handle it with the utmost skill and return us both safely to Mother Earth. Those feelings of admiration and awe, however, did nothing to relax me or help me perform the same maneuvers to his exacting standards. When he handed control of the aircraft over to me, it was as if no one was flying it. When I moved the control stick, I could feel I was making the airplane do something, but it seemed the only maneuver I was able to perform would best be described as a wallow. I could tell when he took the stick and straightened me out, but, when he released his grip and turned it back over to me, it was as if we were both just riding along in an airplane no one was controlling.

Bradney was amazingly patient with me on that first day, and he didn't say too much until we landed and he'd finished conducting his debrief. He recognized my self-confidence was "in the toilet" by the time we were back on the ground. He compassionately reminded me this was my first lesson and advised me not to get down on myself. He offered additional encouragement, saying my performance would improve and I would see myself getting better each day.

On my drive home that afternoon, I experienced a strange mix of feelings. On one hand, I was dejected and felt I had lost all the self-confidence I had mustered up just that morning before the flight. On the other hand, there was a feeling of great thrill from the whole experience as I reviewed in my mind every moment of our flight.

One of the procedures at Saufley was to leave the aircraft's plexiglass canopy open for the takeoff and initial climb. The reasoning behind that was to allow easy egress in the event of a crash. The procedure called for sliding the canopy closed when reaching an altitude of 1,000 feet above the ground, and then, upon arrival back at Saufley, reopening it when entering the traffic pattern for the approach and landing.

When we had taxied out onto the active runway for takeoff that morning, with the cockpit canopy wide open, we both pulled our helmets' tinted visors down. This left our noses, mouths, and lower cheeks exposed to the 80 or 90 mph wind produced by the propeller as we pushed the throttle up and accelerated for takeoff. Once airborne, this hurricane wind in my face brought on a feeling of sheer exhilaration I cannot begin to describe. I felt like a 1930's barnstormer in an old Stearman biplane must have felt. I think I was grinning from ear to ear and was surprised I didn't get back from the flight with bugs in my teeth.

I couldn't get the barnstormer thrill out of my head. Driving home that afternoon, I kept replaying those few minutes when the canopy was open and the wind was blasting my face. It wasn't hard that evening to pump myself back up and tell myself I could do this and things would get better. It all seemed right, and I knew I *had* to do this. I could hardly wait for the next lesson. I may not have impressed my instructor as I'd hoped that first day, but maybe the next lesson would be better.

47

I flew the next two days and loved everything about the flying—from suiting up in my flight gear to the post-flight brief and everything in between. At times I felt like pinching myself because I couldn't quite believe I was getting the opportunity to do all this. I am sure part of my enjoyment was the macho aura of everything we were doing, but it was more than that; I started to feel like flying airplanes was in my blood and something I had to do.

Each flight lesson, over the ensuing weeks, built on the one before it, and the prerequisites for every newly introduced maneuver were the skills learned and developed during previous lessons. The basic flight syllabus called for 12 lessons prior to solo. The twelfth flight, PS-12, would be a checkride prior to solo and given by an instructor who was not the student's regular instructor.

It was possible to "bust" a flight lesson, and one repeat flight was allowed. For any student naval aviator, a second bust would put the individual before a Training Board to decide whether or not the student would be allowed to continue. For a student flight surgeon, a second failed lesson meant the flight training was over, but the medical officer could still be designated a flight surgeon and receive his/her wings. So, for doctors, the experience was something the Navy wanted us all to have, but, if some of us weren't natural-born aces, it was okay; everybody still passed.

My lessons progressed, and we quickly advanced to practicing steep turns, stalls, and spins. Bradney didn't credit me with any landings until Lesson PS-4 on February 15. He was still coaching me and nudging the controls as needed, but he credited me with six landings on that fourth lesson and recorded them in my logbook. On occasion, usually when we were close to the ground, he would take control completely away from me. There would usually be an outburst over the ICS that involved some cursing and would be something like, "WHAT THE #@*! ARE YOU DOING NOW…..sir?" It always struck me as humorous that he invariably stuck the "sir" at the end of each admonishment.

My instructor hammered two frequent reminders into the earphones of my helmet day after day. One of these was, "Trim – trim – trim," and the other was, "Airspeed – airspeed – airspeed." The first of these calls was to remind me to always adjust the trim tabs on the control surfaces (the rudder, elevators, and ailerons) so I didn't have to hold pressure on the controls. This facilitated a light and smooth control of the aircraft. The second mantra was usually given on final approach for landing and emphasized the critical importance of maintaining the proper airspeed for a stable approach and good landing. More importantly, the "airspeed" call might be a warning to correct a deteriorating airspeed that could result in an aerodynamic stall and spin into the ground. The volume and pitch of Bradney's voice when he gave me an airspeed warning always indicated the magnitude of my deviation and how dangerously close I was approaching a stall.

The Navy owned a number of outlying airfields used for touch-and-go landing practice. A couple of these were in Alabama, just outside of Mobile. On a typical flight, we headed for one of those fields to practice landings and, while en route, performed our high-altitude maneuvers. When we arrived at the outlying airstrip, we were frequently the only aircraft in the pattern and had it all to ourselves.

When I was midway through the pre-solo syllabus, I still felt like I was just riding along in the airplane—even when I was at the controls. One morning, as we headed toward the Alabama state line to do some landing practice at one of the outlying fields, I seemed to forget I was flying the airplane. I started daydreaming and looking down at the pretty countryside sliding beneath our wings when I noticed a beautiful lake with several sailboats cruising around on it. I keyed my mic button and said, "Hey, Paul, look at that pretty little lake down there." I had no sooner gotten those words out of my mouth when I felt and heard a terrible crashing blow to the top of my helmet. Bradney had released his seatbelt and shoulder harness, unstrapped his metal kneeboard from his right thigh, then leaned forward and whacked me over the head with it. That was the end of my sightseeing, but I believe my gawking around that day indicated I was starting to feel relaxed and comfortable in the airplane.

When my landings started to improve, Bradney would check the windsock when we got to a field and choose a runway that provided crosswind practice. Those crosswind landings gave me fits. They required, on the approach to the runway, cross-control of the rudder and ailerons in order to keep the upwind wing down and the fuselage lined up with the centerline. If the wind was from the right, for example, it meant keeping the right wing tip down with the ailerons and simultaneously applying opposite rudder. It took a lot of coordination and concentration. The first day we did this, I was concerned he was going to give me a "bust" for that lesson and

186

make me repeat it. When we debriefed that day back at Saufley, he just said, "Your crosswind landings are going to need a little more work, Doc."

On PS-12, my twelfth syllabus flight, I would be scheduled to fly with a check pilot to evaluate whether or not I was safe for solo. I hadn't yet made a decision to solo even if the instructor were to sign me off, but I suspected the choice wouldn't be mine to make since I was doing so miserably. I assumed LTJG Bradney had similar thoughts.

On February 26, I flew twice. When we returned to Saufley at the end of my lesson that day, Bradney asked if I would be his safety pilot while he flew "under the hood" on an instrument proficiency flight. He would sit in his usual position in the aft cockpit but would be under a canopy that snapped down to the rear instrument panel and fly by reference to instruments only. He was required to do this periodically, as were all naval aviators, to meet minimum currency requirements. Since he got essentially no actual instrument time while instructing, he scheduled himself regularly for simulated instrument flights.

My job on the flight was to act as observer, watch for other traffic, and avoid conflicts. Bradney told me to take control of the aircraft, if necessary, to avoid a collision, and I was flattered he would trust me in this capacity. When we got back, he entered 1.2 hours of "special crew" time in my logbook.

On February 27, I completed PS-10, which left only one more scheduled flight with my instructor before my checkride. I thought the lesson went horribly, and I still felt like I was just a passenger and not really flying the airplane. It seemed as though I would need about six more months of instruction before possibly being considered safe to go up on my own. When we arrived back at Saufley that day, I had a serious talk with Bradney in the debriefing room.

"Look, Paul, I don't feel I am anywhere near ready to solo, and we only have one more lesson before my checkride. I'm discouraged," I whined.

"You're doing fine, and you'll be ready. Don't get down on yourself. A lot of students feel what you're feeling at this point," he said with great confidence and assurance.

"Here's the thing, Paul, I never feel like I am really flying the airplane. I think you are a great instructor, but I can always feel a little pressure on the stick when you make corrections for me. I know you're right there, and I don't think you ever completely take your hands and feet

189

off the controls. The only way I'm going to feel confident is to have an entire flight in which you don't touch the controls and I know I'm the one controlling the aircraft the whole time, including landings."

"Okay, Doc. Maybe I have been a little over-protective. We're on the schedule to fly our last flight together tomorrow. I'll try to keep my hands off. How about if I put both hands up on the glare shield? You'll be able to turn your head and see my hands in your peripheral vision. I'll talk to you when I need to, but you can turn your head and see my hands whenever you feel like it. I've done the same thing with other students lacking confidence, just as you are, and it worked well."

When we walked out to the flight line the next morning for Lesson PS-11, I didn't have any more confidence than the previous day. Just before I started to taxi for takeoff, Bradney said, "Turn your head, Doc. See my hands? This is where they are going to be."

I turned my head, and, in my peripheral vision, I could see both of his green flight gloves with the fingers gripping the edge of the rear glare shield.

I doubt he kept his hands on the glare shield for the whole flight, but his little demonstration and assurances were enough to give me the extra confidence boost I needed. I did the takeoff and climb and then performed all the various maneuvers we had practiced over the previous few weeks. By the time we arrived at a practice field in Alabama to do landings, I had completely lost that feeling of being a passenger and hadn't once detected any pressure on the controls from Bradney. I felt I was really flying the airplane for the very first time and even started to have the feeling the craft was an extension of my body—a sensation I had heard described by seasoned aviators.

There was a 12- to 15-knot wind blowing at the field. I double-checked the windsock and set up my pattern for the runway that gave me the most direct cross-component. I side-slipped the airplane down final and touched down gently on the upwind main gear, set the downwind gear down softly, and then the nose gear. I imagine I was smiling and feeling full of myself as I pushed the throttle full-forward for the "go."

I logged nine landings that day—eight cross-wind touch-and-goes, and then one full stop back at Saufley. Every one of the touchdowns was a "greaser." I was smiling as I climbed from the cockpit and then stood on the tarmac wriggling out of my chute. Bradney and I looked at each other. He was smiling too.

The debrief was short and sweet. "Nice job, Doc. I think you're ready. How do you feel?"

"I'm ready!"

49

I would have liked to have celebrated my success of the day with a couple of beers at home that evening, but my exuberance was tempered by the fact I was on the flight schedule the following morning for my checkride. If I successfully passed, I could be taking off on my first solo flight that same afternoon.

I couldn't help but wonder if my sudden demonstration of aeronautical ability and competence was somehow just a fluke. Maybe piloting an aircraft is like playing a sport, such as golf or tennis, I thought. One day you play like a pro, and the next day your game is worthless. My confidence level that evening started ratcheting down as I wondered if I would ever be able to repeat my performance of that day.

Another worry nagged at me as well: even if I somehow pulled off a successful checkride, there was always the possibility of an inflight emergency during my solo flight. Was I ready for that? We had simulated a few of the possible emergencies on each instructional flight. If a real emergency had arisen on any of these flights, I had the comfort of knowing my instructor was right there with me and would likely take control of the crisis and get us both safely on the ground. At this fragile point in my training, I wondered if I was capable of staying calm and methodically accomplishing the items required by the checklist in such a situation.

I knew I would have an oral exam prior to the actual checkride and it would include the emergency checklist. I wanted to get a perfect score on the exam, but, more important, I wanted to be confident in my ability to handle any problem that might arise when I was alone in the cockpit.

That evening, to prepare myself for the big day ahead, I went over and over the emergency checklist, then sat in our living room and had Martha quiz me. Referring to the checklist, she called out the title of each emergency, and then I recited each item and its response by memory: "Engine Fire During Start; Engine Fire After Start; Aborted Takeoff; Low Altitude Engine Failure ……" We went through the entire checklist several times over the course of the evening. Martha was as demanding as LTJG Bradney—correcting me if I said one word wrong.

Martha finally told me it was time to knock it off and go to bed. She wanted to make sure I'd be well rested for my big day. I knew she was right and followed her advice, but I tossed and turned and had a restless night. I lay awake imagining all the things that could go wrong and the possible outcomes. When I left for Saufley Field in the morning, I was exhausted from lack of sleep.

I backed the car out of the garage into a driving rainstorm. The trees were swaying back and forth in a howling wind, and the rain was coming down so hard I had to turn the windshield wipers on the high setting in order to see the road. I arrived at the base and sat in the Ready Room and studied my emergency checklist throughout the entire day. All training flights were cancelled.

50

A series of ugly spring storms churned up from the Gulf of Mexico into the Florida Panhandle for the next nine days. A couple of brief periods of clearing occurred during that time, but only a few abbreviated training flights were launched and recovered before the next wave of wind, rain, and low ceilings arrived, forcing all flight operations at the field to shut down.

My name was on the flight schedule board for my checkride every day, with a different instructor's name next to mine on each of those days. I never met any of them.

After several days of being grounded by the atrocious weather, I had studied the emergency checklist so much I was probably reciting it in my sleep. I finally managed to start sleeping again at night, and that was mostly due to sheer exhaustion. I was beginning to feel rested but had the nagging worry of losing the fragile flight proficiency I had developed. I had flown almost every day before the storms hit, but I knew the longer I was grounded the harder it would be to pick back up the meager flying skills I had so painfully earned. Even seasoned aviators with lots of flight time didn't like being out of the cockpit for more than a few days.

On March 6 it looked as if the bad weather might be coming to an end, and several of my classmates flew that day. I was hoping to be one of them, but, instead of going out for my checkride, I was sent over to nearby NAS Whiting Field for a familiarization flight in the T-28 Trojan.

The T-28 was the aircraft used at the time for student naval aviators to make their first carrier landings. Those were done on the old, semi-retired USS Lexington in the normally smooth waters of Pensacola Bay. The officers in charge of flight surgeon training at NAMI thought it was important for the doctors to at least get an exposure to the mighty T-28 Trojan, even though we weren't required to make any carrier landings.

The T-28 is like a T-34 on massive doses of steroids. It is a monster! The Navy version of the aircraft has a 1450 horsepower Wright-Cyclone radial engine, an enormous engine for the size of the aircraft. Except for its tricycle landing gear, the T-28 looks a bit like the Grumman F-8 Bearcat from World War II, one of the last propeller-driven Navy fighters.

Besides its duty as a primary trainer, the T-28 was being flown in Vietnam by forward air controllers (FACs). This hazardous duty involved flying around the country at low altitude pinpointing strike targets for the jet fighters and attack aircraft, which were often A-4 Skyhawks, A-6 Intruders, F-8 Crusaders, or F-4 Phantoms. The T-28 was armed for this duty with phosphorous flare rockets, and the FAC would often be talking by radio directly to U.S. forces (Army or Marines) involved in a firefight, pinned down by enemy fire, and requesting air support. The FAC would dive on the enemy in the T-28, mark the location for the hostile fire with one or more flares, and then call in the airstrikes. The infantry soldiers on the front lines loved those brave pilots in the T-28s.

Duty as a forward air controller in Vietnam was one of the most hazardous occupations an aviator could be assigned to. When the enemy saw a T-28 in their area, they knew what it meant and tried to take it out. As a result, when one of those aircraft returned to base, it was often streaming fuel from holes in the wing tanks inflicted by ground fire, and it sometimes even had holes in the plexiglass canopy. The aircraft was then on the ground being patched up for a few days before being sent out on another mission.

Several members of my flight surgery class were assigned to Whiting Field and received all their basic pre-solo training in the T-28 instead of the T-34. This arrangement was made due to a shortage of T-34s at Saufley. These docs had actually requested this assignment when the call for several volunteers was made. I think the macho look and size of this magnificent aircraft lured them to it, but most of those fellows admitted they were intimidated once in the cockpit of the beast. Only a couple of them were allowed to solo. I was amazed any of them did. The T-28 was not a beginner's airplane!

My flight on that Tuesday afternoon was short; the T-28 FAM flight totaled 0.4 hours. When I climbed into the front cockpit, I was surprised at how high off the ground I was sitting. That airplane made the T-34 seem like a child's toy in comparison. We made two touch-and-go landings and then a full stop; that was it. The instructor let me follow along gently on the controls in an attempt to give me an idea of what it was like, but he did all the flying. It was a short hop but left an impression on me. The throaty sound of the huge radial engine and the feel of power on takeoff gave me a thrill. I hoped I would get more flight time in the T-28 and wondered if I would ever get the chance to fly one myself. The Navy was already starting to phase out the T-28, and it wouldn't be long until none were left.

51

I drove straight home from Whiting Field that afternoon after my T-28 FAM flight. By the time I turned into our driveway, a new storm system had arrived from the Gulf and it was blowing and raining sideways. All flight operations at Saufley were again canceled for the next two days. I spent my downtime in the Ready Room and studied as much as I could stand, but I was getting bored, frustrated, and discouraged.

Some of my classmates were not as far along on the syllabus as I was for various reasons—cancellations due to mechanicals, a shortage of instructors, and, of course, the inclement weather. We had been told some of us wouldn't finish, but this would not prevent any of us from receiving our gold flight surgeons' wings and reporting to our new operational duty stations on the date ordered. I badly wanted to finish my flight training, although I still hadn't decided whether I would choose to solo or not—even if I was signed off to do so.

When I awoke on March 9, the skies were clear, visibility was unlimited, and a light wind was blowing out of the south—a perfect day to fly. It had been nine days since I had flown the T-34, and I was praying I was on the day's flight schedule.

Martha needed the car for a trip to the commissary to buy groceries and run a few other errands, so she drove me to the base that morning. When she dropped me off in front of the training building, I told her I would call her to come pick me up when I was through for the day.

I walked into the Ready Room with my helmet bag in one hand and my study materials in the other. I looked at the white board and saw I was scheduled for my checkride on the first launch. The check pilot's name, next to mine on the board, was Grocci. A young lieutenant, whom I didn't know, was sitting on the edge of the scheduler's desk. I looked at the brown leather nametag on the front of his flight suit. The tag was embossed in gold with the naval aviator wings, and just below the insignia it said "LT Grocci."

I got LT Grocci's attention and said, "Good morning, Lieutenant, I'm Crawley."

"Well, LT Crawley, let's go brief."

LT Grocci seemed like a pretty laid-back fellow, which was a good thing because I was feeling nervous. The oral exam went well. He asked a few questions about aircraft systems and then had me recite some normal

197

and emergency checklist responses from memory. It almost seemed as if I was over-prepared, and he was apparently satisfied that I knew the material.

Before we left the briefing room, he explained that he would not be giving instruction on this flight or making any corrections unless a safety issue arose. He said once we were in the aircraft he expected me to conduct the flight as if he weren't there. I was to take off and fly to the designated practice airspace and then perform all the inflight maneuvers he requested. After that, he wanted me to find my way to Summerdale NOLF (Naval Outlying Field) in Alabama for touch-and-go landings.

When we got to the airplane, he asked a few more questions about the function of various components as I checked them on my walk-around inspection, and then we climbed in and took off.

I felt a little shaky on the takeoff and initial climb. After being off for nine days, I didn't have the comfortable "at home" feeling in the cockpit I had experienced on my last syllabus flight with Bradney. I settled down and was feeling better by the time we got to the practice area. I performed all the standard maneuvers; none of them were perfectly executed, but, in critiquing myself, I thought I had done a respectable job.

Grocci didn't make any comments after I finished each maneuver, but I knew he was taking notes on his kneeboard, and I would find out what he thought when we got back on the ground and into the debriefing room.

I had just recovered to straight and level flight after an intentional three-turn spin, straight down toward terra firma, when Grocci said, "Take me to Summerdale now, and we'll see if you know how to land."

All of our navigation training until that point had been by a combination of "dead reckoning" and "pilotage." Dead reckoning involves flying a specific compass heading at a specific airspeed for a specific amount of time to arrive at a point on an aeronautical chart. If used alone, dead reckoning is not very accurate, mostly as a result of wind drift and the effects of a tailwind or headwind on the speed and resulting distance calculations. Pilotage is simply flying with reference to prominent ground objects mapped on an aeronautical chart, such as towns, highways, intersections, airfields, water towers, etc. When pilotage is used in conjunction with dead reckoning, it makes an acceptable way to navigate visually in good weather.

I had flown to Summerdale NOLF and done landings with Bradney, so I followed the ground reference points I had memorized and had no trouble finding the field. I checked the windsock, entered the pattern, and started doing my "bounces" (a common reference for touch-and-go landing practice). The first couple of landings were not nearly as nicely executed as those on my last flight, but they were acceptable. I had just completed my third one and was turning downwind for another one when Grocci said, "Make this one a full stop."

My mind started racing and my heart started pounding. Did this mean what I thought it did? When we got on the ground was he going to ask me if I wanted to solo?

I landed the airplane and brought it to a stop on the runway. There were no taxiways to get off on, but the field had no other traffic. I waited for him to ask me if I wanted to solo now.

Grocci didn't "ask" me anything. I had the parking brake set with the engine still running. He said, "Doc, I'm getting out. You turn around, taxi down to the approach end of the runway, take off, and do two touch-and-goes and then a full stop. Pick me up right here, then I'll have you take me back to Saufley."

I wanted to say, "Wait—I am not sure I want to do this—I don't know if I am ready." I turned my head and saw him climb onto the wing and hop down onto the pavement. He didn't give me a chance to tell him I hadn't decided yet whether or not I was going to solo. Didn't he know I wasn't a *real* aviator? I was only a doctor, after all, and doctors weren't required to solo.

It was too late to tell him anything. I was going flying.

52

I slowly taxied the little orange and white airplane toward the end of the runway, where I would begin my takeoff roll. The white stripes painted down the center of the pavement disappeared beneath the nose of the T-34 as I inched toward the approach end. The almost dreamlike effect on me was like watching a movie in slow motion as the trees at the airfield's edge passed by. It felt as if time had almost stopped. The stream of thoughts rushing around in my head was not in synch with all this, and I tried my best to slow everything down. If I taxied slowly enough, maybe I would have the mishmash in my head all sorted out by the time I reached the pavement's end.

I turned around at the runway's end and faced into the wind. I accomplished the run-up checklist and then pushed the throttle up to the stop. As I accelerated down the runway, the thought actually crossed my mind one more time that I still hadn't made up my mind as to whether or not I would solo.

The wheels lifted off, and, with the canopy open and an 80-miles-per-hour wind in my face, I let out a big "yahoo." LT Grocci, standing in the grass at the side of the runway, most assuredly heard my war whoop as I passed 50 feet above him. I was feeling a level of pure exhilaration I had never felt before. He knew that sensation and, no doubt, got a surge of adrenaline himself by being the only witness to this most exciting moment in an aviator's life.

I didn't have to worry about the landing gear. The procedure in the training command was to leave the gear down for touch-and-go landings. This was intended to reduce the possibility of a gear-up landing. So I didn't touch the gear handle.

The sober realization of being all alone by myself in the air for the first time didn't hit me until I leveled off at pattern altitude on the downwind leg for the first touch-and-go; that was when I looked down and saw Grocci, now a small speck, 800 feet below. He was sitting in the grass next to the runway looking up at me, which caused a brief sensation of panic. I got over it quickly by reading and accomplishing the landing checklist. As I started my left descending turn to line up on final approach, I started talking to myself. I tried to anticipate what LTJG Bradney would be saying to me right then. I uttered his mantra, "Trim…trim…trim," and, as I lined up on final, I watched my airspeed indicator like a hawk, saying aloud, "Airspeed…airspeed…airspeed."

By the time I touched down, I was pretty tense and jerky on the controls. My first bounce was indeed a bit of a bounce and not real pretty. I touched on the left main gear, then on the right main gear, again on the left, and then the nose wheel touched and I "wheelbarrowed" for a ways down the runway. At this point, I decided it was time to abort before bouncing off the runway and likely running over LT Grocci. I don't know why he didn't realize he wasn't standing in a very safe place. I pushed the power up and got out of there before it got worse. I later recalled someone telling me the adage that "any landing you can walk away from is a good one." I should have gotten credit for several landings on that one touch-and-go.

Once I was back in the air, I calmed down and loosened up. I tried to pretend Bradney was sitting behind me and talking to me. I did his talking for him and brought the plane around for another one. It was a good one.

By the third landing, my confidence level was growing fast and I felt pretty darn good. When I rolled to a stop next to Grocci, I saw a smile that was probably as big as the one on my face. He looked as though he had enjoyed my first solo flight as much as I had.

He climbed in, and I took him back to Saufley. I then found out the day wasn't over yet.

53

When LT Grocci and I sat down in the debriefing room, I thought he was going to chew me out about my first solo landing, but instead he said, "You made a good decision to abort that first touch-and-go. It was getting ugly after about the third bounce, but you did exactly what you should have done. You had a good checkride. Nice job." That was the extent of the debrief. The lieutenant seemed to be a man of few words. I liked him.

He then took my logbook and started writing. "I'm signing you off for solo," he said. "Go grab some lunch and then go check out an airplane."

He explained that my three solo takeoffs and landings didn't count as my first solo flight. My "official" solo flight would require taking off from Saufley, navigating to one of the outlying Navy fields, practicing a few touch-and-go landings, and then returning to NAS Saufley. He told me I could practice all the flight maneuvers I had learned and then practice landings at any of the outlying fields I had previously been to. He instructed me to plan my flight so I was back at Saufley in two hours or less.

I went to the Ready Room and sat down next to my friend Paul Broadbent. Paul gave me a big smile and asked, "How did it go?" I gave him a minute-by-minute account of my flight and described LT Grocci. I ate a few bites of a sandwich I had brown-bagged from home, but I was pretty keyed up and didn't have much of an appetite.

Student pilots and instructors moved in and out of the room as I picked at my lunch and talked with Paul. By the time I had eaten as much as I could eat, Paul and I were the only ones left in the room. He told me I was going to be one of the first flight surgeons in our class to solo and that he was so far behind he probably would not get the opportunity. He seemed depressed about it and admitted his envy as I was about to depart on my solo flight. I joked, "Maybe you should just climb in the back seat and go with me—how about that?"

I was completely kidding, but Paul's eyes lit up and he said, "I'd love to go with you. Why not? We could walk out to the airplane together, and anyone watching would just think it was an instructor and his student going up." He was serious.

Paul's excitement about this crazy idea made me think somewhat seriously about taking him along on my first solo flight. We talked about it for several minutes and considered the possible consequences of getting caught. We both had the rather naïve idea that, with the war going on and the military needing doctors so badly, nothing much would happen to us. We had both watched the first few episodes of the TV series *M*A*S*H* and saw all the shenanigans Capt. "Hawkeye" Pierce and Capt. "Trapper" John McIntyre got away with as rule-bending military doctors, with little or no consequence. This wasn't Hollywood though, and neither of us considered the reality that we would both likely be court-martialed and our careers finished if we were caught pulling off such a stunt.

I finally came to my senses when I considered that I would be responsible for Paul's life if he accompanied me; just worrying about getting myself back alive was enough. The fact Paul would even consider riding in the back seat on my first solo flight was just one more indication of what a wacky seeker of adventure my new friend was.

I left Paul sitting dejected in the Ready Room as I walked out the door, helmet bag in hand, to go check out an airplane and soar alone into the wild blue yonder.

54

I stood at the maintenance desk and went over every page of the aircraft maintenance log with a fine-toothed comb. I had done this before each syllabus flight, but Bradney's experienced eye was always looking over my shoulder; now I was on my own. I wanted to make sure every "gripe" written up by a pilot had been corrected by maintenance and properly signed off. I took my time. I read a couple of entries for which I didn't understand the write-up or sign-off. The duty maintenance chief petty officer patiently explained them to me until I was finally satisfied.

The aircraft sign-out log, in which LTJG Bradney had always signed for the aircraft, lay on the desk. I wrote in this book for the first time, entering the time and date, the aircraft number, and my signature and service number. I slung one of my parachute straps over my shoulder, picked up my helmet bag, and started toward the door that led to the tarmac. The maintenance chief smiled at me and said, "Have a nice flight, Lieutenant."

When I got to the aircraft, I did the most careful walk-around inspection I had ever done. Once in the cockpit, I went through the pre-start checklist at the same meticulously slow pace.

I then fired up the engine and taxied toward the active runway. With the canopy open and the wind blowing in my face, I could feel the adrenaline flowing through my body. It was a wonderful kind of excitement, both exhilarating and scary at the same time. Several other T-34s joined me in line on the taxiway, but my aircraft was the only one on the field at the time with a sole occupant. The aircraft in front of me and behind me each had a student in the front seat and an instructor in the back. To these other pilots, seeing me alone in my craft must have been the same as if I had a big sign on the side of my plane that read "Student Driver."

The exhilaration I felt as I broke ground on this, my official solo flight, did not quite match what I had felt that morning, but it was, nonetheless, a wonderful feeling. I climbed to 8,500 feet and headed directly toward Summerdale NOLF in Alabama. I had just been there, and I didn't want to risk getting lost by trying to find my way to one of the other outlying Navy practice fields. On the way there, I had an emergency landing field picked out every minute to use in the event of an engine failure. We had practiced every possible emergency over and over again, but encountering such a situation during my solo flight was, nevertheless, a nagging worry I could not get out of my head.

On the way to Summerdale, I practiced a few steep turns and a couple of gentle, power-off aerodynamic stalls. These maneuvers, ironically, increased my confidence a bit. By the time I entered the pattern at the field, I was relaxed on the stick and flew three nice approaches to three smooth touch-and-go landings. I was feeling pretty good when I left the pattern and headed back to Saufley.

I made a full-stop landing at the air station and taxied back to the flight line. I secured the aircraft and headed across the ramp. I had logged one hour of solo flight time and four takeoffs and landings. I signed the aircraft in with no new maintenance "gripes," checked in my parachute at the paraloft, and went back to the Ready Room.

LTJG Bradney was waiting for me. His constant look of grim worry was gone—replaced by a big grin. He shook my hand, congratulated me, and said, "We're going to the Club. You're buying."

I then spotted Paul Broadbent sitting right where I had left him; he was smiling too.

I said, "Okay—we're going to the Club, but Dr. Broadbent is going with us."

55

I was happy Bradney didn't announce to all the flight suits in the club that I had just completed my first solo flight. I had heard stories about guys being expected to buy a round for every table in the bar and was relieved he hadn't put me on display and cleaned out my wallet. That might have put a damper on my celebratory mood. We found a table for just the three of us, and I ordered a pitcher of beer.

I think Paul (Broadbent) was suffering from a bit of jealousy by the time I finished relating, with unbridled enthusiasm, the events of my day. He was full of questions, nevertheless, and seemed to share some of my excitement, if only vicariously. Neither of us said a word about the crazy idea of taking him along as a stowaway on my solo flight and how close we'd come to doing it. I suspect Bradney would have thought both of us were a little nuts if we'd revealed those foolish musings.

Paul and I learned a little more about LTJG Bradney that afternoon. He told us he was a "plough back." This term, he explained, was used to describe an aviator who became an instructor right after receiving his wings; he was "ploughed back" into the training command he had just left as a student, but was now in the role of instructor. Bradney confessed that I was one of his first students and he really didn't have much total flight time logged—less than 500 hours. That still seemed like a lot to Paul and me, but later I realized, with more experience under my belt, it wasn't a whole lot of flight time. Bradney's self-deprecating admissions didn't change my opinion of him in the slightest. I still thought he knew everything there was to know about airplanes and aviation.

He told us that most new aviators would not like receiving orders back to the training command. Most were anxious to get to their fleet assignments as soon as they received their wings. He, on the other hand, said he enjoyed being an instructor. His eventual goal was to become a commercial airline pilot, and he hoped to build multiengine time in the Navy by being assigned to a squadron of P-3 Orions. The P-3, a large four-engine turboprop, is used for anti-submarine warfare, and qualifying in the P-3 would look good on a résumé as would his time as an instructor.

Bradney asked me if I planned to take civilian flying lessons and get my Private Pilot license. He informed me there was a naval flying club at NAS North Island in San Diego, where I would be stationed. He thought the club would provide a great opportunity for me to continue honing my piloting skills. Although I really enjoyed flying, I explained that I had a busy career path in medicine ahead of me and wasn't sure I could fit it in. I hadn't decided at that point whether or not I wanted to take it any further.

After we had finished our beers, I said I was anxious to get home to tell Martha about my solo flight and do a little celebrating with her. I then suddenly remembered Martha had the car for the day. When I mentioned I would have to call her to pick me up, Paul Broadbent offered to drop me off at my house on his way home. I slapped him on the shoulder, and we all got up and headed for the door.

As we walked out of the O' Club, I turned and shook LTJG Bradney's hand, thanking him for putting up with such a challenging student and getting me through the syllabus. I told him I thought he was a great instructor. I didn't know whether I would ever again use any of the skills and techniques he had patiently taught me over the previous few weeks, but it had been an experience of a lifetime that I would never forget.

That afternoon was the last time I saw Paul Bradney. Over my ensuing years in the Navy, I never stopped looking for him, but our paths never crossed again.

Holding Baby Jill next to a T-34 Mentor after my first solo flight
NAS Saufley Field, Florida

March 1973

56

Martha was still out on her errands when Paul dropped me off at our house. I was on my second bottle of Budweiser when I heard her pulling into the driveway. I skipped jubilantly out the front door, waving my bottle of beer over my head.

"Guess what I did today," I shouted as she stepped from the car.

I gave her a big hug and kiss and then opened the rear car door and scooped Jill out of her baby seat. "Guess what Daddy did today," I bubbled at her. She just grinned at me and said, "Dada!"

The three of us celebrated all evening.

I was finished with all my training in Pensacola. I still had to drive to Saufley every morning for the next couple of weeks for a brief check-in, until the rest of my class was released. It was a relaxing time for me, and Martha, Jill and I spent several nice spring afternoons on Santa Rosa Beach.

Most of our class completed all the lessons in the basic flight syllabus, and almost everyone who wanted to solo was able to do so. My adventurous friend, Paul Broadbent, unfortunately did not finish. He had fallen too far behind in his training during the February stretch of nasty weather. I felt badly for him.

On Thursday, March 22, our class of 41 physicians assembled in the auditorium at the main base, NAS Pensacola. We were dressed in our Service Dress Blue uniforms for the formal presentation of our wings. The event was similar to a college graduation; the commanding officer of the Naval Aerospace Medical Institute presided over the ceremony, awarding individual wings and official certificates.

Some of my fellow flight surgeons had family members attending who had flown in for the occasion. Several of the guys came from military families and their fathers or grandfathers were present, wearing their old uniforms, to pin the gold wings on their new young officers. Martha walked up to the podium with me and pinned mine on my uniform. A photographer took a formal picture of each new naval flight surgeon as he exited the stage. Martha posed next to me in front of a dark curtain as the shutter clicked and the flashbulb popped.

The certificate that designated me a U.S. naval flight surgeon was printed on parchment with raised gold print. I had the document properly framed and have proudly displayed it at each of our homes for the many intervening years.

I received another certificate that morning of which I was equally proud. I soon had this document framed for display as well. Also printed on fine paper, it stated:

THIS IS TO CERTIFY THAT ON THIS DATE, THE 9TH DAY OF MARCH, 1973, LT DAVID B. CRAWLEY DID, ALONE AND UNASSISTED, TAKE OFF AND RETURN TO NAS SAUFLEY THEREBY SUCCESSFULLY COMPLETING HIS FIRST SOLO FLIGHT.

Three days after the ceremony, my little family and I pulled out of our driveway in our heavily loaded Oldsmobile station wagon, setting out on our long road trip from Pensacola to San Diego, where I would be stationed for the next two years.

Winging Ceremony - March 22, 1973

57

October 1973

"Hey Doc, would you mind flying straight and level for a little while? I'm not feeling too well." This request came through the earphones of my helmet as I controlled the T-28 Trojan from the front pilot seat. I had just completed a barrel roll; it was about my twelfth one in a row as I tried to make each one a little more precise than the previous one.

This was the first thing Bob had said for some time, and I was wondering why he had become so quiet. I turned my head as far as I could to one side and was just able to catch sight of him in my peripheral vision, sitting behind me in the rear pilot's seat. Bob's face definitely looked a little pale and seemed to even have a slight tinge of green to it.

"Oh, sorry, Bob. How about if we go over to San Clemente Island and do a few touch-and-goes?"

He answered weakly, "Anything—just as long as we stay right-side up."

It was a clear day with almost unlimited visibility. I could see the island, which belonged to the U.S. Navy, and I set a course to make an entry into the traffic pattern. I did three touch-and-goes before Bob finally came up again on the ICS and said, "I'm okay now, Dave; I'll take it and do a few."

I felt a little shake of the stick, his signal to me that he had control, and he confirmed the switchover by saying, "I have the aircraft." With that, I let go of the front control stick and said, "You've got it."

Bob Hawley and I had been practicing aerobatics in the military restricted airspace over the Pacific Ocean, just west of San Diego. When we started out that morning, Bob gave a demo of each maneuver and then let me try each one as he critiqued me. We did a few loops, some aileron rolls, a Half Cuban eight, and then some barrel rolls. We had been alternating control of the aircraft back and forth until Bob said, "Take the aircraft, Doc, and practice whatever you want."

I found the barrel roll to be one of the most difficult maneuvers to perform correctly. The first half of the maneuver involves a climbing turn of 90 degrees of heading change while rolling the aircraft around its longitudinal axis. At the top of the climbing turn, the aircraft should be inverted and on a heading exactly 90 degrees from the original one. The second half of the maneuver is a mirror image of the first half as the roll is smoothly continued, from the upside-down position, and a 90-degree descending turn is made back to the original heading and altitude. If the barrel roll is executed correctly, the pilot rolls the wings level just as he arrives at the original altitude and levels off, and the compass stops turning and indicates the original heading. The maneuver involves precise, smooth coordination between rudder, aileron, and elevator controls. In addition, it is desirable to maintain the same speed throughout the maneuver, which requires close monitoring of the airspeed indicator, advancing the throttles during the first-half's climbing turn and roll, then retarding the throttles during the second-half's descending turn and roll.

The barrel roll requires such a precise degree of coordination of controls that I had a hard time believing it was even possible to do a perfect one, but I decided I would try…..and try…..and try. I have to admit I felt badly that my quest for perfection had made Bob sick. I should have realized something was not right when he stopped talking, but it had gotten so quiet I had almost forgotten he was back there. It was as if I had entered a private world of my own.

Shortly after I had checked in for duty at NAS North Island, I saw four T-28s sitting on the flight line near the station's air ops building. I went into the scheduling office and found that those four aircraft were permanently assigned to the air station to be used primarily for proficiency flying by aviators assigned to desk jobs. I told the first class petty officer at the desk I wanted to log at least some of my monthly flying hours in those T-28s. He took care of me and put me on the schedule for a night flight the following day with an aviator named Joe Hall.

It was 5:30 PM on May 3, a beautiful clear evening, when I pulled into the base ops parking lot for my first flight out of NAS North Island. As I got out of my car, I noticed a tall fellow stepping out of his car at the same time. He was dressed in an olive-green flight suit matching mine. The two of us, with helmet bags in hand, converged on the sidewalk leading to the front of the building. I checked his rank insignia on his "piss cutter" hat and saw he was a lieutenant like me, so there was no required salute, and we each just said hello. As we continued walking toward the door, I looked up at this big fellow and asked, "Are you Joe Hall?"

"Yes, I am," he answered, turning his head to look directly down at my face.

"Well, I'm on the schedule to fly with you tonight."

We both stopped to shake hands as I introduced myself. Joe had a curious smile on his face, and, releasing my hand, he pointed his finger at me, saying "I think I know you."

"I think I know *you*," I said, pointing my finger back up at him.

We stood there on the sidewalk racking our brains trying to figure out where we had met. It didn't take us long to recall we both had gone to high school together at Bishop Miege High in Shawnee Mission, Kansas, a suburb of Kansas City. We had actually known one another pretty well back then. Our meeting again as adults, a long way from high school years and our Kansas roots, was an amazing coincidence.

Joe and I went on a 6.5-hour "round-robin" cross-country flight that night in a T-28, making a fuel stop at Beale Air Force Base in Northern California. While the plane got fueled up, we walked over to the gedunk (snack bar), where Joe introduced me to the "Beale Burger." After chowing down, we obtained an updated weather brief and then took off to resume our cross-country. We landed back at North Island well after midnight. Life is full of delightful surprises at times. Neither of us could have predicted such a serendipitous reunion after all those years, and Joe and I flew many more flights together over the next few months.

By the time fall had arrived, I was well acquainted with four of the naval aviators who flew the T-28s regularly. I had become friends with these guys, and they started calling me when they scheduled a flight to see if I was available to join them. Bob Hawley and Joe Hall were two of those four pilots, and I probably flew with Bob and Joe the most.

All of my new aviator friends seemed like frustrated instructor-pilots who would have been happy to be in the training command teaching budding naval aviators how to fly. All four of these guys apparently loved having a student to teach, and I was willing and happy to be that student. Every flight with one of my new friends was a lesson in which they generously shared their knowledge, skills, and discipline with me, and I couldn't get enough of it.

Being a flight surgeon provided me a welcome break from clinic duties at the dispensary when I went flying. Most mornings I worked in Enlisted Sick Call, Officers' Sick Call, or I did physical exams in the Aviation Exam Room. I scheduled appointments for senior officers or retirees most afternoons, but one or two afternoons each week I was free of all clinic duties and scheduled for "squadron time." That was when I tried to get my flight time in.

The GMOs (general medical officers) attached to the dispensary did not have squadron time and had to be on duty in the clinic five days a week. They were all a little disgruntled about the fact that the flight surgeons didn't seem to pull their equal share of the patient load and got to "go play" a couple of days each week. Whenever I heard any remarks along those lines, I told the complainer I was sure the Navy was still accepting applications for the flight surgery program and he should put in his request. He could then also benefit from the extra pay we received, designated "hazardous duty pay," which was another sore point. My remarks didn't usually do much to slow down the complaining, but I enjoyed teasing them a bit.

Flying the Navy T-28 Trojan
Cross-country flight from NAS North Island to Nellis Air Force Base

November 8, 1973

216

58

North Island Naval Air Station is located on the northwestern end of Coronado Island, and it occupies a little over half the area of the island. The military base shares the island with the City of Coronado, which is spread over the remaining land at the southeast end. The "island" is not a true island, as it is connected to the mainland by a long narrow spit of sand to the south. This connection is known as the "Silver Strand," and it separates San Diego Bay from the Pacific Ocean. The Strand has a two-lane state highway running the length of it, connecting Coronado with the town of Imperial Beach, California.

Near the southwest end of the island, on the shore of the Pacific, is the sprawling Del Coronado Hotel, a National Historic Landmark. The hotel was built in 1888 and is said to be one of the largest wooden structures in the United States. Many famous celebrities have vacationed at the hotel over the years, and it has been the venue for filming a number of Hollywood movies.

Just to the south of the City of Coronado, at the northern end of the Silver Strand, the Navy has another facility known as the Naval Amphibious Base Coronado. This is the West Coast training facility for the Navy's elite Special Forces units known as the SEALS.

When our little family arrived on April 11, 1973, we crossed San Diego Bay to the island on the relatively new Coronado Bay Bridge, which had opened for traffic in August of 1969. Prior to that time, Coronado was accessible only by ferry from San Diego, or by driving around the bay to the south and then north along the Silver Strand from Imperial Beach. At the island-end of the bridge, we paid a 75-cent toll. When we cleared the toll booth, we were on the island. It immediately seemed as if time almost stopped as we entered this little Garden of Eden. I had just negotiated some of California's busiest and most congested high-speed freeways on the east side of San Diego Bay, and I could feel the tension drop away. Martha and I both felt as if we had been magically dropped into a real-life version of Walt Disney's Magic Kingdom.

We rolled down the windows of the car as we toured the quiet streets of our new home. The weather that day was beautiful, with clear skies, light winds, and a perfect temperature of 75 degrees. We hadn't yet learned that this was just another typical Coronado day its residents were used to and generally expected. We sensed a sweet fragrance in the air, wafting from the abundant colorful blooms along the sidewalks and beautifully landscaped yards. We marveled at the amazing variety of trees lining each side of the streets—palm trees, California pepper trees, Norfolk pines, Torrey pines, and the stately white-barked eucalyptus.

We slowed the car to a creep as we gawked at the beautiful houses along the streets of this serene little town. Most were relatively small homes on small lots, but they were all perfectly maintained. We noticed a variety of architectural styles, including English Tudor, New England colonial, Spanish adobe, French country, craftsman bungalow, Italian Renaissance, a few Victorians, and even a couple of contemporaries. Somehow, this mixture of styles seemed to meld together to present a most pleasing picture, making this town seem even more unique.

Coronado appeared to be a little utopia. It had the quaint ambiance of a small town, and, although isolated on an island, it had all the conveniences of a moderate-sized city, San Diego, just across the bridge over the bay.

Before crossing the bridge to the island, both Martha and I were experiencing some negative feelings about being stationed in the bustling San Diego area and were lamenting the fact I hadn't gotten my first choice of duty on quiet and remote Whidbey Island in our beloved Pacific Northwest. By the time we finished our self-guided tour of Coronado, we were beginning to think this place might not be so bad after all.

I reported to the officer of the day at the base to officially sign the log and check in. We then proceeded to the on-base Navy Lodge and got a hotel-style room located right on the beach. This would serve as temporary quarters for a few days until we could find permanent housing.

We started looking for a place to live the next day. We were expecting our second child in a few months, so we wanted to find quarters that would accommodate our growing family. No on-base housing was available for junior officers, so we started looking in the City of Coronado for a home. We considered buying a house, but we quickly gave up that idea when we found real estate prices were way out of our range. Some of the little houses for sale were priced as high as $60,000 or even $70,000, a hefty price tag in 1973 dollars. The mortgage payments would not be possible on my junior officer's salary. We adjusted to searching for a house to rent, and, by the end of the day, we had found the perfect place.

The house was an old, well-built, three-bedroom craftsman-style home at 544 "A" Avenue. The shingled siding was stained dark brown, giving it a woodsy, rustic look—just our style. There was a covered front porch with river-rock pillars and a pretty little shaded front yard. A children's swing set stood in the backyard, just waiting for Jill, and the yard also featured a pretty flagstone patio. The home was situated two blocks from beautiful Spreckels Park, a popular gathering spot for young mothers with toddlers, and it was three blocks from Sacred Heart Catholic Church.

We walked through the home with the managing agent and both fell in love with it immediately. The rent was $225 per month, which was at the upper limit of our budget, but we rationalized that we would save money by living on the island and avoiding commuting expenses. The house was less than a mile from the main gate of the air station where I would be working—an easy bicycle ride away.

Martha and I didn't have to say anything to each other before reaching our joint decision. We hadn't been in the house for more than five minutes when I looked at Martha, she looked at me, and I said, "We'll take it."

544 "A" Avenue, Coronado, California – March 1973

59

I bought a three-speed "English" bike at the Navy Exchange the first week we were in our new home, and I rode it to work at the NAS North Island Dispensary every day. The dispensary was a pre-World War II building, a beautiful, rambling adobe structure with a red-tile roof. Its offices and treatment rooms surrounded a lush central courtyard planted with orange trees, all loaded with oranges. At the rear of the building was an ambulance ramp leading to a small emergency room. My assigned office was at the front of the building, just to the right of the main entrance.

My medical duties at the dispensary were not very challenging. The population I served generally consisted of young, healthy people. None of them would have been accepted into the military service if there was much wrong with them. My work mostly involved performing large numbers of routine physicals and treating minor illnesses. Everything had to be thoroughly documented, and that resulted in a fair amount of administrative paperwork.

Most illnesses I treated seemed to be related to the fact that the majority of my patients were living in close quarters together. Upper respiratory infection was the most common illness, but I saw a significant number of patients with dermatologic problems. After a few months, I could diagnose most common skin rashes when the patient walked into the room. Whenever a young sailor presented with a skin rash, though, primary syphilis always had to be ruled out. Venereal diseases were rampant among this young, predominantly male population. I had a minimum of prior training and experience diagnosing and treating this array of infectious diseases, but within a few months I became a VD expert.

I occasionally treated a traumatic injury of some sort. The Shore Patrol would deliver a sailor who had started a brawl in one of the local watering holes, gotten his clock cleaned, and needed to have his face re-attached. Other times, our ambulance would bring in victims from a car accident, but if it involved any obvious serious trauma, the injured were taken directly to Balboa Naval Hospital, across the bridge in San Diego. I usually encountered these trauma cases when I was the medical officer of the day (MOD), and most of them presented late at night or in the wee hours of the morning.

Our clinic was well staffed, so each of the medical officers was scheduled for duty only three or four times per month. When I served as the medical officer of the day, the enlisted corpsmen treated most of the minor illnesses and injuries, and they even sutured the simple lacerations. Some nights on call, they let me sleep through the entire night, but most of the corpsmen knew when they were facing something a little beyond their level of training and would summon the medical officer from his slumber in such cases.

On my duty nights, I occasionally admitted a patient overnight for observation. Most of the time, this was for acute alcohol intoxication. We had a small ward with a couple of beds for that purpose. Other than that, we transferred patients requiring admission or specialty care to Balboa Naval Hospital.

One morning I arrived at the dispensary for work, parked my bike, entered the front door, and was just rounding the corner into my office when Bea Hamby, our civilian nurse, met me and grabbed me by the arm.

Bea always looked professional in her spotless white uniform dress, white shoes, and with a stiffly starched white cap perched on her head. She was a little animated at all times, but, on this particular morning, she seemed a little more charged up than usual as she asked, "Dr. Crawley, could you come back to Waves' Sick Call and see a patient I've got back there with severe menstrual cramps?"

I set my backpack down on the gray metal bookcase that stood along one wall of my office and picked up the Plan of the Day, which was lying on my desk. I checked the document and said, "Bea, I'm not scheduled for Waves' Sick Call this morning. It looks like Dr. Tulumello is going to be working with you today."

"Doctor, Dr. Tulumello is not here yet, and I need someone to look at this poor girl right away. She is in terrible pain…come on, Doc, let's go." She steered me into the hall.

"Okay, Bea, but our little hyper Italian doctor is going to owe me for this."

The Waves' Sick Call exam room was located in the rear of the building, on the opposite side of the courtyard from my office. As we reached the rear corridor and hurried toward the exam room, I could hear the patient moaning in pain. The immediate thought in my mind at that point was this must be something more serious than menstrual cramps.

When I entered the exam room, I saw Bea had already positioned the young woman for a pelvic exam; she was covered with a paper drape and her feet were up in the stirrups. I didn't like that. I always preferred to sit and talk to a female patient face-to-face, take a medical history, and try to get her comfortable and relaxed before putting her into this compromising exam position. I walked to the head of the table and stood to one side where we could see each other and chat.

Between anguishing cries of pain, I was able to extract a few bits of information. She explained she had a long history of painful menstrual periods, but never this severe. She said her periods had been irregular for several months, but she was vague about when her last completely normal menstruation was. I wasn't getting much information of any value from her and wasn't sure whether that was due to her extreme discomfort or because she was just an unreliable historian.

I finally told her I needed to examine her and requested she try to stay as relaxed as possible. I put on a pair of latex gloves and moved to the other end of the exam table. Bea turned on the goose-neck floor lamp she had positioned there, handed me a vaginal speculum, and then I pushed back the drape covering her perineal area.

My eyes about popped from their sockets; I couldn't believe what I was seeing. I immediately lost all of my professionalism as Bea and I both exclaimed simultaneously, "HOLY #@*!" The metal vaginal speculum fell from my hands and clanked onto the tile floor.

The top of an infant's head was clearly visible with a nice crop of dark hair on the scalp.

I put my left hand on top of the drape over my patient's abdomen and palpated. Judging from the size of the distended uterus, I estimated this was a full-term or near-full-term pregnancy. Bea squirted some lubricant from a tube onto the gloved fingers of my right hand, and I did a careful digital vaginal exam. The cervix was essentially fully effaced and dilated to between nine and ten centimeters.

"Bea, run to the ER and get the emergency OB kit—and please hurry," I ordered. Bea was muttering something unintelligible as she scurried out of the room, and I had no clue as to what she'd said.

While Bea was gone, I asked the young lady when she might have gotten pregnant. She told me, adamantly and in no uncertain terms, that she was NOT and COULD NOT be pregnant. I then had to inform her of the reality that, not only was she pregnant, she was about ready to deliver a baby and the birth would probably occur within the next few minutes. Before she had a chance to get into much of a disagreement over my diagnosis, she began to moan with another labor contraction. Bea came crashing through the door about that time, with two corpsmen accompanying her, carrying an emergency delivery pack and various other supplies.

I gowned up in short order, put on a surgical cap and mask, and quickly re-gloved and sat back down on the stool at the "business end" of the exam table. Everything was then organized and under control, and I was sitting there thinking how fun it was going to be to deliver a baby in the North Island Dispensary—maybe the first such occasion ever. Our patient, between contractions, kept repeating, "I'm not pregnant, I can't be pregnant." I rolled my eyes at Bea over the top of my mask, and I was sure she was thinking the same thing I was. We both doubted this was a case of immaculate conception. I suspect I had a big smile on my face at that point, and Bea could probably "see" that smile despite the fact my mouth was covered by the surgical mask.

Word apparently spread through the dispensary at the speed of light that I was getting ready to deliver a baby in Waves' Sick Call because the commanding officer, Captain Youngman, suddenly bolted through the door in a state of agitation. The captain, who was my boss, immediately informed me I was NOT going to deliver a baby in HIS dispensary. He assured me we were not properly equipped for such a procedure and it would be unsafe.

I responded calmly, "Captain, I don't think we have a choice here. This young lady is almost crowning at the moment. And, sir, I have done a large number of deliveries, have successfully managed a number of obstetrical complications, and I am completely confident I can deliver this baby, successfully and safely, right here in this room." I also argued that I would much rather deliver the baby in this controlled environment than in an ambulance in the middle of the Coronado Bay Bridge.

The argument didn't last long. The captain ordered the corpsmen to get my patient on a gurney immediately, put her in an ambulance, and transport her, with lights and siren, to Balboa Naval Hospital in San Diego. As the young woman was being wheeled out of the exam room, the captain instructed her to keep her legs tightly together, take shallow breaths, and try not to push.

I was crestfallen that Captain Youngman had ruined the only exciting thing I had encountered in my job at the North Island Dispensary. Beyond that, I felt it was a bad decision. I thought I still might get to deliver the baby and knew it might be the only opportunity I would ever have in my career to perform a delivery in an ambulance, but, for my patient's sake and the welfare of the infant, I hoped we'd make it to the hospital.

It was a wild ride, and I did my best to keep my patient calm. When we arrived at the hospital, we rushed through the Emergency Room and straight to the OB elevator. The department had been alerted and the crew was ready for us. I advised them to bypass a labor room and wheel her directly into the delivery room. When we got her in the room, I helped the crew scoot her quickly onto the delivery table.

The OB resident was right there too. I thought he should offer the courtesy of allowing me to perform the delivery, but he was scrubbed and gloved, and I was not, so I guess it wasn't even a consideration.

One good push and the doctor had a healthy-looking 6½-pound boy wriggling in his hands. He ended up having all the fun of bringing a new life into the world, chalking up one more routine delivery to his credit.

The resident clamped and tied the cord, then handed the newborn off to the waiting pediatrics resident to examine.

I wanted to say goodbye to my patient and wish her well, but too many people were in the room and too much was going on. The new mother was just staring off toward the side wall of the room; I think she was in a trance-like state of disbelief and denial. No one seemed to even notice I was still in the room, so I quietly slipped out the door.

We had a much calmer ride in the ambulance returning across the bridge to Coronado. I have to admit I was a little dejected, but I was happy it had all turned out alright for my patient. I never saw her or her infant again and have always wondered how the rest of their lives turned out.

60

Bea Hamby, RN, worked at the North Island Naval Dispensary as a civilian contractor. To say Bea was somewhat of a character would be a serious understatement. I can safely say that all the physicians on the staff, as well as the enlisted medical corpsmen, loved working with her. She had an eternally cheerful disposition, seemed to have boundless energy, and was hilariously funny. On top of everything else, Bea was an excellent nurse.

I enjoyed working with Bea as much as everyone else did. She had a way of making our dull clinic work seem fun. She was always making funny little observations about our patients or telling jokes, some of which were a little off-color. She was also blatantly flirtatious with all the young medical officers, including me. Bea had been married to Dr. Hamby, a cardiologist in Coronado, but was recently divorced and didn't seem at all upset about that.

I recall one morning when she came into my office, sat on the side of my desk, and hiked her skirt up well-above her knees, so that one of her stockinged thighs was right in my face. I wasn't sure whether she was seriously attempting to seduce me, or whether she was just doing this to see my reaction as a zany way of entertaining herself.

Every doctor on staff experienced Bea's flirtations at one time or another. Whenever a few of us got together, we had a good laugh out of her playful behavior. I don't think any of the doctors took her seriously, since she was old enough to have been a mother to any of us. She was a nice-looking woman for her age, but her bifocal glasses were a dead giveaway. None of us knew at the time how old Bea was, but I later learned she was born in 1918, which made her 55 years old in 1973. I don't think there was a medical officer on staff, other than the commanding officer, who had yet reached the age of 30. Besides that, most of the physicians were married, and several of us had small children.

It didn't take me long to learn Bea was a bit of a social butterfly in Coronado. It seemed she knew almost everyone in the town. I found out she was a member of the Coronado Yacht Club and often went sailing with friends who were members there or were members of the San Diego Yacht Club or Southwestern Yacht Club on the other side of the bay.

I started picking her brain about yachting in San Diego, since I had been dying to get a sailboat from the moment we arrived on the island. She had answers for all my questions.

If I bought a sailboat, I wasn't sure how I could make payments on it with my meager military paycheck. Bea suggested I get a moonlighting job at the Emergency Room of the civilian Coronado Hospital. She made some phone calls, provided a recommendation for me, and set me up for an interview. I got the job and started working several nights a week.

We hadn't lived in Coronado quite a month yet when Bea told me about a scheduled weekend boat show to be held in San Diego on Shelter Island. I went to the show and took the big leap, making a down payment on a 27-foot Catalina sailboat. She then hooked me up with a loan officer at the local Bank of California to finance our extravagant new toy.

Boat slips and moorings were at a premium in San Diego; dock space was both limited and expensive. Bea clued me in on a deal the San Diego Yacht Club offered to officers on active duty in the military: the club waved the initiation fee and discounted the monthly dues to $25. The slip fee for the boat was an additional $25 per month. This was a heck of a deal! The San Diego Yacht Club was, and still is, one of the nicest yacht clubs in the entire U.S.

I decided I'd like to join the club and keep our new sailboat there, even though it was off the island and required a drive across the bridge and around the northwest side of the bay. The location had the advantage, though, of a short sail to the mouth of the bay and out into the Pacific Ocean. It seemed ideal, but then I learned the club required a new member be recommended by no less than six other members who were in good standing and had known the prospective member for a minimum of five years. I didn't know anyone, and Bea was not even a member. She belonged to the Coronado Yacht Club.

I had made the deposit on my new boat over a weekend. When I got to the dispensary on Monday morning, I went in search of Bea. I found her in the courtyard smoking a cigarette.

"Bea, I bought a boat this weekend, but I discovered the club requires a new applicant to be recommended by six club members who have known the prospective member for at least five years. I'm sunk!"

"Doctor, did you think I didn't know that? You let me take care of it. I'll get your six recommendations for you. Don't worry," she said, her slight Bronx accent betraying her New York origins. She gave me one of her coquettish winks and flashed a big grin.

228

The following weekend, Bea and I took a drive over to the San Diego Yacht Club. I wasn't sure of our mission, but I trusted Bea and went along with whatever plan she'd concocted to get me in the door of this elite yacht club. Although she wasn't a member, she had a sticker on her car that allowed us swift passage through the club's security gate. The two of us then walked through the club and scouted around the docks until she had zeroed in on and drafted my unsuspecting proxies. All six members were old friends of hers, and each agreed to attest that they had known me for more than five years. Right then, it became crystal clear to me that Bea's San Diego social network was way more far-reaching than I'd ever imagined.

Two weeks later, I was presented at the noon "commodore's luncheon" at the club for the Membership Committee to consider my application. This was a formal affair—men only—and everyone in the room wore a sport coat, most commonly a blue blazer with a white shirt and tie. I wore my Navy Service Dress Blue uniform, which I thought appropriate and coordinated well with the club's nautical theme. After I stood and presented myself, one of my six stoolies stood up and vouched for my fine, upstanding character. I was then asked to leave the room so the committee and the commodore could discuss any apparent character flaws they had detected, and to then take a vote on whether or not I met their impeccable standards.

I stood on a deck outside the dining room as I awaited the verdict, gazing out at all the beautiful sailboats and motor yachts. Only 10 minutes or so passed before I was called back into the room. The commodore announced I was now officially a new member of one of the finest yacht clubs in the world. He then reminded me of their gentlemanly standards of conduct that I was expected to hold myself to in order to remain in good standing. Drinking glasses were simultaneously raised toward me in a group toast, followed by a civilized, gentlemanly round of applause.

When I got back to work the following week, I found Bea so I could report the good news and thank her for what she had done for me.

She gave me one of her trademark winks and a sly little smile and said, "You owe me now, Doc."

San Diego Yacht Club

Years later, after I retired and we started spending winters in Coronado, I began thinking about my experiences on the island back in those early days of my Navy career. In 2011, I picked up the local phone book to see if Bea might still be alive and residing in Coronado. Her name was listed, and her address was an apartment located just three blocks from the house we were renting. Martha and I walked over there and saw her through the window of her first-floor apartment. She was sitting at the kitchen table smoking cigarettes; an ashtray filled with cigarette butts sat on the table. We knocked on the door.

Bea hollered for us to come in. I introduced myself and Martha, and Bea announced that she remembered me well. She then said, "Doc, I'll bet you can't believe I'm still alive." I had to admit to her I was thinking exactly that, and we all three laughed about it. She was 92 years old at the time.

Bea died in her sleep on May 25, 2013, just three days shy of her 95th birthday. She was a wonderful lady who did a lot of nice things for everyone she came in contact with. I will never forget her.

61

On the afternoon of Thursday, June 21, 1973, Captain Youngman, the CO of the dispensary, conducted a special briefing for the air station's staff of flight surgeons. He advised us we would all be on alert the following morning to back up the recovery operation's medical team for the Skylab 2 space mission. The astronaut crew of three was scheduled to splash down in the Pacific Ocean that morning, be plucked from the ocean by helicopter, and flown to the aircraft carrier USS Ticonderoga. We all went about our duties that Friday, June 22, hoping the crew of this first orbiting laboratory would safely return to Earth and the recovery would be flawless. All went well, and it was another normal day at the North Island Dispensary; I read about the successful mission and recovery in the *San Diego Union-Tribune* on Saturday morning.

One Friday afternoon, a few weeks later, I was working late and had just finished up some paperwork in my office at the dispensary. As I was packing my rucksack for the bike ride home, Captain Youngman appeared in the doorway. He said, "Dave, how would you like to go to the Officers' Club and meet the Skylab 2 astronauts?"

My boss informed me that the crew of the orbiting laboratory was back in San Diego, and the CO of the air station had just called and invited him and all available medical officers to a private cocktail party being held in honor of this all-Navy crew of three. Martha was invited too. I called Martha and asked her to call the Reillys and see if one of the girls could come right over to babysit. I told her I would be home shortly and asked her to slip into a nice dress and be ready to go. I pedaled home, changed into my Service Dress Blue uniform, and we were on our way back to the base in no time.

As it turned out, the cocktail party had not been preplanned, and it was, in fact, arranged on a moment's notice by the CO of the air station. By the time he'd called around to the various commands on base to spread the word, it was late, and most of the officers had secured for the day and gone home. I was the only medical officer Captain Youngman found and recruited to attend the party. The result was a relatively small group of people showing up at the club to honor these special guests of the air station.

When Martha and I arrived at the O' Club, we were directed to a small private party room. Upon entering the room, we were surprised to see only about 20 people had come to meet and greet these heroes. Since we were about the last guests to arrive, the party stayed small and I got to enjoy some one-on-one time with each crew member.

The astronauts could easily be identified and distinguished from the other guests in the room by their navy-blue blazers with gold buttons and the NASA logo patch on the left breast pocket. I recognized the mission commander, Charles "Pete" Conrad. Pete Conrad's face was familiar to almost every American at the time because he was frequently seen on network television, sitting next to Walter Cronkite, serving as the technical expert during spacecraft launch sequences. He had logged more than 1,100 hours in space at that point, but I am sure he was chosen for this public media role as much for his vibrant personality as for his spaceflight experience. His friends, associates, naval buddies, and fellow astronauts knew him as a "real pistol," and much of the world had heard and watched live video transmissions from the Moon on Apollo 12 when Pete exclaimed "whoopee" as he cavorted and leapt around on the surface in his spacesuit.

Every guest at the party wanted some face-time with Pete Conrad, and he made a point to introduce himself to each one of us. Martha and I were standing just outside a small circle of awestruck hero-worshipers and were waiting our turn to talk to him when he noticed us. He politely excused himself from the group, slipped between a couple of folks, and extended his hand to me. He said, "I'm Pete Conrad—what's your name?" We shook hands as I introduced myself and Martha, and a new group formed around him. As we talked, it was apparent why NASA liked to put him in front of the TV camera. He was definitely "Mr. Personality."

Joe Kerwin was the mission scientist aboard, and I enjoyed talking with him since he was a naval flight surgeon, like me, and was the first doctor to venture into space. Joe was quieter and not as outgoing and dynamic as Pete. He had a humble and unassuming manner, expressed interest in my life, and he wanted to hear all about what I was doing. I, of course, wanted to know all about him, his career, and the mission he had just completed.

Joe answered a lot of questions I posed about Skylab 2. The space station itself was launched, unmanned, as Skylab 1 on May 14, about two weeks prior to the manned Skylab 2 mission. The astronauts were in space for 28 days—a new record. The mission was Joe Kerwin's first and only trip into space, but it was an exciting one due to multiple technical problems the crew faced and had to solve. He subsequently had a long and distinguished career in the aerospace industry, both with NASA and in the civilian sector.

Paul Weitz was the designated pilot for the Skylab 2 mission, and it was also his first spaceflight. Paul would later command the maiden voyage of the Space Shuttle Challenger in April of 1983, not knowing the spacecraft was destined to explode and break up in flight, with the loss of the entire crew of seven, less than three years later, on January 28, 1986. Paul finished his astronaut career as Deputy Director of the Johnson Space Center in Houston. He retired from NASA in May of 1994.

Pete Conrad would tragically die in 1999 from injuries sustained while motorcycling with his wife and friends in Southern California. Initially, he seemed to have incurred only minor injuries after running off the road on his Harley, but he died several hours later from internal bleeding. He was retired from both the Navy and an executive position at McDonnell-Douglas Aircraft and was 69 years old at the time of his death. When I read about Pete's untimely death in the newspapers, I was saddened by the news, but it gave me an occasion to recall the evening we shared many years earlier at the O' Club at NAS North Island.

Martha and I felt privileged to have gotten to spend a memorable evening with these three impressive individuals. It was easy to see why each had been selected to join such an elite group. As true American icons, they were the best of the best.

I was not only filled with admiration for the three astronauts and, admittedly, a little starstruck that evening, but I was also envious of their exciting lives. I found myself becoming more and more interested in the flight half of my duties and less and less interested in the surgeon portion of the job. I was keenly aware of this growing interest in aviation within me, but I hadn't lost focus on my goal of establishing a private practice of medicine. I reasoned that my choices had been made and my life path was now set in stone. I suspected any second thoughts creeping into my head questioning my career choice would vanish when the Navy finally released me from active duty and I would then be away from this exposure to pilots, airplanes, and astronauts.

62

Monday's child is fair of face,

Tuesday's child is full of grace,

Wednesday's child is full of woe,

Thursday's child has far to go,

Friday's child is loving and giving,

Saturday's child works hard for a living,

And the child that is born on the Sabbath day

Is bonny and blithe, and good and gay.

Before our boat ever arrived in San Diego, we had decided to christen it *Thursday's Child*. We didn't yet know where we would sail off to—or whether we would even go very far—but it seemed like a wonderful name for our new sailboat and could aptly apply to our future lives outside of sailing as well.

The boat was built at the Catalina factory near Los Angeles, and it was finished and delivered to San Diego in early July of 1973. It was trailered by semi to Jack Dorsey Sailboats on Harbor Island where Jack's crew used a crane to launch it into the water. After they stepped the mast and tuned the rigging, Jack and I sailed into San Diego Bay for a shakedown cruise. Once all the paperwork was signed and the U.S. Coast Guard registration numbers were applied to the bow, I motored the boat over to our reserved slip at the San Diego Yacht Club.

The next morning, a Saturday, we outfitted the boat and loaded supplies for an overnight cruise. That afternoon, Martha and I, along with our internship friends, Reg and Karen Williams, sailed out of San Diego Bay into the Pacific Ocean on our maiden voyage. Reg and Karen had flown in from Oregon the night before for this occasion, and they served as additional crew members on this adventurous first cruise.

We had arranged for our neighbor's teenaged daughter, Bridget Reilly, to babysit overnight with Jill. We were lucky to live next door to a wonderful family. Red and Mary Reilly had five great kids, and it seemed either Bridget or Mickey, their two teenaged daughters, was always available and willing to earn a little spending money. So, for our entire stint of duty in Coronado, we never had a problem finding a babysitter when we wanted to get away.

It was a beautiful, clear afternoon when we motored out of our slip at the yacht club; we hoisted the sails as soon as we got out in the bay. Once offshore that afternoon, we enjoyed a steady 12- to 15-knot westerly wind as we clipped along at seven knots on a broad reach and a southerly heading. We cruised about 18 miles south, across the southern border of the U.S., to Mexico's Los Coronados Islands. We dropped anchor in the lee of a jetty on North Coronado, the northernmost of the four islands in the group. By that time, it was 5:00 in the afternoon.

We had just finished furling the sails and coiling the sheets and halyards when we spotted a Mexican patrol boat, with a machine gun mounted on its bow, motoring around the south side of the island. Two uniformed officers were aboard. I had been warned we might expect an encounter like this and might have to offer a bribe to avoid being cited with some contrived violation of Mexican law. I quickly instructed my crew to smile cheerfully and wave at the serious-looking officers. We all pasted artificial smiles on our faces as we talked to each other like ventriloquists through our teeth, without moving our lips, and waved at them like fools. They circled our boat three times, staring at us as if we were caged animals at the zoo. On the third pass, the officer on deck gave us a slight nod and what might even have been a half-smile. The patrol boat then continued on and disappeared around the north end of the island. We weren't sure whether they had decided we weren't a threat to the national security of Mexico or were heading back to get reinforcements. We were all a little edgy for a while after that, but, thankfully, the patrol boat never returned.

Martha and Karen prepared dinner in the galley, and we enjoyed our first meal at the dinette table in the cabin. It was a calm, clear night and we sat in the cockpit after dinner and watched the sun drop spectacularly below the western horizon. As dusk fell upon us, we counted stars as they appeared—one by one—in the darkening sky above. We all felt a chill from the moist salt air and retired early to our cabin berths, with gentle swells rocking us all quickly to sleep.

When I awoke to morning light and peered out of a cabin window, I discovered dense fog had descended upon us. I could barely make out the shoreline, which was probably less than 100 feet away. By the time we were all up and had eaten breakfast, it still looked like pea soup outside, and there was little wind. I was hoping when the sun got a little higher in the sky the fog would lift and the wind would pick up.

Before we made way, I laid out the nautical chart of the area on the dinette table, plotted a course to the entrance to San Diego Bay, and calculated the magnetic heading required to steer. We then hoisted the sails, weighed the anchor, and departed our overnight anchorage.

The shoreline of the northern island quickly disappeared from view, despite the fact we were moving very slowly. It was what sailors refer to as a "real drifter." Our sailboat was moving forward, but just barely.

We were on a port tack, broad reach, so I was able to steer the heading I had calculated. I was glad I had some training in the basic navigation skill of dead reckoning. I learned the technique while sailing with my friend Paul Broadbent in Pensacola and also studied it in ground school at NAS Saufley. Every half hour, I went below and marked our estimated position on the chart based on our speed, elapsed time, and magnetic heading indicated on the compass. This method of navigation is fairly inaccurate, but the extremely accurate and relatively inexpensive electronic method using GPS would not become available for many years ahead. LORAN navigation had been in use on large military and civilian ships since World War II, but those electronic systems were too expensive for the average pleasure-boat owner.

Dead reckoning becomes more and more inaccurate as a means of navigation over time because of wind drift, drift from ocean currents, and variations in speed and heading. Fortunately, I had another way of periodically verifying our position on the chart as we slogged along. I had a multi-band battery-powered radio aboard that had a directional antenna on top. This allowed me to tune in radio stations that had broadcast towers depicted on the chart. By turning the radio to find the "null" point of the signal (the orientation that caused the signal to fade), I could get a compass bearing off of each of three different towers and plot a fix on the map. I then compared my radio fix to the position I had plotted using dead reckoning. The radio navigation was also fairly inaccurate, but the two methods of determining position seemed to be in relatively close agreement as I plotted our course on the chart throughout the day. This gave me a bit of confidence that I at least knew roughly where we were, but I still had a lot of self-doubt. I suspected some major doubts also existed in the minds of my crew as the day wore on, despite the fact I was trying hard to exhibit a confident bravado in order to keep up their collective morale.

The fog never lifted. The visibility varied at times, but I don't think it ever exceeded a quarter of a mile, and we were out of sight of the California shoreline the entire time. I had a foghorn mounted on top of an aerosol can, and I sounded the horn every few minutes to warn any other boats in the vicinity of our presence. We heard other foghorns, but they were somewhere off in the distance, and we never sighted another vessel. I hoped any ships or pleasure boats in our immediate vicinity could see us on their radar, despite the fact we didn't have a radar reflector on the boat.

Just before noon, a pod of dolphins swam by the port side of the boat. Three of them maneuvered right up to the port bow and porpoised along on the crest of the bow wave as they gave us a few squeaky chirps, eyed us, and smiled. They stayed with us for several minutes, but then got bored with our slow speed and quickly shot off ahead to catch up with other members of their pod. This encounter was the highlight of our cruise. We didn't know it at the time, but this experience would repeat itself several times over the next two years of sailing off the coast of Southern California. We would also have a number of "up close and personal" encounters with 50-foot California gray whales as they migrated down the coast, from January to March, on their way to their calving waters off the Mexican Baja Peninsula. A couple of those whale meetings would be in breathtakingly close proximity to our relatively small craft.

A few times that day, we were completely becalmed in the dense fog, and I motored for a while until gentle breezes picked back up again and the sails filled. By the time my charting indicated we were nearing the entrance to San Diego Bay, it was 5:00 in the afternoon, and we hadn't seen anything but water for over eight hours. When I thought we were getting close, I was on full alert. I stared intently across the port bow, looking for a glimpse of light from the Point Loma Lighthouse. I had been hearing the blast from its foghorn for at least two hours, as it sounded every 30 seconds. I didn't ever spot the light, but I did think I caught the sound of a buoy whistle and alerted my crew to listen. They thought they could hear it too, and, a few minutes later, it was clear we were all definitely hearing a whistle and also the occasional barking of seals.

Another hour went slowly by as the whistle (and seal barking) got gradually louder and louder. Then, out of the mist, I saw a flash of light and then a second flash of light. There was one short flash followed by one long flash, a pause, and then another short flash and a long flash. The pattern was Morse code for the letter "A." I knew this was the #1 channel buoy, marking the entrance to the bay. My careful charting had been accurate to within a mile! None of us could quite believe it, but I was probably the most amazed person on the boat. I think I was almost in a state of shock, and concluded I had witnessed a true miracle. We all started clapping and cheering, and Martha, Reg, and Karen slapped me on the back and congratulated me—even though we had yet to get even a glimpse of land.

We ghosted slowly past the red buoy, which had several seals lounging on its round floating base. A couple of them lazily raised their heads and gave us a few extra barks. I plotted the course to the next right-hand red buoy, following the rule of "red-right-return." We left the #1 buoy behind us in the fog, and after a few minutes sighted the next channel-marker buoy. I kept the red buoys on my right to avoid the partially submerged rocky jetty on the channel's east side.

It was 8:00 PM when we finally entered our slip at the yacht club. It had been an interesting first cruise and had been great fun, but it had also been a little stressful with the fog. Not long after that trip, I decided, if we were going to do much more offshore sailing, I needed to invest in some additional safety equipment. Since this was way before the dawn of cellphones, we had no means of communication from the boat. To solve that issue, I bought and installed a Motorola ship-to-shore radiotelephone which allowed us to contact the U.S. Coast Guard directly in an emergency. I also purchased an Avon inflatable life raft that could be deployed quickly by activating a large CO_2 cartridge. We did a lot of ocean sailing after that, and I felt much safer with those items aboard.

I thoroughly enjoyed that first cruise, but had the thought I might like racing even more. I had crewed in enough sailing races to know I liked it, but I had never raced in the ocean, nor had I competed as a boat's skipper. Once again, I was veering from my safe, comfortable and conservative tendencies. I recognized that my friends in Pensacola, and Paul Broadbent in particular, had influenced me to explore new horizons.

Not long after that first sail, I registered for my first race series as skipper.

Plotting the course

Taking a bearing

Martha in the galley of *Thursday's Child*

Sailing back into San Diego Bay

241

63

Our second child, Alice, was born at the Coronado Hospital on October 22, 1973. She was one month premature and was a tiny little thing at 4 pounds, 14 ounces. The delivery was uncomplicated and went smoothly though, and our baby was healthy. Martha recovered quickly and was back on the boat crewing for me as soon as she felt comfortable leaving Alice with one of our trusted babysitters for a few hours.

We started taking Jill sailing with us when we weren't racing. We always had her in a life jacket and attached to the boat with a lifeline. She loved being out on the water with us; it was quite an experience for a two-year-old.

By the spring of 1974, I had skippered our boat through several series of races and collected two trophies—a second place and a third place. The races were sponsored by various yacht clubs around the bay—the San Diego Yacht Club, the Naval Sailing Club, and the Southwestern Yacht Club. All were closed-course races, as opposed to long-distance races. Some of the courses were set up in San Diego Bay, and others were several miles offshore in the open ocean. All of the races I entered were one-design, class-boat competitions—in other words, Catalina 27s racing against Catalina 27s.

I had started out sailing in class-boat racing when crewing for Dr. Harvey Fisher in Kansas, on his Olympic-class Thistle. I had experienced handicap racing in Pensacola when crewing for Frank, the southern gentleman skipper, on his Islander 37, but I much preferred one-design racing. With one-design, the boats competing in a race have the same hull design and are rigged basically the same, and it's more of a contest between skippers and their crews than to see who has the fastest boat. There are still always slight differences in basic performance among boats of the same design, but, regardless of that, it becomes much more of a tactical competition.

Another reason I like the one-design, class-boat racing better is, when crossing the finish line, you immediately know who won. With handicap racing, you have to go back to the club and wait to see the published results after each boat's handicap figure has been calculated.

When sailing and racing as a crew member, I learned most of the racing rules by osmosis. Now that I was a skipper, though, I needed to be sure I had a thorough understanding of all regulations pertaining to the sport. I bought a copy of the NYRU (National Yacht Racing Union) rules and studied all of the right-of-way rules carefully and would review the most important ones before every race.

Things can get a little wild in racing when all of the boats are in close proximity and mixing it up at the starting line and, later in the race, when rounding the marks. It is imperative that a skipper knows which boat has the right of way and may hold its course, and which boat must give way and yield. The immediate environment can become noisy and stressful during some of these close encounters. There is often a lot of screaming by the skippers directed toward other skippers as well as to their own crews. If a skipper thinks one of his competitors may be a little weak in his knowledge of racing rules, he may try to intimidate and bluff the other boat into yielding way to him at a time when the other boat actually has the right of way. I wanted to know all the rules well enough to recognize this type of bluff and not be fooled.

In my very first race in San Diego, another skipper, knowing I was a greenhorn racing skipper, tried to bluff me into yielding to him when turning around a mark. We were both on starboard tacks as we approached the mark, but I was in the boat to lee, we had hull overlap, and I had the right of way. He didn't yield to me, even though I was shouting at him and demanding "buoy room." As we rounded the mark, he came too close, trying to force me below the mark. We didn't bump hulls, but my boat was going faster, and it straightened up as his sails, which were to windward, blanketed our sails. The spreader on my mast caught the leech of his mainsail and ripped it from the trailing edge (the leech) to the leading edge (the luff). His boom dropped down into his cockpit and the race was over for him. I immediately hoisted a protest flag. After the race, the protest committee ruled in my favor, disqualifying him from the race.

The skipper who was disqualified had a bad day. He had to buy a new mainsail, which was an expensive proposition, and he was disqualified from the race to boot. He carried a grudge about it for a while, but he knew it was his fault and gradually got over it. When he finally started speaking to me again, he began calling me "Ben-Hur." This was in reference to the main character in the famous movie in which one of the chariot racers attaches lethal saw blades to his chariot's wheels to disable his competitor's, Ben-Hur's, chariot. When he started this teasing, it was clear he'd taken his disastrous racing experience with me in stride. We could be friends now, and I was happy about that.

I had signed up for a three-race series that spring sponsored by the Southwestern Yacht Club, scheduled for the first weekend in March. It was called the Albatross Series. Two races were scheduled for Saturday and one for Sunday. The racecourse was several miles offshore in the Pacific, and, for the first two races on Saturday, the weather was atrocious. The winds were out of the west at 30 to 35 knots, creating 10- to 12-foot swells.

Martha crewed for me in this race as she usually did, but I also had Bill Jenkins, a young Navy ensign crewing; he was stationed at a radar installation on Point Loma. I met Bill the previous winter when we were both skiing at Heavenly Valley, a ski area near Lake Tahoe, and happened to board a chairlift together. I found out he had some formal sailing instruction while a student at the U.S. Naval Academy at Annapolis, and that he was also currently stationed in the San Diego area. He had never done any racing, but he jumped at the chance to crew for me. We started practicing as soon as we both got back to San Diego. After a little practice and a couple of actual races, Bill turned out to be a fantastic crewman.

As we maneuvered around behind the starting line in the wild weather that Saturday, I kept changing my mind about sail configuration. I decided to put a reef in the mainsail (meaning it is partially lowered and the excess sail folds secured around the boom). I then took down my small foresail (the 120 percent jib) and replaced it with my large genoa (150

245

percent) which was really designed for use in much lighter winds. When we crossed the starting line, we had the only boat with this sail configuration. The other boats in the race had hoisted their mainsails all the way up and were using their smaller jibs as foresails. Since I was probably the most inexperienced skipper racing that day, I had serious thoughts about whether or not I'd made a wise move. It was a risky decision.

The boat was crashing through the cresting rollers and moving like I had never seen it move. Martha, Bill and I all wore foul-weather gear, but our chins were dripping with saltwater from waves crashing over the bow and smashing us in the face. I wondered if we might have overpowered the boat and hoped it all stayed together. My fears were realized when a stainless-steel fitting on the mainsheet traveler failed during the race and the mainsail began luffing violently as we lost control of the boom. I stayed at the tiller while Bill made a fast and efficient jury-rigged repair and everything came quickly back under control. We were lucky; another boat was dismasted that day and had to be towed in by the Coast Guard.

Our boat, *Thursday's Child,* was first across the finish line, with second-place finisher, *Go Devil,* sailing in next, and third place going to *Bonnie Jean,* several boat lengths back.

As we maneuvered behind the starting line for the second race, I was wondering if we should drop out because of the damage to the mainsheet traveler. Bill beefed up his temporary repair and assured me it would hold, so we decided to stay in. We stayed with the reefed mainsail and the genoa, and, once again, we were the only boat using that configuration. We easily won first place in the second race as well. My risky idea paid off!

The winds and seas were much calmer on Sunday for the third race, and we did not do nearly as well. We came in sixth for that race, but our 1-1-6 scores still gave us a first place for the series. We were all ecstatic about our first-ever first-place win. The trophy was a beautiful etching of an old sailing ship in a teak frame. It had been hand-crafted by one of the artistic members of the club whom we had been racing against.

Yachting news was plastered all over *The San Diego Union-Tribune* on Monday that week. Gerry Driscoll, skipper of the 12-meter Intrepid, was practicing with his crew all weekend for America's Cup Race, and the newspaper featured a prominent article which primarily highlighted their drills in the stormy weather. Yachting results from around the nation were announced in the same article and included some other rather well-known luminaries in the sport—Dennis Conner, Ted Hood, and Ted Turner. In the same article that included these yachting heavyweights, there was a paragraph about the race series in which I had just won a first-place trophy. I was thrilled to see my name mentioned, but, to my great disappointment, the reporter got my first name wrong.

"Perhaps the fastest growing racing fleet in the area is the Catalina 27 group. Yesterday, 11 of the Midget Ocean Racing Association racers competed as a class with <u>Dick</u> Crawley's Thursday's Child scoring a narrow victory. Crawley scored 7½ points off a 1-1-6 series. Only ¼ point back was Bonnie Jean with M & M's another ¼ point back."

I thought: oh well, at least he got my last name right. As a relatively novice skipper in the world of yacht racing, I didn't deserve to have my name on the same page as these famous sailors, and I knew that. This realization and honest appraisal, however, didn't keep me from showing off the article to all of my relatives, friends, and pretty much anyone else I could wave the blurb in front of. I clipped the article and pasted it in our scrapbook with the hope that when my grandchildren and great-grandchildren discovered it someday, they wouldn't ask, "Who the heck was 'Dick' Crawley?"

Sailboat racing involves a lot of tacking back and forth, adapting to rapidly changing tactical positions, and making critical, sometimes split-second, decisions. There are risks involved, especially with ocean racing. One decision at a critical time can determine whether the race is won or lost. I had no way of knowing the tacks my life would take in the years to come or predicting I would one day reach a crossroads requiring a decision that would change my entire future.

Racing in the Pacific on *Thursday's Child*

64

By January of 1974, I had done a lot of Navy flying with my four favorite T-28 pilots—Bob Hawley, P.J. Newman, Joe Croteau, and Joe Hall. Each of these aviators enjoyed sharing his knowledge of aviation with me, generously sharing "stick time," and pushing me to hone new piloting skills. I spent a lot of time under the hood—a canopy-like affair covering the cockpit—as those guys gave me instruction and practice flying on instruments.

While I thoroughly enjoyed the lessons these aviators were giving me, the fact that these hours of flying were unofficial started bothering me. I wasn't a designated naval aviator, and, other than my solo flight in Pensacola, I wasn't allowed to check out an aircraft and go flying as the pilot in command. I was getting hooked on aviation, and it seemed it was in my blood. I had the itch to earn some aviation credentials of my own in the form of a civilian Private Pilot license.

One afternoon in January, before those spring sailboat races had started, I drove over to Lindberg Field (now San Diego International Airport) and visited an aviation supply store located on the opposite side of the field from the passenger terminal. I bought a home study course to prepare for the FAA Private Pilot written exam. I studied the book for a couple of months, did all the exercises in the accompanying workbook, and completed the practice tests included in the kit. I took the FAA written exam in early March and passed.

The San Diego Naval Flying Club was located on the base at NAS North Island. As soon as I passed the written test for my license, I went over to the club, joined, and signed up for an official lesson. On March 31, I took my first lesson in a Cessna 150. After the second lesson, my instructor signed me off for solo flight.

I had an exciting first solo in the Cessna 150 when I developed engine trouble while practicing maneuvers in our practice area just north of Brown Field, near the Mexican border. The aircraft would not hold altitude, so I headed for the field and declared an emergency over Brown's tower frequency. After I landed and was rolling out, the engine quit completely before I could taxi clear of the active runway. The tower closed the runway until two mechanics arrived from a nearby hangar and helped me push the plane off the runway.

Martha drove over to Brown Field that afternoon and picked me up. The engine was repaired after a few days, and my instructor and I went back over, picked the aircraft up, and flew it back to North Island.

By mid-May I was doing my required solo cross-country flights. I completed all the required dual and solo flights by mid-July, and I passed my Private Pilot checkride with an FAA examiner on July 15.

On July 27, I took my first passenger for an airplane ride: my brave wife, Martha. We flew over to Santa Catalina Island, ate lunch there, and then flew back to North Island. I am not sure whether her demonstration of trust and confidence in my abilities was real or just for show, but I believe it was misplaced and perhaps a little foolish. She really should have flatly refused to go up in a single-engine airplane, over an expanse of open ocean, to land on a short mountain-top island airstrip, with a new and very inexperienced private pilot at the controls. As I look back on that flight today, I am not sure whether to admire her for her courage and blind trust in me that day or to question her sanity.

Martha's judgment (and mine) came into question again when, on September 20, 1974, we took off in a Cessna 172 from San Diego and flew 1300 miles up to the Expo '74 World's Fair in Spokane, Washington. We confidently left our children with our two trusted babysitters, Bridget and Mickey. We miraculously made it back home alive from that daredevil junket as well, and no one will ever be able to say we weren't an adventurous young couple.

I wasn't sure what I was going to do in the future with my new Private Pilot license or where all this would lead, but I was already starting to think about getting an instrument rating. Then what?

My first passenger—A crazy daredevil named Martha

Lunch date to Santa Catalina Island
July 27, 1974

65

Shortly after I started duty as the air station flight surgeon at NAS North Island, I was assigned additional duty as the command flight surgeon for the Commander of Naval Air Pacific (COMNAVAIRPAC). Rear Admiral James Stockdale assumed the command soon after he arrived back in the U.S. after being incarcerated for seven years as a POW in North Vietnam. The admiral was the senior-ranking officer in the infamous prison camp known as the "Hanoi Hilton." Coincidentally, Admiral Stockdale, his wife Sybil, and their four boys lived directly across the street from the house we rented in Coronado. We often watched as his driver, in a shiny black car with flags on the fenders, picked him up at his home each morning and dropped him back off in late afternoon.

I considered it an honor to be the physician on the admiral's staff. I already knew a lot about this fine officer and had great respect for him, but I had no idea what my orders meant as far as duties and responsibilities as the Command Flight Surgeon. I don't think the admiral himself or any of his aides knew what I was supposed to be doing either. I did stop by his office a few times in hopes I could visit with him and offer him a chance to enlighten me with what he expected. Every time I made such an attempt, his secretary informed me he was in a meeting or off somewhere else on the base.

Admiral Stockdale did come to my office at the dispensary on a couple of occasions to ask for some medical advice, and I made sure he knew he could come see me anytime without an appointment. That little courtesy was the only way I could think of to serve him as a member of his staff. I suspected there was more to the job, but I never found out what those duties might be. I saw the admiral socially from time to time at neighborhood parties and also at an occasional official function at the base. He never said anything to me that might indicate I was falling down on the job—whatever that job might be. I finally stopped worrying about my new assignment and just worked at the dispensary treating patients, doing what I'd been trained to do.

On June 12, 1974, I received a new set of orders from the Navy that added additional duties. These orders transferred me to the Fleet Aviation Survival Operational Training Group Pacific, known by the mother of all acronyms: FASOTRAGRUPAC. My new duty was to serve as the Fleet

Survival School physician. This was in addition to being the staff flight surgeon for the admiral.

I continued to work at the dispensary for two or three weekdays after that, but, on weekends, I spent Friday, Saturday, and Sunday at a simulated POW camp in the Anza Borrego Desert, east of San Diego, as pilots and other flight crew completed the land phase of survival training. The course was known as SERE School, which stands for survival-evasion-resistance-escape, and the training was designed to not only teach land survival techniques, but also to give the crews a realistic exposure to the experience of being a prisoner of war. My job, while disguised in the uniform of the camp guards, was to observe the training activities and assess the risk potential for serious injury or death to the participants, as well as to provide medical care in the case of an injured student or instructor. It turned out to be a stressful assignment.

As the camp physician, it was hard for me to watch some of the simulated tortures being administered to our own naval aviators, but, I must admit, most of it was well controlled and designed to produce mental stress rather than to inflict physical pain. I understood the training had to be realistic in order to be effective, but I did occasionally have to pull an instructor aside and tell him he was getting a little carried away. Whenever a student got injured, I felt somewhat responsible; for that reason, I didn't like the job at all.

The camp was a sprawling complex and looked precisely the way I imagined a prisoner-of-war encampment would look. It closely resembled such camps as portrayed by Hollywood movie producers. There was a long serpentine dirt driveway leading from a California state highway to the compound. The turnoff was marked by a rather forbidding sign that simply read "Restricted Area—Property of the U.S. Government." The drive led to a guardhouse at the compound's entrance, and the entire area was surrounded by a tall metal fence topped with razor wire. None of the crudely built ramshackle buildings of the compound were visible from the highway.

One modern-looking building, which was a fairly well-equipped medical dispensary, stood just outside the compound's entrance gate. The dispensary served as my overnight quarters when I was on duty at the camp. There was a private bathroom in the facility, but it had no separate sleeping quarters. I slept, feeling somewhat imprisoned myself, on a portable metal bed shoved up against one wall of the emergency treatment room. I slept there alone—I guess you could say in solitary confinement—

apart from the other personnel. My only connection to the camp at night was through a "squawk box" mounted on the wall near my bed; this intercom connection was utilized to contact me if a medical problem arose inside the camp. One night in that room, I had a remarkable experience during which I was the one who had to use the squawk box to call out for help. I will never forget the events that unfolded that night.

A sparsely populated community of people resided on scattered plots of private land in the hills surrounding the Navy compound. Those folks were many miles from the big city and modern medical care, but most were aware of the existence of our Navy dispensary and knew they could come to us in an emergency and be treated. I was only at the facility on weekends, but one or two medical corpsmen staffed it during the week.

On the aforementioned memorable night, I was on duty and sleeping in the dispensary when I was suddenly awakened at about 2:00 AM by fierce pounding on the double doors. As I opened my eyes and tried to orient myself, I heard a woman screaming in terror on the other side of the entry and calling frantically for help. I turned on the lights, quickly slipped on my shoes, shuffled across the floor in my rumpled green scrub suit, and hurried to unlock and open the door.

A beaten-up old sedan was parked in the drive just a few feet from the door, and the screaming woman was leaning into the vehicle's back seat through the open rear door. When she heard the dispensary door unlatch and open, she jerked her head toward me and cried, "My daughter has been shot in the head—please save her!" The woman stepped aside and I leaned into the back seat.

The car's dome light was on, and I saw a little girl, dressed in pink pajamas, slumped over in the seat. She appeared to be 10 or 12 years old. The child was not moving, and I saw fresh blood all over the left side of her head. I gently picked her up in my arms and carried her into the dispensary and laid her on the examining table in the middle of the room. The child's mother, between anguished sobs, said, "It was an accident…oh, a horrible accident."

As I placed the young girl on the table, I organized my thoughts and reviewed in my mind the ABCs—airway, breathing, and circulation. I checked her airway and her breathing simultaneously by putting my ear in front of her mouth. There did not seem to be any obstruction. I could hear her shallow breaths and feel the warm air as she exhaled onto my cheek. I put my stethoscope diaphragm on her chest, confirmed breath sounds, and listened to her steady heartbeat while placing my fingers on the side of her neck and palpating a strong, steady carotid pulse. I had determined the child was alive and stable—at least for the moment. My mind was working at warp speed, thinking of what to do next.

I ran to the squawk box on the wall, pushed the button, and hollered for help. I told the duty officer I needed a corpsman immediately. I then raced back over to my patient and applied a blood pressure cuff to her left arm. As the cuff squeezed her arm, I thought I detected a tiny flutter of her eyelids. Her blood pressure was 125/80—completely normal.

I next made a cursory exam of her head and found a bleeding wound in the left parietal area of her scalp consistent with a bullet entry point. I needed to determine how much brain damage this poor little girl had sustained, so a careful neurological exam was the next step. I pinched the skin of her shoulder to test for response to pain—one of the most basic levels of consciousness. She immediately opened her eyes and looked at me. I asked if she could hear me, and she nodded her head. I asked her to tell me her name and she told me, in a barely audible voice, her name was Emily. I asked her how she felt and she told me her head hurt and she felt a little sick to her stomach. I asked her to squeeze my hands and wiggle her toes. Her strength and movements seemed normal. I was just finishing testing all her cranial nerves when my medical corpsman blasted through the door.

I quickly briefed the corpsman on what I knew so far and suggested he try to calm the child's mother. She was, at that point, standing on the other side of the table, sobbing and babbling, with both hands held to her mouth. He led her to a chair against one wall and did his best to calm her while I completed my exam.

The result of the neurological exam was completely normal. I found no sign of any neurological deficits whatsoever. I couldn't understand how anyone could have a gunshot wound to the head and show no indication of brain damage. What was I missing?

When the corpsman returned to the treatment table, I asked him to set up an IV with Ringers Lactate solution. I found a suitable vein above the patient's right wrist, slipped a Jelco intravenous catheter in, taped it down, and started a slow drip.

There was an x-ray machine in the dispensary, and I asked the corpsman if he was trained to take x-rays. He assured me he was trained and experienced and had used that particular machine on one or two occasions. I ordered a skull series.

The skull x-rays were also completely normal with the exception of a lead bullet lodged in the soft tissue outside of the skull on the right side—the opposite side from the obvious entry wound. There was no bullet hole in the bone of the skull. How could the bullet have ended up on the other side of her head, directly opposite the entry wound, without penetrating the skull and passing through her brain? I was baffled and immediately accused the corpsman of mislabeling the film with regard to left and right. He assured me the labels were correct. I was totally flummoxed.

I went back to my little patient's side and re-examined the wound. It appeared the bullet had entered at an upward angle. I found a linear area of tenderness and bruising that extended up over the top of the scalp and down the other side of the head. Just above and behind her right ear, I found a tender, hard lump where the bullet had apparently lodged. The slug had miraculously tunneled along the surface of the skull, under the scalp, from one side of the head to the other. This explained the puzzling lack of any signs of brain damage. The bullet hadn't gone *into* her brain, it had amazingly gone *around* it. I was practically ecstatic when I explained this fantastic news to Emily's mother.

The corpsman set up a suture tray for me. I shaved the hair around the entry wound and the area of the imbedded bullet on the opposite side, then injected the area around the entry wound with local anesthetic, cleaned the wound thoroughly, and closed it with two sutures. The bleeding essentially stopped. I then moved to the right side of the head where I could feel the bullet. I injected that area with local anesthetic and made a small incision with a #15 Bard-Parker scalpel blade to expose the bullet. I grasped the lead foreign body with a curved hemostat and easily removed it. I thoroughly irrigated the wound and then sutured it closed.

While the corpsman and I were busy working on her scalp, the mother, who was by then relatively calm, explained how her daughter had been shot in the head. She told how her six-year-old son had found their loaded 22-caliber rifle in a closet, starting playing with it, and had accidentally shot his sister. I didn't ask why the child had access to a gun, why the gun was loaded, or what the kids were doing awake and apparently unsupervised in the middle of the night. I thought it was pointless to ask any of these questions, since it was doubtful I would have received satisfactory answers.

Our little patient was "as good as gold" throughout this ordeal. She shed a few quiet tears but proved to be a brave little trooper and hardly made a peep. When, lastly, my corpsman gave her a tetanus booster shot, we were done.

In the first few minutes of this emergency, I assumed I would just be stabilizing this patient, summoning a helicopter, and evacuating her by air to San Diego. My first impression also included the thought that she probably would not be alive for long. Instead of that dire scenario, I found myself, two hours later, removing the IV and walking her out the door to her mother's car. I instructed her mother to take the child to their family doctor in five days for removal of the sutures. I told her what to look for as far as signs of infection, but I assured her I had thoroughly cleaned both wounds and that it is unusual for scalp wounds to get infected, due to an extensive blood supply.

The corpsman and I went back into the dispensary after they drove off and conducted an informal debriefing session. Our conversation was rich with superlatives, including, "Amazing, unbelievable, incredible, miraculous...." After such a nerve-wracking ordeal in the early morning hours, we couldn't have predicted a more fortuitous outcome, and it was an experience I knew neither one of us would ever forget.

When the corpsman left and went back to the compound, I turned out the lights and crawled back into bed. For the rest of the night, I lay on my back staring straight up at the dark ceiling as my mind replayed the entire sequence of events over and over again. I didn't get another wink of sleep that night. I was "wired."

I never heard a word from little Emily or her mother after that. When they drove away from the dispensary in the wee hours of the morning, it was the last I ever saw of them. I only hoped their family was as thankful as I was that this near-tragedy had such a happy ending.

That case was a memorable experience, but not because I had rendered any lifesaving treatment; I hadn't. All I had done was provide minor wound care. I had nothing to do with the little girl's survival from a gunshot wound to the head, and I almost felt like a bystander—a witness—possibly a witness to a miracle. Of course I was thrilled with the outcome, but the stress it had elicited in me in the first few minutes of the emergency was almost unbearable. How many more high-stress moments like this would I be able to withstand during my career ahead?

66

The summer of 1974 got busier for us when we found out the Catalina 27 Association had designated San Diego as the location for their national regatta that fall. A series of three races were scheduled to be conducted offshore in the Pacific in early September. Each of the local chapter cities on the East Coast and West Coast would be allowed to send three or four boats, depending on the size of their respective fleets.

Our San Diego fleet was awarded four entries for this national race, and eliminations started in June to decide which boats and their skippers would participate. Six separate elimination races were scheduled during the summer. The top four boats would represent San Diego in the National Catalina 27 Regatta. Martha and I registered *Thursday's Child* for the series.

In order to be free for the scheduled weekend races, I had to trade some shifts with other flight surgeons to provide medical coverage for my Navy SERE School duty. Dr. Ed Clark and Dr. Joe Tulumello agreed to cover for me at the survival school in exchange for my assuming some of their night-call duty at the dispensary; it worked out, and I was available for all the race days.

Bill Jenkins and I crewed the boat with just the two of us through the eliminations. Frank Radford won the six-race series in his sailboat, *Pursuit*; I expected that. Frank was a good sailor and had well-cut sails and a fast boat. I had been looking at the stern of his boat all year, so I wasn't surprised he won. Bill and I placed fourth, and we qualified as one of San Diego's four entries to the nationals.

After that, Bill and I trained in earnest for the big race, which was scheduled for the first weekend in September. We had been doing fairly well all year against some experienced sailors and both thought, if we could just get a little more speed out of the boat, we had a chance to win the regatta. We discussed several issues of interest and concern.

My sails were cut for stronger winds than San Diego typically experienced, so the sails especially hurt us in light winds. I also knew I wasn't much of a light-wind sailor—certainly not as good a sailor in light winds as Frank Radford. I couldn't afford to buy new, custom-made sails, so we just had to pray for strong winds on race day.

Hull speed was something we might be able to improve, though. I had heard that Jerry Driscoll, skipper of the *Intrepid* in the 1974 America's

Cup race, had developed special bottom paint for racing. The paint contained graphite and he called it "Graph-Speed." I called his boatyard, which was located on Shelter Island, and scheduled my boat to be hoisted out and painted with this mysterious concoction the week before the big race. I was warned that the anti-fouling properties of his paint, which prevented barnacles from accumulating, were minimal and the protection didn't last long. This meant I would have to have the boat hauled out of the water again, after the regatta, and have it repainted with a conventional bottom paint that lasts up to a year. It was an expensive proposition, but I decided I could just schedule a few more nights of moonlighting in the Coronado Hospital ER to pay for it.

Another area lending itself to possible improvement was changing our starting technique. Whenever we got a bad start at the beginning of a race, we both had noticed it was difficult to make up for it, and it greatly diminished our chances to win. Conversely, if we got a nice start, we always did well. So, we needed to figure out a way to be the number one boat to cross the starting line every time.

If you watch the start of a sailboat race, as soon as the five-minute warning horn sounds, you will see all the boats running downwind, away from the line, and then jockeying for their positions before lining up and heading back toward the starting line. The plan is to arrive just short of the line right before the start gun fires. Crossing the line before the gun is a false start and requires maneuvering back behind the line again to restart. So, you want to get there on time, but you definitely don't want to arrive early.

I had been thinking a lot about the starting procedure. I thought I had figured out a technique to almost always arrive at the line upwind of the other boats, on a starboard tack, and be first to cross after the gun. I had not seen my procedure described in any book nor had I seen any other racers try what I had in mind, but I ran my plan by Bill and he thought it just might work. Instead of heading downwind with the rest of the pack after the five-minute warning horn sounded, we would head off on a crosswind reach to the right of the committee boat for about two minutes and 20 seconds, then come about and reverse our course back toward the right end of the line. By doing this maneuver, we could completely avoid the congested jockeying for position in "the pack," as we came in to ambush them all at the starboard end of the line. It was a bold maneuver to try. It would probably be a little unnerving until the last few seconds, when we rounded the stern of the committee boat to come parallel with all the other boats. We would count on there being an open slot, at least the width of our hull, to sneak through between the nearest boat in the pack and the committee boat. If there was not enough room between the most upwind starboard tack boat and the committee boat, we would have no choice but to fall off the wind and duck behind the stern of that boat; we then could, hopefully, slip between the number one and number two boats. The biggest problem with my plan was there was no way to practice it and do a test run ahead of time. Our first experiment with my idea would have to be at the start of a real race.

I entered the boat in one more race before the nationals. It was the Sixth Annual Jack Dorsey Fly a Kite and Sail Race. This race was open to any sailboat of any type and had been set up with the whimsical idea and rule that each crew was required to keep a kite flying in the air above them, controlled from the cockpit of the boat, throughout the race. The race was scheduled for Sunday, August 25, the weekend before the Catalina 27 National Regatta.

The Fly a Kite and Sail Race was really fun and much less formal than the races I was used to. Way too many boats had turned out for this event and the real possibility of a collision was worrisome to me. I wasn't sure which skippers knew the right-of-way rules and which ones didn't. The popular mayor of San Diego at the time, Pete Wilson, was an honorary official on the committee boat and pulled the trigger on the starting gun. The atmosphere was light and festive throughout the race. The air was rich with the sounds of laughter and some folks threw water balloons at the other boats.

My crew for this race was Martha, Joe Hall (my old high school buddy and naval aviator friend), and Joe's wife, Cindy. Cindy was in charge of the kite, and she got it flying high before the start. Martha and Joe handled the jib. The kite was in the air when we crossed the starting line, but I quickly realized I had my hands full steering the race course, staying on a heading that kept the kite airborne, and maintaining enough separation from the other boats to keep the kite from getting snarled up in their rigging.

The kite flew well on the upwind and crosswind legs of the race, but when we started sailing downwind, there wasn't enough relative wind to keep it aloft. Our kite, to our dismay, slowly wafted down and into the bay before we reached the finish line. Once the kite was down, it was against the rules of the race to launch it again. So, we crossed the finish line without a kite aloft and were disqualified. Cindy was crestfallen, but I explained it wasn't her fault the kite had crashed and that it was all in good fun anyway. By the time we pulled into our slip at the yacht club, Cindy had shed her guilt about the kite, and we all expressed what a wonderfully fun day it had been.

The day after the kite race, our boat was hoisted from the water, and work was started to prep the bottom and finish it with Jerry Driscoll's Graph-Speed. Jerry's crew told me I could expect the hull speed to increase by about one knot. That didn't seem like much, but over several miles of a race course, it could definitely give us the edge we needed.

While our boat was in dry dock, Martha and I went to the boatyard to watch the progress. We soon found ourselves admiring a beautiful ketch perched on cradles next to our boat. It appeared to be about 50 feet in length and had a deep green hull with polished teak rails and spars. I asked the technician in charge of our boat who owned this beautiful yacht. He told me the owner was Roy Disney, Walt's brother, and he invited us to go aboard for a tour. We took off our shoes and he led us up a ladder and onto the polished teak decks. It was a gorgeous craft and perfectly maintained. We went below and found a teak chart table in the salon with a panel just above it which was crowded with the latest state-of-the-art instrumentation. They included wind and air temperature indicators, a chronometer, a knot meter, multiple navigation instruments, and a myriad of engine gauges. The face of each dial and gauge was painted with a picture of Mickey Mouse, and the indicator hands were Mickey Mouse hands.

The national regatta opened the following weekend, Saturday, August 31. Twenty boats had registered, including the four of us representing the San Diego fleet. Two races were scheduled for Saturday and one for Sunday. Only 14 of the 20 boats registered showed up at the starting line for the first race, which was several miles offshore. Sailing conditions on both days were perfect, with steady winds of 10 to 15 knots out of the west and average swells. I would have liked stronger winds, but that was the hand we were dealt that day and we'd just have to make the best of it.

Martha had not been racing with us much that summer, but I insisted we needed her as a third crew member for the nationals. She was good at it, we needed her extra help tailing the winches, and I didn't want her to miss out on the excitement of this big event.

Since Bill wasn't with us for the kite race, we still hadn't gotten a chance to try out our new starting technique before the national regatta. It seemed a little crazy to be trying something new like that in the most important race I had sailed in so far, but both Bill and I felt pretty confident it would work.

The technique did work! We were the first boat to cross the starting line in the first race on Saturday. The second to start, just to our lee, was Frank Radford in *Pursuit*. Frank had no idea what we were doing as we raced in toward the side of his boat as he approached the starting line. He hollered, "No barging!" at me. I yelled back, "Turning up, hold your course," as I saw there was a slot for us to slip through between his boat and the committee boat. I gave the command for Bill and Martha to harden up on the jib as I pulled in the main and turned up until we were close-hauled and on a parallel course to Frank, just a few feet away. If Frank had been required to alter his course because of our maneuver, it would have occurred right in front of the judges, and we would have been disqualified.

We started each race using the same technique, and we were the only boat to use this somewhat unorthodox method. When we approached the line for the second race on Saturday, we had to duck behind the most windward boat and assume the second-place starting position; there wasn't a slot for us to slip into, but we adapted quickly to the situation and still managed to get a great start.

We couldn't notice much difference in speed from the high-tech bottom paint, but I was glad to have any slight advantage it might be providing.

When the last race was over on Sunday and the standings posted at San Diego Yacht Club, Frank Radford, in *Pursuit*, received the first-place trophy, Bob Combs from San Francisco took second place, Dave Sargis was third, and our *Thursday's Child* was awarded the fourth-place trophy for the national regatta. So, three of the four winning boats were from our San Diego fleet.

We would have liked to have won, but all of us were happy to have placed. Our trophy was a beautiful mahogany serving tray with a sterling silver rim, an engraved medallion in the center, and four pewter wine goblets with sailing ships etched around the outside of each one. I took my crew out for a celebration dinner in Coronado that evening. We were proud of what we had accomplished, and we all raised a toast to ourselves as a team and to *Thursday's Child*.

67

I got called out on a number of SAR (Search and Rescue) missions during the two years I was stationed at NAS North Island. I welcomed these opportunities to break away from the clinic for a few hours and saw them as another advantage of being a flight surgeon instead of a general medical officer. A few of these search-and-rescue events on which I served were Navy missions, but most were conducted by the U.S. Coast Guard.

The San Diego Coast Guard Station did not have a flight surgeon attached, and so they would call the air station and make a request for one of us to join the crew when they had a mission that might involve a victim with an injury or medical condition. The Coast Guard Station was located just across the bay from NAS North Island, and, when a SAR was launched, they would make the short flight across the bay in one of their rescue helicopters to pick up one of the air station's flight surgeons.

I enjoyed the sense of adventure these missions provided, even though I never felt very comfortable flying in helicopters. The fact that they required much more maintenance than an airplane concerned me. I thought they had way too many moving parts whirling around, any one of which had the potential to fail at any moment. I also wondered how such a contraption could fly at all. My helicopter pilot friends explained that the rotor blades on top were actually wings—rotary wings. They didn't look like wings though—they were way too skinny! Wasn't this design similar to the one Leonardo da Vinci tried that turned out to be a total failure? I was especially concerned about all this when I was assigned to go out the door and hang from a cable in a horse collar underneath the machine. If it was going to crash, it seemed as though it would be much better to be inside than to have the aircraft coming down on top of me. Whenever I got back from one of these escapades, I always felt as if I had cheated death one more time.

One memorable mission was on New Year's Eve, 1973. It was a Monday and a normal work day for me, but the CO was in a holiday mood and said we could take off early for the day as soon as morning sick call was over. I was just getting ready to head home at about 11:30 AM when I got the call from the Coast Guard. I was the duty flight surgeon for the day.

The initial report indicated there was a medical emergency aboard a large cargo ship that was about 200 miles off the California coast. A crew member had been found unconscious in his bunk and could not be aroused.

Someone in the chain of communication had raised the concern he might be in a diabetic coma.

I closed the door of my office, took off my uniform, and dressed in my flight gear, which I kept stowed in a parachute bag behind my desk. I grabbed my helmet bag and the rest of my equipment, ran outside, and jumped into the ambulance that was waiting for me with the engine running. The corpsman at the wheel drove me to Base Operations. As we pulled up in front of Ops, the Coast Guard's Sikorsky HH-52A amphibious helicopter was touching down on the ramp on the opposite side of the building.

I passed through the building and out the double doors that opened to the tarmac. The aircraft was idling with the rotors turning. A crewman in full flight gear came toward me, in a stooped walk, from the helicopter. The main rotor blades on top are located so high above anyone on the ground that there is no reason to stoop and duck, but I always felt the need to walk that way too whenever I entered or exited one of these machines when the engines were running and the main rotor turning. The crewman glanced at my leather name tag and then gave me a friendly and informal salute that I returned in a similar fashion. He turned around and hustled me along to the open door of the helicopter, we both strapped in, and we were up, up, and away.

Our flight to the ship was at an altitude of 500 feet. Helicopter pilots, for some reason, always like to fly low. Maybe it is so they won't have as far to fall if something goes wrong. Airplane pilots like lots of altitude so there is plenty of time to run emergency procedures and formulate a plan in the event of a problem. There is a saying, "neither altitude above you nor the runway behind you will do you any good." I had flown enough of these missions, though, to know this is the way helicopter pilots operate.

We had been in the air almost two hours when we got a visual on the ship. It was churning along, on a northerly course, at a good clip in heavy swells. One of the helicopter's crewmen opened the sliding door on the right side so we could all get a good view of the vessel. We circled it three times, hoping to be able to pick a safe spot to lower me onto. Cables, booms, masts, stacks, and cranes were everywhere—from stem to stern. We cruised along at an altitude of 100 feet. Just over the stern, we saw a small structure with a shed-type roof on it that appeared to be made of tin or some other type of light metal. The aircraft commander was in radio contact with the captain of the ship and asked him if that structure would support a person's weight; he was assured it would be fine.

My helmet was connected to the communications system (ICS) and I could hear the discussion about the potential landing site. I unstrapped and moved up behind the two pilot seats and put my head between them where I could get a good view of my planned landing spot. The structure had open sides, and it was basically just a roof supported by four skinny metal poles. I could see the upper half of the ship's two huge propellers turning as they powered the ship and appeared when the stern reached the top of each swell. I noted that the shed roof had a slight slant to it, sloping downward toward the back of the ship and those giant meat choppers. I didn't like the scene below at all, and I told the aircraft commander that over the ICS, but we didn't see any other alternative.

I advised the crewman acting as the hoist operator I would keep the horse collar on when my feet touched the roof while I made a quick evaluation of whether or not the structure would support me. I also had to see if there was enough traction to keep from sliding off into the ship's huge propellers below. If either of these issues presented a problem, I would give him a hand signal to immediately pull me back up. With this being the plan, I slipped the horse collar over my head and shoulders, and out the door I went.

The plan fell apart the second I hit the shed's tin roof. There were at least a half-dozen burly seamen who had all climbed up to the edges of the roof to be in position to grab me by the ankles as soon as I was within reach. In an instant, I felt strong hands all over me; I couldn't have stayed in the horse collar if I had tried. I flung the horse collar off immediately as I was unceremoniously yanked off the roof and plopped onto the deck. It took me a few moments to recover and get on my feet and then find my sea legs on the pitching deck. A crew member supported me on each side and hurried me to the superstructure where we entered a hatch. Neither of the two seamen uttered a word until we got inside, and when they finally spoke, it was in some foreign language I could not understand. It sounded a little like Russian or some variation of Russian.

We navigated a labyrinth of passageways, hatches, and ladders before reaching a crew sleeping room several decks below the one we had descended from. As I followed along, carrying my flight helmet in my left hand by its chin strap, I started wondering how in the world I was going to get my patient up into the helicopter. We would have to strap him into a Stokes litter and then lift it to the top of the dangerously flimsy shed roof. I couldn't think of any alternative, and I was also dreading the thought of climbing back up there myself to be lifted off the ship as it porpoised and plunged through the ocean swells.

The two crewmen and I entered a tiny cabin with gray steel walls, studded with hundreds of steel rivet heads. A tiny porthole on the outside wall was strapped open, allowing the salty sea breeze to blow in. The compartment was lit by a single flickering fluorescent tube on the ceiling. A bunk was attached to one bulkhead wall, and there I found my patient propped up on a couple of pillows. He was, surprisingly, awake and alert—not at all in the serious condition I had expected to find him. A third crewman was sitting in a chair next to the bunk. He sprang up when we entered and waved an empty liquor bottle in front of me, tipped it up to his lips to mimic guzzling it down, and then pointed to my disheveled and sheepish looking patient. I immediately realized these idiots had called out the Coast Guard for an alleged life-saving mission for a sailor who had passed out due to alcohol intoxication.

I looked at the three and asked, "Anyone speak English?" They all looked at each other with puzzled expressions. I tried pointing at my mouth and saying, "English...English," in a much louder voice. Talking loudly seemed to help, as one of the two who had escorted me down said, "I speak a little." It was English, but heavily accented.

My main concern was we had gotten an initial report this fellow might have been in a diabetic coma. I starting saying, "Diabetes....diabetes. Ask him if he has diabetes." My translator seemed to understand that word. He started jabbering back and forth with the patient in their language, and I did hear the word "diabetes" mentioned several times. The patient shook his head each time he was asked. I then tried to have him ask the fellow why he had passed out, using a combination of words and my own sign language. This initiated another unintelligible discourse among them. When they finally finished, my translator looked at me and said, "Him drunk...go to sleep....no diabetes."

I unstrapped my medical kit, got out a stethoscope and blood pressure cuff, and did a quick exam. I then packed up my gear and waved bye-bye to my patient, who smiled weakly at me. I looked at my escorts and pointed up. They looked at each other as if they didn't understand, so I pointed at my chest and started flapping my arms up and down like a bird. They both laughed out loud, and we started our trek back to the main deck and the fantail of the ship.

The helicopter was still hovering over the stern where it had dropped me. I gave a hand signal for the crewman to drop the horse collar as I fearfully climbed a stepladder placed next to the metal shed roof. I think all the ship's crewmen surrounding me knew how precarious this perch was, and they never let go of me until I had the horse collar secured around my torso. I had to be careful not to get a foot tangled in the excess cable of the hoist which accumulated on the shed's roof whenever the stern rose with the swells, but I didn't stay there long. As soon as I had a death grip on the horse collar, I signaled frantically and spasmodically with a "thumbs up." I got to the top of the hoist and lots of friendly hands pulled me back into the safety of the cabin. The machine I always considered so dangerous suddenly seemed like a wonderful safe cocoon.

Everyone was quiet on the return flight. It was after dark on that New Year's Eve night when we landed back at NAS North Island. I called Martha to drive over and bring me home. We went back to the base on New Year's Day and picked up my bike, which was still in the bike rack at the dispensary.

A few months later, I got a package from the Sikorsky Helicopter Company containing a fancy certificate that conferred on me the "Igor Sikorsky Award" for outstanding service in a lifesaving mission aboard a Sikorsky helicopter. I thought of this award as an ironic joke considering the entire circumstances of the mission. There were no lifesaving efforts performed that day. I found out later the company only awards a few of these commendations every year and I should consider it a great honor to have received it. I might have actually deserved an award on some of my other missions, but this was definitely not the one.

68

Not long after I had literally risked my life to drop onto the cargo ship to examine an intoxicated seaman, I got an invitation to participate in another air-sea rescue with the Coast Guard. This one was to be a night operation, and the weather was atrocious. A high pressure system, associated with a cold front, had moved into the area behind a deep low; gale-force winds gusted to 60 miles per hour and the ocean waters were tumultuous. A relatively small pleasure yacht was somewhere out in the wild ocean waters off of San Diego that night, and it had made a distress call to the Coast Guard because of a female passenger who couldn't stop vomiting. The mission plan was to drop me from a helicopter onto the craft and determine whether the woman was just suffering from seasickness or something more serious.

Whenever I received a call for my services on a Coast Guard mission, I didn't directly talk to anyone from the Coast Guard. They called the naval air station, and the duty officer called me. As he described the nature of the mission that night, I immediately began to question the sanity of it and made a decision pretty quickly to refuse to go. The duty officer was shocked by my response. He told me he was going to contact the other flight surgeons stationed at the base and find a substitute for me, but he warned me of the consequences I might face for refusing this duty. He did contact all of my peers, and each of them, in turn, also refused to support the mission.

I listened to the wind howling as I tossed and turned in our bed for the remainder of the night; I was unable to sleep because I was racked with guilt. I felt sorry for the poor seasick passenger on the yacht, but I also had the feeling she was out on the ocean with a bunch of idiots. The storm had been forecast for days. Why would anyone with a brain take a boat on a "pleasure" cruise out into such weather?

I had to take the car to work the next morning because the storm was still raging. All the streets en route to the base were strewn with palm fronds and other debris. When I arrived at the dispensary, I went straight to the office of Captain Youngman, the commanding officer, to acknowledge my failure and find out if I would be court-martialed for dereliction of duty. I explained to the captain's secretary, Naomi, why I was there, and she told me he already knew all about it. I swallowed hard, and, at that point, I think my knees started shaking.

271

After a couple of minutes, the captain called me into his office. He stood, smiled, and greeted me as he extended his hand for a shake. Before I could get any words out of my mouth, he said, "Dave, you made an excellent decision last night. I wouldn't have gone on such a crazy, dangerous mission either. That was good headwork. You can always count on me to back you up on any decision you make like that."

Navy custom is to never salute when indoors or when you don't have your cover (hat) on. I nevertheless gave him a crisp salute and said, "Thank you, sir." He asked me if there was anything else I wanted to discuss, and, when I told him that was all, he dismissed me. I was so relieved by his support of my decision, I felt like skipping back to my office. I never heard another thing about the incident, and I don't know whether or not the rescue flight was even launched that night. If someone had died on the boat in the storm, *The San Diego Union-Tribune* would have published a front page story, but there was never a mention of it. If there had been an article, it likely would have highlighted the fact that some unidentified flight surgeon had cowardly shirked his assigned duty. I was happy there was never a mention of the incident in the media and hoped the female passenger on the yacht was safely ashore and would be choosier about whom she ventured out to sea with on future voyages.

Not long after that incident, on a spring day in 1974, I deployed on another rather memorable rescue. The Coast Guard received a call from a cruise ship, located over 300 miles offshore, reporting an ill passenger aboard who needed to be evacuated for treatment. The ship was the Royal Viking Star, and it was cruising from Norway to Tahiti by some circuitous route. The ship's physician had determined the elderly male patient had an acute surgical abdomen and should be transported to a major medical facility ashore as quickly as possible. The Coast Guard dispatcher advised the ship that their location was near the limit for a helicopter to reach and return on a load of fuel, and he suggested the captain set a course at maximum speed toward San Diego to minimize the distance.

When our rescue helicopter got within radio range of the ship, the pilots made contact, related our precarious fuel situation, and told the crew to have the patient on deck and ready to go. When we sighted the ship, the pilots told me to be ready to be lowered onto the deck and warned I would have a maximum of 20 minutes to evaluate the situation, obtain information about the patient, and get him and myself back aboard.

It was a beautiful, clear, crisp day, and the Royal Viking Star, with its almost blinding-white finish, looked elegant cutting through the waves.

The ship was massive in size, yet appeared sleek and streamlined too. As we approached the ship, we made a 180-degree turn back to the east so we could match the vessel's speed and course. We saw several suitable landing spots to lower me onto, but the patient was on the large open deck at the bow, lying supine on a stretcher and surrounded by the medical staff and other crew. I would land there.

The pilot put the helicopter in a sideways crab over the bow, enabling him to see the superstructure out his right side window and maintain the same relative position to the ship as he matched its forward speed. The crew in the helicopter cabin opened the big sliding door on the right, and I swung out in the horse collar. As I was lowered to the ship, I saw hundreds of passengers lining the rails and windows on all the forward decks with cameras and binoculars trained on me. This was probably the most exciting moment of the cruise for those folks!

The hoist operator tried to time my landing so I was not going down at the same time the bow was rising on a swell, since that would double my impact force with the deck. He did a nice job, but it still required a parachute-type landing. I bent my knees, rolled to the deck, and flipped off the horse collar, as I had been trained to do in Pensacola. When I was on my feet, I walked over to the central area of the bow where the patient lay. An IV pole was attached to the stretcher, and a drip was infusing.

A tall, thin, blond Norwegian doctor and two attractive, young Nordic-looking nurses attended the patient. They were all dressed in crisp, white uniforms. An elderly woman in a light blue dress stood at the side of the stretcher and held the patient's hand. The medical attendants spoke perfect English, so it was easy to get a brief history of the man's illness. They had also prepared copies of his medical chart for me to take with him. It was all organized and efficient.

As soon as I felt I had the information I needed, I told the doctor we needed to get his patient aboard the helicopter as soon as possible, since our fuel situation remained critical. At that point, the patient's wife said, "If you are taking him, you are taking me. He is not going anywhere without me."

I spent little time arguing with the lady. She expressed herself firmly and clearly, and that was that. I warned her she would have to be cabled up into the helicopter and asked her if she was willing to accept the risk. She again stated that either she was going too, or he was not going.

The crew on the helicopter didn't know what I was arranging, and I had no idea how close we were to the maximum gross weight limit for the aircraft or how much additional fuel burn the extra weight would incur. I gave the hand signal for the Stokes litter and it was lowered to the deck. We transferred the patient to it, strapped him in, attached the cable hook, and the flight crew hoisted him up.

The crew then started to lower the horse collar for me. I made an "X" with my arms and signaled for the two-man rescue basket to be lowered. The crewman in the doorway at first looked confused, but he understood what I was requesting, complied, and lowered the basket.

We helped the elderly woman into the basket, placed her cane across her lap, and then loaded their three suitcases into the opposite side of the basket. The flight crewmen hoisted her up and got her aboard, but by the time they lowered the horse collar for me, I was looking at my watch. I had gone several minutes beyond my allotted time. When I ran over in a frantic hurry to grab the horse collar, I got a terrific electrical shock that almost knocked me down; I had forgotten to let the steel cable touch the deck first, as I had been trained to do, in order to discharge static electricity. I somehow recovered my senses, pulled the horse collar over my head and shoulders, and was hoisted aboard. I just hoped we still had enough fuel to make it back to San Diego.

On the return trip, I wasn't able to provide much medical care other than to take vital signs every 15 minutes and check the IV flow. This was before the days of electronic blood pressure cuffs, and it was difficult, with a standard BP cuff, to even obtain an accurate reading because of the noise. Helicopters are extremely noisy. I could only get a rough idea of the systolic pressure by watching for a needle flicker on the gauge as I slowly deflated the cuff. We had placed earplugs in the patient's ears as soon as we had gotten him aboard, so I couldn't even converse with him, but I had equipped his wife with a headset and was able to talk to her and get a little more medical history through my helmet system.

We had been airborne for over 5½ hours, and it was dark by the time we touched down on the lighted helipad at Scripps Memorial Hospital La Jolla. A nurse and two orderlies came out and helped us lift the Stokes litter onto a wheeled gurney. As we walked into the Emergency Room, the nurse told me their doctor needed to talk to the physician who was reportedly attending on board the helicopter and wanted to know where he was. I said, "That would be me." She eyed me up and down for a few seconds, taking in my flight suit and survival gear and said, "Oh!"

I didn't spend much time in the ER. I told the physician assigned to the patient what I knew, handed him the records from the ship, and then I hustled back out to the idling helicopter. We immediately took off on the short flight to North Island to drop me off.

We had been airborne about two or three minutes when an amber "low fuel" light came on. It stayed on until we touched down in front of the ops building. On previous missions with the Coast Guard, the pilots just sat idling for a couple of minutes while I jumped out, and then they took right off to fly back across the bay to their home base. On this particular night, they shut down and called for a fuel truck. The aircraft commander told me the amber light comes on when there is about 20 minutes of usable fuel remaining. I was happy to have made it safely home again. It had been an eventful day.

I felt a little guilty as I headed off for home after leaving the rest of the crew waiting for the fuel truck at the end of the long mission. I was probably at home and in my bed asleep by the time they finally took off again.

I called Scripps La Jolla the following day and was connected to the nursing station where my patient was being cared for. I identified myself to the charge nurse and asked for an update. She told me the man had been taken directly to surgery the night before, and he was found to have an infarcted kidney caused by a clot in the respective renal artery. The affected kidney was removed, and the patient was stable and beginning a satisfactory recovery. The nurse also told me the man's wife could not stop talking about being hoisted aboard the helicopter. She told the staff it was the most exciting thing she had ever done in her entire life.

A few weeks later, I started thinking about all the people on the Royal Viking Star who had been taking pictures of our rescue operation, and I wondered if I might be able to obtain some copies. I wrote to the headquarters of the Royal Viking Line in San Francisco to see if any of the ship's crew had taken any photos. I got a reply from Warren Titus, the president of the company, thanking me for my participation in the operation, and I found a pack of pictures enclosed that had been taken by the ship's official photographer. The entire rescue was well documented, but I particularly liked one in which I was hanging beneath the helicopter in the horse collar. When I look at the photo today, it brings back memories of that mission and a few other exciting ones.

Air-Sea rescue in the Pacific
The Royal Viking Star cruise ship

Spring - 1974

69

I had a sudden surprise on Wednesday, December 4, 1974, when I received TAD orders (temporary additional duty) to the *USS Ranger* for a one-week period to serve as an additional flight surgeon for the ship's medical department. The aircraft carrier's mission that week was carrier qualifications for pilots checking out in new equipment (aircraft type). Due to the increased risk of an aircraft incident or accident during the scheduled training evolutions, the senior medical officer (SMO) on the carrier had requested an additional flight surgeon to supplement his regular medical staff. My orders were issued on short notice, and I was scheduled to depart for the ship two days later, on Friday, December 6.

One worry I always had about being in the Navy was I might, at some point, be assigned sea duty. Those assignments typically involve deployments of nine to twelve months at sea, separated from home and family. If I had been a bachelor, I might have looked at sea duty as an exciting adventure and a chance to see the world, but I had a wonderful wife and two small children, whom I was very close to, and I couldn't imagine such a long separation. Orders for the dreaded sea duty had unexpectedly arrived, but it would be for only one week, and I could handle that just fine. I looked at this as another great adventure and an opportunity to escape from my generally boring duties at the NAS North Island Dispensary.

A flight crew of squadron VR-30 flew me to the carrier. The unit's nickname was *The Providers*, and its primary mission was to fly personnel, supplies, and mail to and from aircraft carriers at sea. The flights were made on a daily basis whenever a carrier was at sea and within range. For these operations, the squadron employed two aircraft types: the C-1 Trader, a twin engine propeller plane with reciprocating radial engines, and the C-2 Greyhound, which is powered by twin turboprop engines. Whichever aircraft was flown for a given mission, the operation was known as the COD (the acronym stands for "carrier on-deck delivery"). My official naval flight logbook reminds me the aircraft used for the COD that morning was a C-1. We had mail and one other passenger aboard for the flight to the ship that Friday morning. When I climbed aboard the aircraft at North Island, I wore the same flight gear as I did for a flight in the T-28, but I felt a little weird carrying my brown Samsonite carry-on suitcase as I stepped through the boarding door and stooped into the cabin.

The *USS Ranger* was about 100 miles offshore when we departed the air station, and the flight to the ship was a short one. The weather was beautiful, with clear skies and unlimited visibility. I could see the *Ranger* through the windshield when we were still 30 or 40 miles away as I stood in the cockpit doorway between the two pilots. When we entered the downwind leg of our approach, I returned to my seat under the overhead wing, on the port side, and snugged up my seat belt and shoulder harness. I looked down at the ship through the porthole window and thought it looked like a toy in a bathtub. It didn't appear to be nearly big enough to land an airplane on, and I had a hard time wrapping my mind around the fact we were actually going to do that. It seemed surreal. The C-1 does not have ejection seats, and I took another look at the exits and went over in my mind how to open them in the event we ended up in the water.

Once we turned final approach, I could no longer see the ship, since my seat faced toward the rear of the aircraft. All I could see was we were getting closer and closer to the water, until, all of a sudden, I saw the aft end of the ship's flight deck go by, and then the island superstructure came into view. I thought we had missed all of the arresting wires and were going around for another try, when I was slammed into the back of my seat as we came to an abrupt stop. We had trapped a three-wire on our first approach. When I stepped out onto the deck that day, I arrived in a whole new world. A sailor grabbed me by the arm and whisked me and my suitcase quickly over to a hatch that led into the relative safety of an interior passageway. My exposure to the dangers of the flight deck that morning was brief, but the environment's hazards to life and limb were almost tangible; I was relieved to step through the hatch.

My medical duties on the ship were minimal. We conducted a couple of hours of sick call every morning, and I was expected to spend some time in the squadron Ready Rooms with the pilots before they launched. Other than that, I was generally free to explore the ship; I was all over it—the bridge, the hangar deck, Aircraft Maintenance, Flight Operations, Pri-Fly (Primary Flight Control), "Vultures Row" (a balcony with an excellent view of the flight deck), and the LSO (landing signal officer) platform.

The pilots were qualifying for carrier operations in F-4 Phantoms, A-7 Corsairs, and F-8 Crusaders. I carried my camera everywhere I went on the ship and captured lots of pictures as aircraft catapulted off the deck, flew the final approach, touched down and "trapped" the wire, and as they occasionally "boltered"—bounced off the deck after missing all three wires.

I spent a lot of time on the LSO platform standing directly behind the landing signal officer. That was the best place on the ship to get good pictures of aircraft on final approach and as they trapped (or boltered). I got some great shots. The LSO is always a highly experienced carrier pilot who has been specially trained and qualified for this critical positon. During flight operations, he is in direct communication with the pilot when an aircraft is on final approach. He offers verbal instructions when corrections are necessary to the aircraft's attitude or flight path, and he expects the pilot to immediately make the corrections advised. He communicates with the pilot via a headset but can also signal with large paddles in the event of a radio failure.

When I stood on the platform watching the LSO direct the approaches, I wore a headset as well so I could hear the banter. I heard things like, "You're a little low—add power…line-up, line-up; you're right of course—come left." As the aircraft got closer and closer to touchdown, the calls were more frequent and the LSO's voice became more emphatic. Getting low on short final was the most dangerous deviation and generated the most dramatic commands from the officer. In such a case, he would shout into his boom microphone, "Power…power…power." If the pilot didn't make an immediate and appropriate correction, he would command, "Wave off…wave off…wave off," and activate a flashing red light on the approach end of the deck. The wave-off is a mandatory command, and the pilot is required to go around for another try, regardless of whether or not he agrees with the decision. If the aircraft touched down but missed all of the wires and failed to trap, the LSO would call, "Bolter…bolter…bolter," to let the pilot know he was not going to come to a stop on the deck—he was going flying again.

A large safety net is located in front of the LSO platform for everyone standing there to dive into if it looks like there might be a ramp strike. The net funnels its occupants to a chute leading several stories down to one of the lower decks. I suspected it would be too late to dive into the net by the time anyone realized an aircraft was actually going to crash into the back of the ship. I believe the net gave us all a false sense of security; nevertheless I was glad it was there.

The ship cruised up and down the California coastline as it conducted day and night flight operations all week. The conditions were relatively calm seas the entire time, and we were always within approximately 100 miles of Miramar Naval Air Station or North Island, so any pilot who didn't get aboard had a "bingo" (alternate) located on solid ground. As an extra precaution, an A-3 tanker was airborne at all times for air refueling, and a helicopter hovered on station with rescue swimmers aboard. The qualifying pilots completed 1,700 arrested landings that week. I don't know how many bolters occurred.

All of these pilots were previously carrier-qualified as an initial requirement to receive the wings of a naval aviator. So they had all done this before, but in different equipment. Despite the fact the weather and sea conditions were ideal all week, plenty of tension existed in the Ready Rooms at all times, especially before the night launches. I spent most my evenings hobnobbing in those Ready Rooms with the pilots, and, at times, I felt more like a chaplain than a flight surgeon. My role was to observe and attempt to detect signs a pilot's nerves might be getting the best of him, but I found most of the aviators just sat quietly before their launch and didn't seem to be inclined to share their thoughts and fears with me or anyone else.

In each squadron Ready Room, I was constantly watching for an opportunity to harangue the commanding officer in each unit into adding my name to the flight schedule to fly with one of his qualified pilots. Some of the instructors were scheduled for proficiency flights, and I was dying to go along with one of them. Each of the COs, in turn, told me they would try to fit me in, but it was a busy week and it never happened. I thought I would finally get to experience a CAT (catapult) shot anyway when they flew me off the ship, but that would not be in one of the high-performance fighters or attack aircraft.

On December 10, I went up in the rescue helicopter, an SH-3D Sea King, to watch the flight operations from there. I logged 3.3 hours of flight time, which counted toward my monthly minimum. While we were airborne, we watched an F-8 on approach, and then, as it touched down, I saw a large piece separate from the aircraft, shoot across the deck, and land in the water. The aircraft trapped the wire but slewed to one side, stopping close to the edge of the deck. One of the main landing gear wheels had broken off on touchdown. The pilot was fine, there was no fire, and none of the deck crew was injured, but the aircraft had sustained major damage. It sat on the deck tipped over on one wing. The deck was cleared quickly, and the damaged plane was taken on one of the elevators down to the hanger deck below so the rest of the airborne aircraft could be recovered. That was the only accident that occurred that week, in the over 1,700 arrested landings. It was a coincidence I happened to be up in the helicopter when the accident happened and watched it from above. I was extremely thankful no one got hurt.

One morning when I was seeing patients in sick call, I evaluated a sailor with abdominal pain whom I thought might have an acute appendicitis. I found the senior medical officer, who was also a board-certified general surgeon, and he examined the patient as well. He felt my diagnosis was correct, and since it was only a short flight to Balboa Naval Hospital, he thought the safest thing to do was to load the sailor into a helicopter and medevac him for surgery there. The skipper of the ship told the SMO he would have to deal with the problem because he wasn't going to interrupt the flight schedule to launch a helicopter.

So, that afternoon, I scrubbed into surgery with the senior medical officer, and we removed the sailor's inflamed appendix. The SMO had never done major abdominal surgery at sea before, and he was notably nervous. He checked the surgical packs carefully to make sure he had all the instruments required before we made the first incision. No anesthesiologist was aboard, so the dental officer administered a general anesthesia. I thought that was the most worrisome issue for the procedure, but the dentist seemed to emit an aura of robust self-confidence, and no problems arose from the anesthesia. The SMO and I had to strap ourselves to the operating table during the procedure in order to remain steady while the ship rolled and pitched in the swells, and we had a few instruments fall off onto the deck. We could hear aircraft pound onto the deck above us with each landing as we cut, clamped, stitched, and tied. Our patient did fine post-op, and we medevaced him to shore the next morning.

By the time the aircraft qualification period was complete at the end of the week, I felt as if I had been gone from home a long time. A huge H-46 tandem-rotor helicopter, known as the "Flying Banana," transported me back to North Island. About 20 other personnel were passengers on the same flight and taken ashore.

I never got my CAT shot, but I wasn't too disappointed. I was just happy to be back at home. I had really missed my wife Martha and our two babies. It was the longest I had ever been gone from them. I had friends in the Navy who had been at sea and away from their families for months and months, but I sure wasn't cut out for one of those nine-month deployments. I was so proud of myself for putting on my "big-boy pants" and somehow toughing out my one week of sea duty.

My "bus ride" to the USS Ranger

Arriving aboard on December 4, 1974 in a Navy C-1 "Trader"

70

The same December week that I got orders to the *USS Ranger*, I also received an official-looking letter from BUMED (The Bureau of Medicine and Surgery). I knew it contained something important because "Airmail" was stamped in red on the outside of the envelope. The letter inside, dated November 27, contained a bunch of acronyms, numbers, and codes that I couldn't understand or decipher, as was the case with all my official military orders. It was just a letter, though—not orders—but it looked as if it had been written in something resembling hieroglyphics. I somehow gleaned the fact I could expect to receive PCS (permanent change of station) orders in January to NAS Whidbey, Oak Harbor, Washington.

NAS Whidbey had been my first choice of duty when everyone in my class at the Naval Aerospace Medical Institute was making their selections. Now that I had finally been awarded my dream assignment, I wasn't real excited about it. Martha and I had made the most out of our tour in Coronado, and I don't think either of us would have minded at all staying there to complete the rest of my three-year service obligation. I had applied for a residency in orthopedic surgery at Balboa Naval Hospital earlier in the year. I had been accepted into the program and was scheduled to start the following July, but I decided not to take the position. I changed my mind for a number of reasons, but the decision was primarily due to the fact I was 29 years old, had a family to support, and was getting tired of being in training. Also, the residency had a year-for-year payback period to the Navy, and I was anxious to get out into civilian practice and start earning a living.

Martha and I had been discussing where we wanted to start my medical practice and "hang my shingle" when I completed my obligated military service. One of the nice things about being a physician is you can probably make a living anywhere you choose; the whole world was wide open to us. It was a great feeling, but we kept thinking more and more about the little town in North Idaho with the beautiful French name of Coeur d'Alene. We had visited the pretty little logging town frequently when I was an intern in nearby Spokane, Washington, and we both thought the lake on which it was situated, Lake Coeur d'Alene, had to be the most beautiful inland body of water in the entire United States.

My relatively short tenure as a small-town physician in Grand Coulee, Washington, right after internship, had given me a taste of what it was like to be a general practitioner in rural America. That experience made me aware of the rewards as well as the personal hardships of that type of practice, but I thought the satisfaction of really making a difference in a community would far outweigh the sacrifices I knew I would have to endure. I had decided I wanted to be a country doctor, and this looked like a great place to live, raise a family, and have the type of medical practice I envisioned. Coeur d'Alene would one day become a major tourist destination and a popular retirement locale, but, at the time, it was a small lumber mill town. The population was mainly comprised of loggers, mill workers, and miners. They were just the kind of salt-of-the-earth folks I wanted to take care of. This became our working plan for when I finally completed my required military obligation.

Martha, by this time, had happily settled into her life as a young mother in Coronado. She loved the local climate, and she had made a number of friends, joined a book club, and set up an informal babysitting pool with other young mothers. Those women would bring their toddlers in strollers to the city swimming pool together and visit on the edge of the wading pool, while the kids splashed and played in the water. Martha also took our two children to nearby Spreckels Park almost every day; there she fed Alice her infant formula and watched Jill chase the pigeons while she chatted with her friends. Martha didn't want to leave Coronado at all, but official orders were coming down the pike, and we had no choice. I had a couple of months to ease both of us into the idea that this would be another good transition for us.

Duty on Whidbey Island would get us back to the Pacific Northwest for a few months prior to my projected release from active duty, and that would make it more convenient to further explore Coeur d'Alene and other cities and towns in that part of the country, scoping out practice opportunities. By the time my official orders arrived, we were both adjusted to the idea of leaving Coronado and were looking forward to a new adventure.

It was mid-January, 1975, when I received my official orders to NAS Whidbey Island, with a report date of February 21, but, after receiving the letter of advance notice in late November, Martha and I had already started making plans for the move.

One of the first things we had to consider was what to do with our precious sailboat, *Thursday's Child*. We both loved the boat, but we knew we either had to sell it in California or somehow arrange to have it shipped on a semi from San Diego to Oak Harbor, a distance of over 1,300 miles.

The protected waters of Puget Sound are known as a sailor's paradise, with the many secluded anchorages in the San Juan Islands as wonderful weekend destinations. With that in mind, both of us wanted to take the boat with us to Whidbey Island, but we came to the realization that the cost of moving it was beyond our means. Another problem was that I was still making payments on the boat with extra money I was earning by moonlighting at Coronado Hospital, and no moonlighting jobs were available at my new duty station. I thought briefly about sailing it up the coast, and it is only because the Navy did not allow enough travel time to complete a voyage by sea that I was forced to abandon that option—a blessing in disguise. We finally resigned ourselves to the fact we would have to sell *Thursday's Child.*

One evening in early January, Commander Ralph Gaither, the commanding officer of the SERE school, invited Martha and me to his home in La Jolla for dinner. I had gotten to know Commander Gaither pretty well, since I was under his direct command as the flight surgeon for the survival training, and he was always present at the compound on the same weekends I was there. Ralph was a naval aviator who was shot down in an F-4 Phantom over North Vietnam on October 17, 1965, and was a prisoner of war for almost eight years. He was released on February 12, 1973, in Operation Homecoming. Ralph and his wife, Bobbi, planned to entertain us that evening as a farewell before we departed San Diego for Whidbey Island. We had a wonderful evening with this fine couple, and Ralph gave me a signed copy of a book he had authored about his years of imprisonment. He also showed us some letters he had written home to his parents in which he told of his dream of buying a sailboat, if and when he was ever released. When I heard that, I told Ralph I might have a deal for him.

Ralph bought our sailboat from us with a partner, George Coker, and the two friends became joint owners. George had been a fellow POW at the "Hanoi Hilton" with Ralph, and he had also been dreaming of owning a boat someday when he returned home. Ralph and George made me a fair offer, and I was able to pay off the remaining loan on the boat with the proceeds of the sale. Martha and I hated to say goodbye to *Thursday's Child,* but we were both happy it would be enjoyed by such deserving patriots. I wished I had been in a financial position to just give them the boat, but that was not an option; I knew, in any case, nothing could compensate them for what they had endured.

In late January, I flew up to Whidbey Island to check out the housing situation. Once again, I was informed that no government housing was available for junior officers, but I found a wonderful three-bedroom rental house just outside of Oak Harbor, and I made deposit to hold it until we arrived.

Our little family aboard *Thursday's Child*
David – Jill – Alice – Martha

The San Diego Yacht Club – December 1974

71

It was the second week in February when we loaded up the Olds station wagon again, this time with a family of four, said goodbye to Coronado, and crossed the bridge to head north on Interstate 5. We spent our first night on the road in Sacramento.

On the second day of our journey, we left the San Joaquin Valley of Central California behind us and continued on the interstate highway up the fertile Sacramento Valley and on into Oregon. We arrived at the Washington State Ferry Terminal in the little town of Mukilteo, north of Seattle, late in the afternoon on our third day out of San Diego. The car ferry carried us across Puget Sound from Mukilteo to the little town of Clinton on the south end of Whidbey Island.

Western Washington has an extensive state ferry system to transport vehicles and passengers between the mainland and the Olympic and Kitsap Peninsulas, as well as to islands in the Sound—Vashon, Bainbridge, and Whidbey. Some of the areas served are accessible only by water, while others can be reached by land, but only via a long, circuitous route. The ferries are part of the highway system in Washington. We were on State Highway 525 when we arrived at Mukilteo, and the highway appeared to terminate at the ferry terminal, but it actually continues with the same highway number from the Clinton Terminal on the island side. This intrigued me, and it made our new island home seem remote, isolated, and exciting.

Our little family of four put on our coats and traipsed up to the passenger deck and out onto the open bow for the 20-minute voyage across this narrow part of the Sound. It was almost dark, and gusty winds were whipping up white caps on the water. Martha and I stood tightly together on the rail, holding the kids in our arms. Inhaling the salty marine air made me feel invigorated, healthy, hardy, and confident as I watched the lights on the shore at Mukilteo fade behind us and the lights of Clinton get brighter and brighter. I was excited to get to my new duty station.

Whidbey Island is about 55 miles long from the south end to the north end, where it connects to the mainland by the Deception Pass Bridge. It took us almost an hour to drive from Clinton, at the south end, to Oak Harbor, near the north end. We found a motel room in the little town of Oak Harbor for the night.

The next morning, we stopped at the Koetji Real Estate office and picked up the keys to our new home. We drove north and east a few miles out of town to the new Polnell Shores development. Our house was located on a terraced hillside just above the eastern shore of the island. It was an attractive, newly constructed three-bedroom rambler with a nice big yard. On a clear day, the large windows in the living room would provide a killer view of the east sound and the snow-capped Cascade Mountains. We would be able to enjoy Mount Baker to the north, Glacier Peak to the east, and Mount Rainier to the south—three of the four highest mountain peaks in the state. On this particular February day, however, the home's spectacular view was completely obscured. It was cold, cloudy, rainy, and windy. We could just make out the edge of the water below us at the bottom of the slope, but that was all.

When we pulled into the driveway, we found a car already parked there. The real estate agent who was managing the rental, Bob Huddleston, and his associate, George Churchill, were unexpectedly there. They had inspected the house, started the furnace, and built a fire in the wood-burning fireplace. The two helped us get our utility accounts set up and provided us with all kinds of information about the community. Bob and George checked on us periodically over the next few days until our furniture arrived from San Diego and we were settled in. Thanks to these two fine gentlemen, we couldn't have had a warmer welcome to our new community. Their neighborly, above-and-beyond efforts confirmed for us the kind of support we had envisioned for ourselves in moving to a small town.

72

The medical facility at NAS Whidbey is more than a simple clinic. It is actually a small hospital with a well-equipped emergency room, an operating room, outpatient clinics, and physical therapy. In 1975, the hospital had departments of family medicine, pediatrics, surgery, obstetrics, anesthesia and aviation medicine, and it housed a limited number of inpatient beds where patients could be admitted for overnight hospitalization. Although we were well staffed and equipped for a small military hospital, the facility had no Intensive Care or Coronary Care Unit. This limited our capabilities somewhat and meant any patients with critical injuries or serious medical illnesses had to be evacuated by air from the island. In those cases, the flight surgeon on call was assigned as a special crew member and provided care and monitoring of the patient en route.

Although I worked in several of the clinics, my official assignment at Whidbey was to an operational aviation squadron, and I would split my time between the hospital and the squadron. I was officially the squadron flight surgeon for VAQ-129, the EA-6B Prowler replacement air group (known as "the RAG"). The squadron was the West Coast training squadron for the Prowler. After a student "graduates" from the RAG, he has completed training and receives an assignment to a regular fleet squadron operating that aircraft.

The EA-6B is a twin-engine jet aircraft that flies at subsonic speeds but is extremely maneuverable and routinely operates from aircraft carriers deployed at sea. Its mission is electronics counter-warfare. The onboard electronic equipment is designed to jam enemy radar and antiaircraft tracking capabilities. The Prowler has a single pilot seat and three seats occupied by non-pilot naval flight officers (formerly known as bombardier/navigators). In the EA-6B community, these officers are specially trained to operate the jamming equipment and are referred to as ECMOs (electronic counter-warfare measures officers). The four ejection seats in the aircraft are configured such that there are two side-by-side front seats and two side-by-side rear seats. There are separately operated clear canopies over the front and rear. The left front seat is the pilot's seat and is equipped with the only set of flight controls. The ECMO occupying the right front seat performs co-pilot duties by reading checklists, assisting with navigation, operating the radios, and accomplishing, with the pilot, any

289

required inflight emergency procedures. The rear-seat ECMOs operate the jamming electronic equipment.

I didn't know any of this stuff about the airplane or its mission when I checked into the squadron. In fact, I don't think I had ever seen an EA-6B Prowler at that point.

The commanding officer of VAQ-129 was Commander "Johnny" DiLoreto, a gregarious little Italian from New York. The CO welcomed me into his office on my first day, and we sat and talked for a few minutes. I liked him immediately, and it soon became apparent everyone in the squadron thought the world of him. While I was there, he called Lieutenant Commander Dave Pate, the operations officer, into his office and told him to give me an orientation to the aircraft and issue the additional personal flight gear I needed for the Prowler. Johnny wanted to take me flying. I needed my own personal torso harness (which attaches to the ejection seat fittings), a G-suit, a new survival/flotation vest, a new flight helmet, and an oxygen mask with a mini regulator. I already had the rest of the personal flight gear I needed. With all these new goodies, it was as if Christmas had arrived early.

Dave Pate and I hit it off right away. He was in charge of flight scheduling and made sure my first Prowler flight was with him. It didn't take me long to realize what a popular guy I was. All the flight instructors wanted the "doc" to fly with them. At first I thought this attraction was a result of my magnetic personality, and it took me a while to figure out the real reason.

Naval aviators and naval flight officers (NFOs) are almost paranoid when they show up in the Aviation Exam Room for their annual flight physicals. They are all aware of the strict physical standards for aviators and realize they can be grounded for any deviation from these requirements. By sucking up to the flight surgeon and cultivating a friendship, they thought I was more likely to sign off one of my aviator buddies, even if he was one or two pounds overweight or his blood pressure was a millimeter or two above the maximum. They all knew I had a lot of power over them with regard to their continuing flight status, and it eventually became obvious to me why they each tried to get me on the flight schedule with them, wanted to sit next to me at the squadron's all-hands meetings, and encouraged me go to the O' Club and drink beer with them on Friday and Saturday nights. They might have to cash in on this relationship at some point, and most of them realized that cultivating a working friendship with the doc was like money in the bank. I figured this all out, and it was okay with me.

I went on my first flight in the EA-6B on March 17 with Dave Pate. He gave me a good ride with lots of aerobatic maneuvers he thought I would enjoy. I was impressed and did enjoy it, but not as much as he expected me to. The flying I had done in San Diego from NAS North Island in the T-28 was much more fun because I always had a set of controls and got to fly it. In this fancy, high-tech jet, I was merely a passenger. I felt like I was just on a wild carnival ride each time I went up.

During my six-month tour at NAS Whidbey, I only flew on seven more training flights in the EA-6B. The rest of my required flight time was logged on SAR missions and medevacs in Navy helicopters.

On July 21, I went on a flight that was a little more interesting than the rest. It was a daytime training flight of two jets on a formation low-level, going east across Washington, into the Idaho Panhandle, south into Central Idaho and then back through northern Oregon and southern Washington to NAS Whidbey. The squadron's rule for flying a low-level restricted us to a minimum altitude above the terrain of 500 feet. Most of the pilots didn't consider 500 feet to be low-level flight at all, so the rule was flagrantly violated. On this particular flight, I recall looking up at treetops going by as we hugged the ground and sped along at speeds approaching 600 miles per hour, wing tip to wing tip. We covered a lot of real estate that day in a short time and completed the circuit in 2.8 hours of flight time.

On our descent into NAS Whidbey, we got a call from Squadron Operations over the UHF com radio. The message ordered all of us to report to the commanding officer's office as soon as we had secured the two aircraft. None of us had any idea what it was all about, but we figured we must have done something bad.

Commander DiLoreto had received a call from the airport manager in Grangeville, Idaho, to report a near midair collision involving a civilian aircraft and two EA-6B Prowlers. He told the commander our two aircraft had come screaming through the traffic pattern at the airport while a Cessna 172 was in the pattern doing touch-and-go landings, and we had flown *under* the Cessna when it was on a downwind leg to land.

The CO called us each in, one at a time, to hear our individual stories behind his closed office door so he could compare them for inconsistencies. I was first to be summoned. None of us knew we had experienced a near midair at the Grangeville Airport that day, and no one on the flight had seen the airport or the Cessna in the pattern. That was both good and bad. It was good because we had nothing to hide, but it was bad because none of us eight airmen had seen the airport or the other aircraft. I think the commander wanted to talk to me first because he assumed his flight surgeon was the least-likely crew member to lie to him. Fortunately, I didn't know anything, and I swore to him we were never below 500 feet above ground level. I am not sure he believed me in that regard. After we had each "testified" separately that we hadn't seen anything, it was apparent to him we were all telling the truth about the near-disaster with the Cessna.

I don't remember any serious consequences from our reckless and dangerous transgressions that day. Commander DiLoreto did suspect we were flying lower than the required minimum altitude and reiterated the restriction. He reminded us that everyone in the aircraft is responsible for knowing exactly where we are at all times and that we all need to have our "heads outside the cockpit" looking for traffic when flying a low-level. He told us he would write a letter of apology to the manager of the Grangeville Airport and assure him nothing like that would ever happen again.

Navy EA-6B Prowler

73

The call schedule at Whidbey Island Naval Hospital was the lightest I had experienced since starting medical school. The facility was well staffed, and I was medical officer of the day only three or four times per month. Even when I was on call, the duty was generally pretty easy. A comfortable sleeping room was provided for the duty doc, and I occasionally experienced a call night in which I banked a full eight hours of uninterrupted sleep.

The medical corpsmen were competent treating most of the minor problems and frequently didn't even awaken the doctor on call. They could almost always distinguish between a minor, self-limited illness and something more serious that an MD should evaluate. Some of the medical officers were so confident in the corpsmen's abilities that they pre-signed pads of blank prescriptions so they wouldn't be awakened for a signature. When I was on duty, the corpsmen on call with me invariably asked if I would pre-sign prescriptions for them, but I never felt comfortable doing that and requested I be awakened if a prescription drug seemed indicated. That reluctance on my part likely saved the life of a naval aviator's wife late one night.

The pilot brought his young wife to the hospital with cramping pain in her abdomen. The corpsman on duty with me happened to be one I thought was very competent, and I had a lot of faith in him. He evaluated the patient and diagnosed a bad case of gastroenteritis. He advised her to stay on clear liquids for a few days and wrote a prescription for an anti-diarrheal known as Lomotil. He then brought the prescription into the sleeping room for me to sign. I was in a sound sleep when he gently shook me awake. He described the problem to me and said I could just sign the prescription and go back to sleep. I asked a few questions, and it sounded like nothing serious, so I was tempted to just put my "John Henry" on the paper he held out to me, roll back over, close my eyes, and go back to sleep.

I let out a long sigh, yawned a couple of times, and said, "I'd better come take a quick look at her."

I shuffled out into the hall wearing the rumpled green surgical scrub suit I had been sleeping in, and I was still yawning and trying to wake up when I walked into the examining room. As I entered the room, my eyes focused on the face of a pretty young woman who was lying on her back on the exam table, covered with a sheet. Her face was the same color as the sheet. I was suddenly wide awake and the adrenaline was flowing through me. I took one of her hands in mine and looked at her nail beds. They were white too and didn't fill with capillary blood when I pushed on them and then released. I pulled down her lower eyelids and saw that the conjunctiva, which reflects on the back side of the lid, was also pale and bloodless. At this point, I was no longer yawning; my mind was going at warp speed. What was going on here? This definitely was not a case of simple gastroenteritis.

I felt for a pulse at her wrist; it was rapid and thready. I looked at my watch and started counting and came up with a rate of 120 beats per minute. I put a blood pressure cuff on her. Her BP was 70/40—very low. I put my hand on her abdomen and she moaned and asked me not to do that. She had signs of diffuse peritoneal irritation, and it had to be blood causing that irritation. I knew at this point this patient had massive internal bleeding into her abdomen. I needed to get a little more history, but I was already pretty sure I was dealing with a ruptured ectopic (tubal) pregnancy. I told the corpsman to get me an IV set up and to call the gynecologist on staff, the anesthesiologist, and the Operating Room crew.

One of my biggest worries at that point was that we didn't have a blood bank at the hospital, and the young woman had already lost a lot of blood. A rapid infusion of a normal saline IV solution would likely correct her volume loss and temporarily bring her blood pressure up, but she needed some whole blood to replace what she had lost. We drew a blood sample and determined her blood type, then called the civilian hospital in Anacortes, Washington, to see how many units of the that type they had in their blood bank. There would be no time to do a full cross-match, and we would just have to get the appropriate type on the way and hope it was a compatible match. The hospital, located 20 miles north of Oak Harbor, had five pints of blood that matched her type, and I told them to send me all five ASAP via Washington State Patrol with lights and siren.

I started an IV with a large-bore needle and catheter and ran normal saline in, with the stopcock on the tubing wide open. I could then finally talk to the patient and take a medical history. When I asked her about her menstrual history, she told me she had missed her last period, and the one before had been unusually light. She had no previous pregnancies, but she told me that she and her husband had been trying. This all fit with my working diagnosis of a ruptured ectopic pregnancy. The remainder of her medical history was unremarkable, and she stated she hadn't eaten anything all day nor drunk any liquids for several hours. That was good and would make the anesthesiologist happy.

When the anesthesiologist arrived, we wheeled the patient to the Operating Room. She shed a few tears when she said goodbye to her husband just outside the OR's double doors. I patted her on the shoulder and assured them both that she would be fine—a statement I wasn't very confident about. The OR techs arrived shortly after that, set up the laparotomy tray of instruments, and started prepping the skin of her abdomen. The anesthesiologist organized his cart and assembled his gear while we waited for the gynecologic surgeon to come in from home.

The gynecologist on staff was newly assigned to the hospital, and we had not yet even met one another. This required him to put blind faith in the diagnostic acumen of a general physician whom he did not know. He wouldn't even have an opportunity to do his own assessment, as time was of the essence and surgery could not be delayed. When he arrived, we both immediately started our surgical scrub while the anesthesiologist put the patient to sleep. The surgeon's first contact with the patient was when he made a transverse incision across her lower abdomen. I had started all this in motion and sincerely hoped my diagnosis was correct. No ancillary tests had been conducted—no x-rays or ultrasounds—and no one had provided a second opinion. Even if there had been some test to confirm the diagnosis, there just wasn't time. The young woman was bleeding to death.

The GYN doc was a good surgeon. He got into the peritoneal space quickly, and we found it filled with a massive amount of blood. We both swabbed and suctioned the blood to gain exposure, and then we quickly discovered a ruptured left fallopian tube which was producing a fountain of red liquid in a pulsating stream. The surgeon placed clamps on either side of the torn passageway, and that immediately stopped the hemorrhage. We looked across the table at each other and both took a deep breath; everything was now under control. The gynecologist had been in the hospital less than 10 minutes at that point. We asked the anesthesiologist how our patient was doing, and he informed us he had already infused one unit of blood, one of those that had been rushed from Anacortes, and had started a second unit. He said her vital signs were stable and it looked like she was going to make it.

We excised the jagged remnants of the left fallopian tube and removed the ovary as well. The young woman would be happy to learn she was still capable of becoming pregnant, as the opposite tube and ovary were still intact and appeared to be perfectly normal.

We kept our patient in the hospital for several days, and she recovered uneventfully. The news of this incident spread through the VAQ-129 squadron spaces like wildfire, and over the next few days, I was treated like a hero. Commander DiLoreto even called me into his office to personally thank and congratulate me. It was obvious everyone understood what a close brush with death the young woman had survived.

I have often thought what a different scenario would have played out if I had left a pad of pre-signed prescriptions with my corpsman that night. I don't even like to think about it.

74

By the time early signs of spring began appearing on the island—crocuses and forsythia blooming and buds sprouting on the twigs of giant maple trees—Martha and I were getting attached to our life on Whidbey. I enjoyed coming home from the hospital every evening during the last days of winter, when the wild winds and driving rain made our little home a cozy abode. Almost every night, I would put on my rain jacket and venture out into the weather to split firewood. Jill usually insisted on coming with me, and she would fill her little red wagon with kindling and then pull it to the back door. We could hear the waves crashing in on the rocky shore, just below the house, and I think it made us both feel tough and hardy to be out there braving the elements. Once the fire was blazing, Martha and I would sit relaxing by the hearth and drink a beer or glass of wine together while we compared events of the day and the kids played with their toys on the carpet. On some of these cozy evenings, the winds were so fierce we wondered if the roof was going to lift right off of the house. It was exciting!

Martha and I loved how quiet it was in our home and neighborhood most of the time; the only sounds we could hear were the sounds of nature: the wind, the ocean, and the rain pelting against the windows. The stillness was interrupted, however, for several hours at a time during flight operations, when the whine of jet engines could be heard as pilots made their final approach to the air station. Our house was directly under the traffic pattern when one particular runway was in use. We became accustomed to the sound, though, and it really didn't bother us. At the main entrance to the base, a sign was posted for the public, painted in blue and gold, that read, "Please pardon our noise. It is the sound of freedom." I always liked that sign because it reminded me of the importance of what I was doing.

As the days grew longer and it was still daylight when I arrived home, Jill and I often hiked down a path behind the house leading to the water's edge, while Martha prepared our evening meal. The trail wound down a forested hillside through future homesites, but the trees had not yet been cleared nor any homes yet built between our house and the rocky beach. It was our private waterfront wilderness that we enjoyed every day. When we got to the beach, Jill poked along, inspecting every interesting pebble and shell she came across and filling her pockets with treasures. As spring eased into summer, the four of us, with Baby Alice in a Gerry Pack carrier, hiked the trail and spent time at the water's edge on warm, sunny weekends.

My obligated time in the service was quickly winding down, and my release from active duty was projected for September. Martha and I began to think that starting a civilian medical practice on Whidbey would not be a bad life at all.

Three GP's had established private practices in Oak Harbor, and they were all on the staff of Whidbey General Hospital in Coupeville, a tiny town a few miles south of Oak Harbor. I had met those doctors—John Teays, Warren Howell, and Robert Goetz—and I thought highly of each of them. I especially connected with John and Warren, who were in practice together. John was a pilot and owner of a Cessna 210, and he took me flying with him one day. Martha and I invited John and his wife over to our house one night for cocktails, and then the four of us went out to dinner in Oak Harbor. I asked John that night if he and Warren might be considering a third partner in the practice. He said he didn't think they were ready for that, but he would talk to Warren about it.

I first met Dr. Goetz one night in March, shortly after we had arrived on the island. A serious car accident occurred on Polnell Point near our house that evening. It was a one-car rollover that resulted from a young male driver going too fast to negotiate a curve. I heard the crash from our home and went to assist. I was still wearing my Navy uniform from work that day as I helped the emergency personnel at the crash site with the extrication of the driver from the vehicle. It was particularly tricky since the victim had a fracture of his cervical spine with injury to his spinal cord. I attended to the patient in the ambulance on the way to the civilian hospital in Coupeville, where Dr. Goetz was waiting for us. I stayed at the hospital and helped him evaluate the patient for his injuries, and the two of us studied the spinal x-rays together. We identified a serious fracture of the second cervical vertebra. The young man had a worrisome loss of sensation and muscle control on one side of his body, and the following day Dr. Goetz transferred him to Harborview Medical Center, a renowned Level-1 trauma center in Seattle.

I stayed in touch with Dr. Goetz to follow up on the patient, and I found out he had completely recovered, with no paralysis and no sensory loss, indicating he only had a contusion to his spinal cord. The doctor was very complimentary of our stabilization of the patient's spine at the scene of the accident, since the type of spinal fracture he sustained was unstable and could have resulted in permanent paralysis. The good doctor was so appreciative that he wrote a letter to Admiral Tierney at the base to thank the Navy for this assistance. I later received a letter of commendation from the admiral.

I was humbled and somewhat embarrassed by the attention I received for my role in this emergency. I thanked Dr. Goetz for sending the nice letter, but I told him the real credit belonged to the EMTs who had expertly removed the victim from the mangled vehicle with great care and professionalism, whereas I felt as though I had just been along for the ride.

On March 20, three days after playing a good-Samaritan role at the car accident, I drove off the island to the little airport at Bayview, Washington, to start taking the next level of flying lessons in order to qualify for my instrument rating. My official Navy flying consisted of just riding around in the EA-6B, and, after going on a flight with John Teays, in his airplane, I was anxious to get back into an aircraft I could actually pilot myself. I decided to start working on some advanced ratings. I paired up with an affable (and hilariously funny) retired Navy chief petty officer, an FAA certified instrument flight instructor named Dick Boslough. Apart from being quite a character, Dick proved to be an excellent instructor. All of my lessons with him were in a rented Cessna 172, and every flight was "under the hood," as I controlled the aircraft with reference only to the flight instruments. I flew at least once a week and completed 23 instrument flight lessons with Dick, flying out of Bayview (now Skagit Regional) and Anacortes Airports, between March and September. I didn't have any idea where this additional flight training would lead or what exactly I was going to do with it, but I knew I really liked it.

By early summer, the idea of staying in Oak Harbor and joining a practice, or starting one of my own there, had faded. By that time, I'd cemented a good relationship with all three of the general physicians in Oak Harbor as I put out feelers for civilian practice opportunities, but none of the three had a heavy enough patient load to consider adding an associate. I could open my own solo practice, but it appeared it would be tough to get up and running. Dr. Teays pointed out to me that the majority of the population on the island was somehow associated with the Navy base, and most of those folks were eligible for medical care at the naval hospital. The three private physicians in Oak Harbor seemed to be able to easily handle the limited patient load generated by those seeking civilian care, and a fourth GP would likely have trouble staying busy.

Martha and I set our sights back on Coeur d'Alene, the beautiful little town in North Idaho we had fallen in love with while I was interning in Spokane. I made a couple of trips over to put out feelers. I was disappointed when I got a cool reception from most of the doctors in private practice there. They all seemed almost paranoid about the idea of a new practitioner coming into town, and I sensed they were afraid I might steal all their patients away. Almost without exception I was told, "Coeur d'Alene doesn't need another doctor." But I wasn't discouraged and didn't let this unwelcome treatment deter me. We were going to Idaho!

On my second trip to Coeur d'Alene, one of the docs suggested I talk to a fellow by the name of Dick Eggleston, who apparently had an extremely busy solo practice in the little town of Post Falls, 10 miles to the west. He thought Dick might be open to taking on an associate. I ran right out to Post Falls and sat down for a chat with Dick in his office. We hit it off right away, and—bingo—I had found the opportunity I was looking for. We could still live in Coeur d'Alene, where the hospital was located anyway, and I would have just a short commute to the office in Post Falls. Our plans were all coming together. The next trip to North Idaho was with Martha to look for a house.

75

By mid-August, with about a month of obligated military service remaining, I had found a medical practice to join, bought a house in Coeur d'Alene, and made the arrangements for the transport of our household goods to our new home—courtesy of the United States Navy. There was one task yet to be accomplished before I could examine my first patient in my new civilian practice: I had to be granted a state license that authorized me to practice medicine and surgery in Idaho.

I had taken and passed the National Board of Medical Examiners examination, which is given in three installments over several years while in training. The state of Idaho accepted this certificate, as do most states, in lieu of passing their own written exam, but Idaho also required an oral interview in person before the State Board of Medicine. The board was next convening at the State House in Boise on Tuesday, September 2, the day after Labor Day. I had to figure out a way to get there.

I had developed a good relationship with the squadron's commanding officer, Johnny DiLoreto, by then. I thought I had been doing a pretty good job as the squadron flight surgeon and was wondering if I dared ask him to fly me to Boise for my interview on the day the board convened. I knew the flight schedule was busy with training flights, and it was doubtful an airplane and crew would be available to do something like this. Besides, I was being released from active duty shortly and would no longer be affiliated with the squadron, so there was no incentive, and certainly no practical reason, for him to grant such a request.

I sat down with the CO in his office one morning in August and nervously began explaining the requirement for a personal interview for my license. I had barely started my pitch when he interrupted me and said, "Doc, what day and what time do you need to be there? We'll fly you over."

I sat there speechless, with my mouth hanging open, as he scribbled a note on a piece of paper. He handed it to me and said, "Give this to Pate, and tell him to take care of it. Is there anything else, Doc?"

"No sir. That's it. Thank you, sir. I mean, thanks a lot, sir." He smiled, stood up, handed me the scrap of paper for Lieutenant Commander Pate, and we shook hands across his desk.

I did have a concern and possible request, but I saved my question for Dave Pate. I had to take a coat and tie along to change into for my interview, since I certainly couldn't show up in a baggy, olive-green Nomex flight suit. Also, I would have to bring my medical school diploma and other documents along, and they were all nicely framed behind glass. I had no idea how I could take these things with me in the EA-6B. There was no baggage compartment, and I couldn't have anything on my lap while sitting in an ejection seat. I asked Dave Pate if he had any ideas to solve this problem.

"Doc, that's no problem at all. You can bring a suitcase. We'll just have maintenance hang a baggage blivet on the bird. Just put everything in a piece of luggage, and we'll load it up for you."

I didn't know what a baggage blivet was or where it was attached to the airplane, but that didn't matter, and I didn't want to ask him. I added a new word to my Navy vocabulary and would find out what a blivet was on the day we departed on the flight.

Dave told me they would fly me into Mountain Home Air Force Base, about 50 miles southeast of Boise. I asked him if he had been there before and whether or not he knew if there was bus service from the base into the city. I was thinking a 100-mile round-trip cab ride might be more expensive than just purchasing an airline ticket from Seattle to Boise. He said, "Don't worry about ground transportation. The skipper told me to take care of that. We've got you covered, Doc."

On the morning of September 2, a pilot, two ECMOs, and I walked across the tarmac toward the line of EA-6Bs sitting on the ramp. I had my little brown Samsonite carry-on in one hand and my helmet bag in the other. I noticed one aircraft in the line had what looked like a torpedo or a bomb attached to the bottom of the fuselage between the two main landing gear struts. I immediately knew that was the plane we were taking, and I also then knew what a baggage blivet looked like. There was a plane captain standing by, and, when he saw us approaching, he ran up and took my suitcase from me. I followed him under the aircraft and watched as he opened a door in the side of the blivet, loaded my bag into it, and re-secured the door.

As I watched my suitcase being loaded, one of the ECMOs told me that other types of "external stores" can be carried by the same centerline attachment point, most commonly an auxiliary fuel tank. He also informed me that the pilot, in an emergency, can jettison any of the external stores, including the jammer electronic pods hung under the wings.

"I hope we don't have an engine failure today," I joked, "because earning that diploma was a lot of work, and I would hate to have it jettisoned and end up on the side of a mountain in the Cascades." I told the pilot, seriously, that I would appreciate it if he didn't do any aerobatics or pull any G's so the glass in my certificate frames wouldn't get broken.

We landed at Mountain Home a little over an hour later and secured the airplane in front of the air terminal building. A dark blue official U.S. Air Force car with a driver sat on the tarmac waiting to take me to Boise. I think the driver was a little shocked when he saw the two silver lieutenant bars on the collar of my flight suit. He was used to carting around Air Force colonels or generals. I doubt if he had ever been ordered to spend half a day chauffeuring a young Navy lieutenant. I asked my driver to stand by while I went to the restroom and changed into my suit with a white shirt and tie. I packed my flight suit back into the suitcase with the diplomas and we were off for Boise.

When we got to the statehouse, I asked the driver if he could give me a telephone number where I could reach him when I was ready to return to the base. He said, "Sir, my orders are to wait for you here until you are finished with your business."

I found the office of the Idaho State Board of Medicine and checked in with the secretary. I only had to wait a few minutes before being called into the conference room where the board was in session. I left my suitcase with the secretary and walked in with my framed certificates under my arm. The chairman of the board had my file on the table in front of him and knew from having reviewed it that I was still on active duty at NAS Whidbey Island. The first casual question he asked with the intent, I am sure, of relaxing me was, "How did you get over here from Whidbey Island?"

When I explained I had just flown in aboard a Navy EA-6B Prowler, that was all they wanted to hear about. When I first walked into the room, the six panel members looked extremely bored and almost ready to fall asleep; now they were all alert and looking at me with riveted intensity and interest. They asked a string of questions about the aircraft: how fast it went, how many airmen it seated, and whether or not it had ejection seats. One of the doctors asked if I had ever flown upside down. The chairman wanted to know why I had changed out of my flight gear for the interview. He said they all would have enjoyed it much more if I had shown up in my flight suit. I apologized for disappointing them.

Prior to my interview, I had expected I would have an oral exam, with questions being asked in turn by each of the various medical specialists sitting around the table. I knew these guys wanted to be sure I was competent to practice medicine, and I thought I would have to convince them of that before they approved my license. The fact I was a military physician who flew around in high-performance jet aircraft seemed to fascinate them to the point that they lost their focus on why I was there. Their questions came fast and furiously, but none had anything to do with my knowledge of medicine and surgery. They were all questions about aviation. I had run their train right off the track, and they never got it back on.

When I arrived back at the air terminal in my Air Force car, I found the other three crew members at a pool table in the facility's snack bar. I apologized for making them wait so long for me—it had been a little over three hours—but none of them seemed the least bit upset. I went to the restroom, changed back into flight gear, and packed my suit into my suitcase for the flight home.

It was mid-afternoon when we touched down at NAS Whidbey. That was my last flight in an EA-6B Prowler. I stopped by Commander DiLoreto's office while I was still in my flight gear and thanked him again. He said, "Doc, it was just another training flight we had to do anyway. It wasn't anything special."

That flight *was* special to me, and I have never forgotten Commander Johnny DiLoreto. I took care of his boys, and he took care of his flight surgeon.

76

The long-awaited day when I would "hang my shingle" and begin my private practice finally arrived. I left our new home in Coeur d'Alene on a morning in late September, 1975, and drove 10 miles west to my office in Post Falls to see my first patients. I was 30 years old and had finally finished all my training and obligated military service. On that first day, I was excited about my professional life that lay ahead, felt full of confidence, and was anxious to get started on this new chapter.

Martha and I realized our financial situation was dire; we had very little money. However, with such a promising future, we were filled with optimism, and neither of us was worried. At that time, physicians in the military were awarded a $15,000 retention bonus about a year before being discharged. I spent $5,000 of that on a second car I would drive to work, but we managed to save the rest. This meant our total savings was about $10,000, and we would have to live on that until the money from the practice started rolling in. We had purchased a $40,000 house with a 100 percent VA loan, which, fortunately, required no down payment. The house payments and all our other living expenses would have to come from our savings for a while.

Dr. Eggleston and I weren't really partners in the medical practice. We considered ourselves solo practitioners with an expense-sharing agreement, which included a shared office building. We both preferred this type of an arrangement, at least to start out. We planned to alternate night call and cover for each other on days off and vacations. We split the office rent and the employees' salaries, and I paid Dick a rental fee each month for the office equipment he owned but we both shared. I got a small business loan from a local bank for another $10,000 to pay my share of the office overhead until my income covered these expenses.

Many of Dick's patients were loggers or mill workers and their families. A significant number of our patients had no insurance, and their medical expenses came right out of pocket. We had to keep our fees affordable for these hard-working folks, and both of us used the same fee schedule. An office call was $6 and a house call (which we both did) was $7. We charged $250 for a delivery, which included all of the prenatal care for the full nine months, the postpartum office exams for the mother and infant, and, if the newborn was a male infant, it included the circumcision.

When I arrived at the office that first morning at 8:30 AM, the parking lot was already full. After entering through our private door in the rear of the building, I passed behind the reception desk and saw every seat in the waiting room was taken, despite the fact it was a fairly large room. My first day was obviously going to be a busy one, and I was ready to go to work.

I didn't see a single patient that day—or the next day, or the next. I sat behind the beautiful new oak desk in an impressive new leather chair (I had bought this furniture using my borrowed money) and read articles in my medical journals all day. I could hear the receptionist telling an occasional patient that he or she could avoid a long wait if they would like to see Dr. Crawley. The response was always the same: "I'll just wait for Dr. Eggleston."

After sitting behind my desk for the entire first week, all of my enthusiasm was gone. By the time I got home every evening, I was almost in tears.

Dick suggested I place a practice announcement in the local paper, *The Post Falls Tribune*. At that time, it was considered unethical for a physician to advertise for his services, but an unpaid announcement in the media was considered acceptable. A reporter from the paper came over to the office and snapped a picture of me sitting behind my fancy desk in my fancy chair, and then she took a few notes for an article. The announcement didn't seem to help much, but I did see two or three patients during my second week of practice. Each of those folks probably got the most thorough exam they had ever experienced at a doctor's office.

After a few weeks of doing almost nothing every day, I was discouraged. I was bored with what had become my daily routine, and, beyond that, our financial situation was looking bleaker by the minute. Martha understood my concerns, could see my unhappiness, and never complained about her meager household budget, but any illusions Martha had formed regarding the life of a typical doctor's wife had evaporated. Neither of us expected a profession in medicine would make us wealthy, and that was not why I had become a physician, but neither of us had been prepared for what we were experiencing those first few weeks. It certainly wasn't what I had envisioned.

Late one afternoon, I waited for Dick to finish with his last patient of the day, and I strolled over to his corridor on the opposite side of the building. I walked into his office and plopped down in one of the chairs across from his desk and let loose on him with all my frustrations and worries. I rattled on and on while Dick just sat there with a thoughtful look on his face as he listened to my complaints. I'm sure there was some anger in my tone as I clearly implied most of this was his fault. I told him I knew he was seeing some of his patients in the ER on nights I was on call for him. I suspected this was because many of his patients refused to see the doctor on call (me) and insisted he come in, but I told him that had to stop. Dick just sat and listened without arguing with me or trying to refute any of my heated accusations. In fact, he didn't say a single word until he was sure I was through talking.

Finally, when he was pretty sure most of my tirade was over, he said quietly, "David, I need some time off. Donna and I are long overdue for a vacation. We have a week-long trip planned for early December, and you will be on your own. I think that will give you the boost you need."

77

Dick called me at home on a Saturday morning in early December to let me know he was heading out of town and I was in charge. That call was unnecessary because I would have known almost immediately he was gone. It wasn't five minutes after I hung up the phone from talking with Dick that all hell broke loose. I was quickly on my way to the ER. My life was suddenly turned upside down.

Whenever I was home that week, the phone rang almost continuously, day and night. I ran back and forth from our home to the hospital several times each night. When I was at the office, I was at least an hour behind schedule seeing patients, and the waiting room was standing room only for most of each day. I made trips from the office to the hospital once or twice a day, and each time I got back to the office I felt like I was hopelessly behind. Many of the patients complained about their long waits. I saw several of Dick's patients in the hospital Emergency Room each day, I admitted a few people to the hospital with fairly serious illnesses, and I delivered five or six babies—most of them at night. By the end of the week, I was walking around like a zombie. I missed several evening meals with Martha and the kids, and, by mid-week, I was so sleep-deprived I felt like I could barely function.

This was the life of a solo practitioner in a small town, and it was the life Dr. Eggleston had been living for several years before I had joined him. How did he do it? He seemed to thoroughly enjoy this life and even thrived on it. For the first time, I wondered if maybe I wasn't cut from the same mold, and I started to question whether this was the life I wanted. Be careful what you wish for, I thought.

I put some badly needed fees on the books that week in the accounts receivable column. That improved my outlook and relieved some of the worry over finances, but few of the charges were paid within a reasonable time frame. Our patients were in no hurry to pay their medical bills, and both of us were admittedly pretty poor businessmen. We never demanded payment at the time of service and rarely turned over unpaid accounts to a collection agency. It would be several weeks or months before I received any actual cash for what I had put on the books during that busy week when Dick was gone.

After Dick returned from his trip, I dropped back into my sluggish routine at the office, but my associate finally started relinquishing most of his after-hours emergencies to me on the nights and weekends I was on call; that helped. Over the next few weeks and months, I got gradually busier as some of his patients became used to me, and I attracted some new patients of my own to the office.

By the end of my first year in practice, I was starting to see light at the end of the tunnel. It seemed I had turned the corner. My accounts receivable had grown appreciably, and some cash was finally starting to trickle in. Our austere living had stretched the borrowed money and savings out as far as possible, but there was little left to stretch any further. I was hoping my patients would start paying their medical bills a little faster so I wouldn't have to go back to the bank and grovel for another loan.

By midway through my second year as a family physician, I was seeing all the patients I could comfortably see each day. I think the office staff thought there was something wrong with me when they compared the number of patients I was able to see hourly with the number Dr. Eggleston could examine and treat. Dick was smart and figured things out quickly, but I also realized that he had treated most of his patients for years. He knew their medical histories by heart, so it took him little time to get them in and out. For me, I had to start from scratch with every patient; each was new to me, and it took me a while to get to know them and learn the background information I needed to make a diagnosis and treat them properly. Regardless of this awareness, I realized I would probably never feel comfortable seeing as many patients in a day as Dick, and I really didn't want to see that many anyway. I felt as if I had reached the point at which my schedule was as full as it could possibly be.

Dick and I both diagnosed and treated a wide variety of medical and surgical problems. It was a true general practice that was just starting to be referred to by the increasingly popular term of "family practice." Whenever I met someone new socially and they asked me what my specialty was, I liked to respond, "The skin and its contents." The joke frequently fell flat when the person would say, "Ah, so you are a dermatologist." We both were dermatologists, though, at times, as we were also internists, cardiologists, obstetrician-gynecologists, ear-nose-throat doctors, neurologists, surgeons, urologists, orthopedists, gastroenterologists, and pediatricians. We both tried not to refer a patient to a specialist unless the problem was clearly beyond our expertise or capabilities. We wanted our office to be one-stop shopping for medical care. The wide variety of medical problems made each day both interesting and challenging.

310

Family medicine had recently been designated a specialty; residency programs were being established at major medical centers, and the American Board of Family Practice was formed to examine and certify applicants in this newly formed branch of medicine. Doctors who were already out in general practice could count an internship and a certain number of hours of practice in lieu of the required three-year residency training program. Doctors who met these requirements were allowed to "challenge the boards" and take the exam to become board certified. Physicians who qualified in this manner were grandfathered in. This alternative to the residency had a cut-off date after which the only way to be eligible for the exam was to complete the residency. My hours of practice in the military counted toward the grandfathering requirements, and I was eligible to take the test. Dick and I both qualified, took the rigorous exam, and both passed. We were then Board Certified Family Physicians. There wasn't any change in what we did after that; we just called ourselves family physicians from then on instead of general practitioners, and we each had a new diploma to hang on the wall. I don't believe any of our patients knew about this added credential or even cared, and I don't remember any of my new patients asking me whether or not I was board certified.

As my practice got busier and busier, my family and personal time suffered. After a few months into my second year, I was rarely eating any meals with Martha and the kids. Several days in a row sometimes passed without me seeing them awake. I left in the morning before they got up, and when I returned in the evening, they were all in bed asleep.

On a typical weekday, I got up at 5:30 AM (if I wasn't already up from a night emergency) and left the house around 6:00 to drive to the hospital and make rounds on my hospitalized patients. This often included examining an obstetrical patient or two in labor or checking on my newborns in the nursery. When I finished rounds, I typically headed to the office in Post Falls, which we opened for business at 8:30 AM.

After morning rounds, I sometimes had a surgical case to perform or to assist on in the OR. On those days, I usually knew about it ahead of time and had the receptionist avoid scheduling office patients until my estimated arrival time at the office. Sometimes the estimate was accurate, and sometimes it was way off and caused the office to be in more turmoil than it normally was.

I often didn't see my last patient in the office until 5:30 or 6:00 PM, and that was on an easy day. When I finished, I headed back to Coeur d'Alene to make evening hospital rounds at Kootenai Memorial. I sometimes had an admission history and physical to dictate and orders to write for a patient I had earlier sent from the office to be admitted. It wasn't unusual for me to see a patient or two in the Emergency Room and to have a couple of more obstetrical cases show up. I rarely got home before 9:00 PM and occasionally I worked through the night without ever coming home at all.

Dick and I both scheduled a day off each week. My day off was Thursday, and it gave me a much-needed break to try to recover from a grueling schedule. I always looked forward to it, but I was often too tired to enjoy it much. It seemed as though it was never a complete day off anyway, since I always made the usual morning rounds on my hospital patients, just as Dick did on his day off. We also each made our own rounds on our weekend days "off."

We both volunteered at a WIC (women-infants-children) clinic in Post Falls every Thursday morning. This was a health and nutrition program administered by the federal government for low-income people, but it was fully staffed by volunteers. It mostly involved doing well-baby physical exams and administering immunizations. We alternated this coverage, so it occurred on my scheduled "day off" every other Thursday. The reality was: neither of us ever had a complete day off without leaving town.

By the fall of 1977, I was starting to question my choice of becoming a family practitioner in a small town, and at times I was even wondering if I should have become a physician at all. I hated the long hours, associated physical fatigue, and lack of family time, and I had little in the way of a social life. There was another major factor contributing to my increasing unhappiness with my life and profession, and I was gradually becoming aware of it.

Someone once described being a passenger on an airplane as "hours and hours of extreme boredom, punctuated by occasional moments of stark terror." Medicine is a little like that. Despite the occasional interesting and challenging case, most of the patients I saw had minor self-limited illnesses that would most likely resolve without any treatment at all, or they had a problem that dictated a simple "cookbook" solution I barely had to think about. So, much of the time, I found what I was doing was unchallenging, uninteresting, and even boring. Then there were the hypochondriacs who seemed intent on driving me completely nuts. I spent hours upon hours ordering myriads of tests on some of these individuals, attempting to determine whether or not the patient was suffering from a real physical illness. This is not at all what I expected when I decided on a career in medicine.

As my unhappiness and frustration were building, I started trying to figure out what I could do about it. It seemed like a noose was tightening around my neck, and I wondered if I was permanently trapped in this living purgatory.

Throughout that stressful first year of practice, I never stopped thinking about flying. I hadn't completed the course for my instrument rating back on Whidbey Island, and I worried about losing the pilot skills I had worked so hard to develop. We had been in Idaho over a year when I finally drove out to the Coeur d'Alene Airport on one of my Thursdays off. I didn't feel as though I could afford to pay for an aircraft rental and instructor yet, but, as a military veteran, I was eligible for educational benefits through the GI Bill. The program covered 90 percent of the cost of flight training when enrolled in an approved course of instruction leading to a Commercial Pilot certificate.

I had no idea what I would do with a Commercial Pilot license. It would involve a lot more instruction and a lot more flying than I had been thinking about but would include the instrument rating I wanted. I was determined to somehow find the time to do it, and I thought I might be able to squeeze enough out of our family budget to pay my 10 percent share. I just had to find an operator that offered the program.

The Coeur d'Alene Airport was a sleepy little airfield with three paved runways laid out in a standard triangle configuration. Two small FBOs (fixed base operators) on the field rented airplanes and offered instruction. I felt a little discouraged upon seeing the dilapidated condition of the buildings at both of these businesses. It appeared they were both operating on a shoestring budget—just as Martha and I were at the time.

The airport had no air terminal or commercial airline service. I was nevertheless hoping I would at least see a little airplane taxiing, taking off, or landing that day, but there was no activity whatsoever. It was exciting, though, for me to just see a number of single-engine private aircraft tied down on the tarmac as I imagined myself climbing into one, taxiing out, and taking off.

Harold Rhodes, the owner of North Idaho Aviation, was a nice old fellow who had been flying airplanes since before I was born. He was vague about his flight instruction program and if and when he might have an instructor available. He didn't know anything about the GI Bill for flight training.

The other FBO, a few hundred feet south on the tarmac, was Coeur d'Alene Airways. It was owned and operated by a couple who were also senior citizens—Charlie and Sophie Starr. I found Sophie asleep on a couch in the office of the facility that morning. I couldn't even imagine anyone wanting to sit on that couch, let alone take a nap on it. It was covered with about an inch of dust and worn so badly that a couple of springs poked out through the mohair fabric. Sophie yawned and directed me to the door leading to the hanger, where I found Charlie working on the engine of an old Cessna 182.

Charlie told me, to my utter amazement, he was approved by the Veterans Administration to offer flight training under the GI Bill. He said he only had one part-time flight instructor at the moment, a crop duster named Jerry Squibb. Jerry worked for various owners of large farms in the Eastern Washington Palouse country, and he gave a little flight instruction on the side to make ends meet. Charlie gave Jerry a call, and a week later, I took my first flight lesson in more than a year.

Jerry and I went out that day and practiced takeoffs and landings, stalls and stall recoveries, 720-degree steep turns, and slow flight. Those maneuvers were all intended to rekindle my stick-and-rudder skills and get me back in the saddle after a year's absence from the cockpit.

Jerry Squibb was a bit of a maverick, but he was a wonderful instructor and I liked him a lot. I had no idea that, just a few years later, Jerry would be the student and I would be the instructor as I tested him for his FAA-required biennial flight review.

I somehow managed to get to the airport several times a month after that to continue my flight training. I went through several different flight instructors in 1977, as Coeur d'Alene Airways was sold to a new owner, reorganized, and became West Aire. The new owner was quickly approved for flight training under the GI Bill, so I was able to continue taking instruction without interruption.

I passed the FAA written test for my instrument rating early in January. On April 9, I flew a fully instrumented Cessna 182 to Spokane for a two-hour instrument pilot checkride given by an FAA examiner. I passed the oral exam and flight test, and "instrument rating" was added to my Private Pilot certificate.

I passed the written test for my Commercial Pilot certificate that summer, and, by fall, I had logged all the required hours of dual instruction and solo flight required for the flight test. On November 2, I flew a PA-28-200 (Piper Arrow) to Spokane for my checkride. The test had to be completed in a "complex" aircraft that had a variable-pitch propeller and retractable landing gear, and the Piper Arrow met those requirements. I passed the oral exam and flight test and was granted a Commercial Pilot certificate with an instrument rating for single-engine land aircraft. I could then legally fly for hire.

My flying was a wonderful respite from the stresses of my medical practice, but it wasn't enough. I needed more time off to fly and to spend time with my little family. Daughter Jill was now five years old and Alice was three. I wasn't getting to spend nearly enough time with them and see all the rapid changes in their growth and development that Martha witnessed every day. The flying was now taking me away from them even more, and that made me feel guilty about the one leisure activity I had a passion for and enjoyed the most.

Something had to change. Martha and I started discussing my unhappiness in late-night conversations and exploring what, if anything, we could do about it. Martha never begrudged my flying, knowing how much it meant to me, but she was getting tired of our life the way it was and also wanted it to change.

In the fall of 1977, Dick and I began discussing the idea of investing in the practice in the form of a medical building we would have constructed and jointly own. We were also considering forming a legal partnership and incorporating. We talked to a business consultant, hired an architect, pored over blueprint designs, and requested bids from a local contractor. I was excited about this for a while, but after a few weeks, I started getting cold feet. I felt the noose getting tighter around my neck.

As the end of the year approached, I made a decision about what I would do.

79

Whenever patients of mine or Dr. Eggleston's presented at the hospital Emergency Room, the ER nurse on duty would call whomever was on call. If I was on call and the illness or injury was something clearly minor, I might give the nurse orders over the phone to provide temporary treatment until the patient could be seen in our office. If it was a serious medical emergency or involved severe trauma, the nurse would do her best to keep the patient alive and stable until one of us got there.

The specialty of emergency medicine was just starting to evolve in the mid-'70s, and most hospitals did not have in-house physician coverage of their emergency rooms, with the exception of large metropolitan hospitals with training programs. In those institutions, ER patients were treated by relatively inexperienced interns or residents (who, in most cases, were minimally supervised). This system was starting to change at about that time.

All physicians on the medical staff at Kootenai Memorial Hospital were required to serve once or twice a month as "duty doctor of the day" for the hospital's Emergency Room. If a patient who did not have a personal physician presented at the Emergency Room, the duty doctor was contacted. ER call duty was an opportunity for a physician just starting out in practice, such as myself, to recruit new patients, as follow-up visits were generally done in the physician's office.

This system frequently failed to provide the best treatment for patients arriving for emergency care. The doctor on call for an emergency at night had to wake up, get out of bed, get dressed, and drive to the hospital. This delay in treatment could obviously be critical in some cases. Another downside was that a person might arrive at the ER with a myocardial infarction or a fractured hip, for example, to be initially examined and treated by a psychiatrist or dermatologist who happened to be the duty doctor.

In the spring of 1977, a young physician from the little town of Sandpoint, Idaho, 45 miles to the north, started showing up at our hospital on weekends to provide in-house coverage of the ER. Dr. Jim Arthurs was a busy general practitioner in Sandpoint, and he was experiencing some of the same stresses and frustrations I was going through at the time. He was looking for a way out. He decided to test the waters to see if he might be able to make a living as a hospital-based emergency physician. The hospital administrator drafted a loose contract with him to provide this coverage at the times of his choosing but refused to hire him or pay him a salary. He was simply allowed to provide this service, but he was required to bill any patients he treated and be 100 percent responsible for his own collections.

On the seemingly random nights when Dr. Arthurs covered the ER, I found myself occasionally asking him to see and treat one of our patients who presented there. It was a wonderful luxury to hang up the phone, roll over, and go back to sleep knowing the patient would receive competent care without me. A few of the doctors on staff were possessive of the patients whom they considered "belonged" to them, and those physicians were resistant to abdicating their care to Dr. Arthurs. Another factor was that some of the patients initially were adamant that only their private physician provide their care, and they did not want to be treated by a doctor they had never met.

There was a lot of talk at hospital staff meetings about whether or not Dr. Arthurs should be allowed to infringe on the doctor-patient relationships these physicians had worked so hard to cultivate. A cadre of doctors felt threatened by Dr. Arthurs and feared their practices would evaporate as patients realized they could get all of their medical care at the Emergency Room. Balloting on this issue was finally conducted, and Dr. Arthurs was allowed to continue. My thought on this matter was that it was a big hullaballoo about nothing. Life as a family physician might even be bearable for me if the hospital had full-time, in-house physician coverage of the Emergency Room.

Shortly after the medical staff gave a thumbs-up to Dr. Arthur's arrangement, a second physician joined him and started covering some of the nights and weekends in the ER when Dr. Arthurs was not available. Dr. Paul Shrum was a semi-retired general practitioner who returned to his home in North Idaho after serving several years as a physician for the U.S. Foreign Service. He was an interesting fellow who had been assigned to various U.S. Embassy posts all over the world prior to his retirement. He had an adventurous second career similar to that of my friend, Paul Broadbent, whom I had met in Pensacola. With Dr. Shrum on board, Coeur d'Alene then had two emergency room physicians.

Late one afternoon, Dr. Eggleston called me into his office to sign the construction contract for the new office we had planned. I knew once I signed those papers it would be difficult to extricate myself from a life in which I was becoming more and more miserable. That evening, I told Dick I had changed my mind about the building. I then made what I thought would be a shocking announcement to him: I was leaving the practice and becoming the third emergency room physician at Kootenai Memorial, joining Drs. Arthurs and Shrum.

As it turned out, Dr. Eggleston wasn't surprised by my announcement at all. It apparently had been obvious to him how unhappy I had become. He listened to all I had to say and then quietly accepted my decision. He didn't try to talk me into staying and said he would support me in any way he could. I had been talking to Dr. Arthurs and Dr. Shrum for several weeks about my plan, but I had been dreading this moment of announcing it to my partner in practice and dashing all the plans we had made for the future. The tension melted away from me when I saw his reaction, and I appreciated his support and understanding more than he could ever realize.

80

Practicing steep turns in an airplane is intended to hone basic flying skills and perfect stick-and-rudder coordination. A steep turn is defined as a turn in which the angle of bank is 45 degrees or more. There is probably no such thing as a *perfect* steep turn, but the pilot attempts, throughout the turn, to stay at the same precise angle of bank, maintain a constant airspeed, keep the slip/skid ball indicator centered with coordinated rudder inputs, and roll out of the turn on an exact, predetermined heading. The maneuver takes focused concentration, coordination, and good power control, and it also requires a rapid instrument scan. Whenever I was dissatisfied with my performance at the completion of a steep turn, I could repeat and practice it until it was acceptable. I was now making the first steep turn in my professional career, but if this one didn't turn out as expected, I wasn't going to have the luxury of a do-over. As Martha often reminded me, "Life is not a dress rehearsal," and I hoped to get it right.

I rolled into my first career turn on January 1, 1978, when I worked the first shift of the new year at Kootenai Memorial as an emergency room physician. After that, Jim Arthurs, Paul Shrum, and I alternated shifts to cover the ER 24/7. We worked a 24-hour shift, from 8:00 AM to 8:00 AM, so it meant being on duty for 24 hours and off duty for 48. It wasn't as grueling as it sounds, though; we had an on-call room with a bed and, at least for the first few months, I often was able to take catnaps in between treating patients at night—sometimes for several consecutive hours. A 24-hour shift can seem interminable, but I had two days off out of every three and felt my quality of life had improved dramatically. The best thing about it was: when I was off work, I was *really* off. Patients no longer called our home in the middle of the night, and, when I heard a siren wailing from the comfort of my bed, I no longer tossed and turned waiting for the phone to ring and summon me to the hospital.

As the residents of Coeur d'Alene and the surrounding communities became aware the hospital had a physician on duty in the ER at all times, we became busier and busier. It was like that memorable line in the movie *Field of Dreams*: "If you build it, they will come." The catnaps at night in the on-call room became shorter and shorter, and it was soon apparent that we needed to find another associate to join our ranks.

Dr. Mike Carlson, a young family practitioner from Spokane, became the fourth emergency room physician to join our group. This made it possible to trade shifts on occasion and to enjoy a vacation for a few days at a time. With four of us on staff, I wanted to start working 12-hour shifts instead of 24. We tried that for a while, but no one liked it. We all preferred to work longer shifts in order to allow ourselves more consecutive days off.

We formalized our group as a legal entity and incorporated under the name Kootenai Emergency Physicians, but the corporation was only an instrument to contract with the hospital for our services. No money flowed through the corporation, and we all continued to operate financially as independent contractors. That meant each of us had separate billing services and were responsible for collection of our individual physician fees. I hired a bookkeeper who worked out of her home to complete health insurance claim forms and send out monthly statements. I scribbled a fee code on each patient's record and then dropped off copies of all of my shift's ER records to her on my drive home after the shift. She did a good job, and after a few months, my collection rate stabilized at almost 80 percent. That was about the same as I had been collecting in my office practice, and I was pretty sure that was about as good as it would ever get.

When all four partners were in town, we each worked one day on and three off. My first day off was pretty much a waste. I got home, ate a little breakfast, and then collapsed into bed. During the school year, the kids were gone and the house was quiet. And in the summer, Martha frequently took the kids to a park or a beach on the lake, allowing me some quiet rest time. I usually awoke at about 4:00 in the afternoon, played with the kids for a while before dinner, and then went right back to bed for the night. I never had any trouble sleeping all night, even though I had been asleep most of the day. On the second day off, I felt better, but I didn't feel recovered enough to do much. On my third and last day off, I was back to normal and felt great—then I went back to work the next day and started the roller-coaster cycle over again.

One day I mentioned to Martha how nice it would be to have a popcorn popper to set up in the ER nurses' lounge and fire up late at night when things occasionally quieted down. She went right out to Coeur d'Alene's Modern Drug and bought the latest model for me. I took it to the hospital at the start of my next shift, but it was a busy day and I never had time to even open the box it was packed in and set it up. I just stuck the popper in its unopened box underneath the desk in our on-call sleeping room and then completely forgot about it.

When I came in for my next 24-hour shift three days later, I looked for the popcorn popper under the desk where I had left it, but it wasn't there. Paul Shrum was just finishing his shift, and I asked him if he had any idea what had happened to it. He told me that the previous evening, an anonymous bomb threat had been telephoned in to the hospital and a police bomb squad had been quickly dispatched to investigate. In their search, they discovered a "suspicious" unopened package under the desk in the ER on-call room. They didn't want to take a chance on opening the package, so they took my popcorn popper out to the corner of the parking lot and blew it up. It was such a hilarious story that I couldn't be too upset about it. I sent Martha back to Modern Drug to buy a new popper.

Aside from having more time off and freedom for my personal life, I found I was no longer bored with what I was doing. I enjoyed the high-energy atmosphere of the ER during times we were dealing with victims of severe trauma or treating patients with critical medical issues such as cardiac arrest. All four of us knew we were saving lives and realized what we were doing was important and really mattered in the larger scheme of things.

The variety of injuries and illnesses I faced made it a challenging job, but that kept things interesting. I still saw some patients with rather routine minor problems that could have been treated in a doctor's office, but I didn't seem to get bored with these non-emergencies; the minor problems allowed me some much-needed moments of respite between episodes of high drama.

I had a new lease on life, I was happy again, and I started spending a lot more time at the airport.

81

The new-found freedom I experienced after becoming a full-time emergency room physician allowed me to spend more and more of my off-duty leisure time in the cockpit. By doing most of my flying during the day while the kids were in school or otherwise occupied, I no longer felt guilty about neglecting my family to pursue my passion; at last we were a family again and able to spend a lot of quality time together. We went to the beach on the lake, played at the park, went out to lunch, took day hikes, and we even went on a couple of family backpacking trips in the Cascade Range of Western Washington.

After I earned my Commercial Pilot certificate, I started driving over to Spokane to fly out of Felts Field. West Aire seemed to be rather poorly managed and had lost its certificate for VA-approved flight training under the GI Bill. Felts Field Aviation, on the other hand, was a successful FBO with an approved flight school curriculum where I enrolled for more advanced ratings and certificates. Over the next few years, I earned my FAA basic Flight Instructor certificate, Instrument Flight Instructor certificate, multi-engine land rating, and single-engine seaplane rating. I also passed the written exam to become a certified FAA ground instructor for basic, advanced, and instrument.

Shortly after I got my basic Flight Instructor certificate, I started working as a part-time flight instructor in Coeur d'Alene for West Aire, while at the same time still working on more advanced ratings out of Spokane. I was starting to accumulate more coveted flight time while my students footed the bill, and I even earned a little extra money as a bonus. I quickly found that giving flight instruction improved my flying skills more than any of the past instruction I had received. Demonstrating basic flight maneuvers to a student demanded perfection, and then critiquing a student, as he or she took the controls and attempted the same maneuver, made me more aware and critical of my own skills. It became clear to me that flight instructing was making me a better pilot.

One of my first flight students was James B. Crowe, a local builder who was running on the Republican ticket in the 1978 Idaho gubernatorial race. Jim had a Private Pilot license but was relatively inexperienced, having logged few flight hours. I gave him some instruction in a Cessna 210 he had purchased and planned to fly around the state on the campaign trail. After a few lessons, he decided piloting his new airplane was a little beyond his skill level, and he hired me to fly with him as he travelled the state. As Jim wisely put it, I was there to keep him from killing himself. This was a wonderful early opportunity for adding to my total flight time. I admired Jim's aspiration for the highest state office, but it was a crowded slate, with seven Republican candidates. John Evans, the Democratic incumbent, beat Jim and the other candidates in the gubernatorial race and reclaimed his seat.

I had a few friends who were private pilots and flew their airplanes around as a hobby. They took their buddies up to do a little sightseeing or fly somewhere for lunch. I never enjoyed that type of pleasure flying much; I liked doing work with an airplane. If I got paid for flying, I knew I was accomplishing something, and it made me feel like a professional pilot. I wanted to do more commercial flying besides just giving flight instruction, but that required more total flight time. I needed more multi-engine time before I would be considered qualified and insurable to fly charter, corporate, or contract flights. The magic numbers for total time seemed to be a minimum of 1,000 to 1,200 hours, and 500 was generally required for multi-engine pilot-in-command time.

I spent as much time as I could in the cockpit, with the goal of building my total flight time to a respectable level and increasing my multi-engine time. During the winter of 1979, I got a contract with a regional Piper aircraft distributor in Vancouver, Washington, to ferry new Piper Tomahawk single-engine trainers across the United States for delivery from the factory in Lock Haven, Pennsylvania. That winter, I made the 3,000-mile flight three separate times between Lock Haven and Vancouver, and I also delivered a new Tomahawk from Chicago to a buyer in Coeur d'Alene. The aircraft's typical cruising true airspeed was only about 90 knots, and since the flights were all from east to west and against the prevailing winds, each trip was a long ferry. I had to make lots of fuel stops, and because I didn't fly at night, each trip took three or four days to complete. The Tomahawk was not equipped or suitable in any way for instrument flight, so all the flights had to be conducted in visual meteorological conditions and in accordance with visual flight rules (VFR); it was low and slow. Before I took off each day, I carefully planned the flight, with special attention to the forecast weather along my route.

I was amazed at the casual attitude the people at Piper Corporation had regarding pilot qualifications for these ferries. When I made my first trip to Lock Haven, I had never laid eyes on a Piper Tomahawk, let alone flown one. I sat in a small office at William T. Piper Memorial Field and read the entire operating manual from cover to cover. Hundreds of airplanes were tied down just outside on the tarmac—all brand-new Piper Tomahawks. When I finished studying, I walked alone out to the airplane I was assigned to ferry, did a preflight walk-around, and then climbed in and familiarized myself with the controls and instruments. The Hobbs Meter, which shows cumulative running time on the aircraft's engine, indicated 0.3 hours; so it appeared as if they had tested the new engine for a few minutes. There was no instructor and no checkride. I taxied out, took off, and made three touch-and-go landings in the pattern before turning west for my transcontinental flight.

I actually delivered five aircraft that winter because I talked a couple of my private-pilot friends into going with me to pilot two additional aircraft on one of the trips.

Dr. Harold Thysell was a Coeur d'Alene family practitioner who had a Private Pilot license. He was in his late 50s at the time and had been a P-38 fighter pilot in World War II, flying bomber escorts out of North Africa on missions to Germany. Harold was an excellent pilot and an interesting character; he had logged a lot of flight time and owned his own private airplane, a Cessna 182.

Pat Flynn was the other pilot I invited. He was a nurse anesthetist at the hospital. Pat held a Commercial Pilot certificate and had a few hundred hours of flight time under his belt.

Harold, Pat, and I flew three Tomahawks in close formation across the country. It turned out to be an ill-fated adventure when we got caught in a major winter snowstorm and had to land in Billings, Montana. We stayed in a downtown hotel as the blizzard raged outside and the snow piled up day after day. We never got bored as we waited out the storm, though. Harold kept Pat and me entertained every minute. After getting up each morning, we studied the weather. If we came to the conclusion that there would be no chance of flying that day, Harold would suggest we go to the hotel bar and start the day with a glass of peppermint schnapps. We then wiled away a few hours in the bar as Harold regaled us with hilarious stories until early afternoon. We then would go back to our rooms and take naps before going out to dinner.

After three days of snowing heavily, with no end in sight, we decided it was time for us all to get back to work. We gave up, left our airplanes in Billings, and flew back to Spokane on a commercial Frontier Airlines flight. After the storm subsided, I took a few days off from the Emergency Room and made two separate trips back to Billings to retrieve two of the Tomahawks, mine and Harold's, and deliver them to Vancouver. Pat also made a trip back to pick up and deliver his aircraft.

Those Tomahawk ferries provided a nice boost to my total flight time, but multi-engine flight time was much harder to come by. Most of my multi-engine time was logged by going along on charter flights as a second pilot. I knew all the qualified multi-engine charter pilots at West Aire, and they all gave me a little "stick time." I didn't get paid for those flights, but I could legally log the segment of time during which I was the sole manipulator of the controls.

One of the pilots I paired up with was Al Hall. Al was a retired naval aviator who had recently moved to Coeur d'Alene. As the most experienced pilot on West Aire's staff, Al was the designated chief pilot. He often put me in the left seat of the Cessna 414 and let me fly an entire charter flight, while he sat in the copilot's seat and coached me. The Cessna 414 is a fairly sophisticated pressurized twin-engine aircraft, so it provided wonderful experience for me and added to my credentials. In 1980, I got to know Al better when he and I flew Idaho Senator Frank Church on a trip during his re-election campaign. Al and I quickly became good friends, and he became my aviation mentor over the next few years. I admired and respected him as an aviator and a fine person. He was from Georgia and a true southern gentleman. Al politely taught me many things, both in and out of the cockpit, about aviation and life in general. I flew with Al every chance I got, spending many hours in the air together, and the multi-engine flight hours recorded in my logbook started gradually increasing.

Our gaggle of Piper Tomahawks
Ferrying from Lock Haven, PA to Portland, OR – April 1979

82

On March 30, 1980, Al Hall and I flew an air ambulance flight in the Cessna 414 from Coeur d'Alene to the National Institute of Health Medical Center (NIH) in Bethesda, Maryland. The patient was a young Coeur d'Alene woman whom I had treated for cardiac arrest at Kootenai Memorial Emergency Room the previous week. We were transporting her to NIH for emergency open-heart surgery. The story of her survival is the most memorable event in my entire medical career, and I believe it is probably the most dramatic life-saving care any of us on my ER team ever provided.

I was sleeping soundly in our on-call room on the night of March 22 when one of the staff nurses called me over the intercom. She told me an ambulance was en route with a patient in cardiac arrest onboard. She then told me the victim was reportedly a young woman who was only 24 years of age.

A patient with cardiac arrest arriving at the ER always started my adrenaline pumping, so it didn't take long for me to transition from a deep sleep to being wide-awake and alert. As I shuffled toward the treatment room used for cardiac emergencies and where the cardiac "crash cart" was located, I puzzled over the rarity of such a young person suffering a cardiac arrest. My first thought was drug overdose—probably an attempted suicide. We treated several drug overdoses each week, and they almost always presented late at night. Those cases were invariably messy and unpleasant to deal with, but they rarely resulted in cardiac arrest before arriving for treatment.

When I pushed open the door to the large treatment room, I saw it was already bustling with activity. My team was gathered around the white sheets of a yet-unoccupied gurney. The large swing-arm surgical light was turned on and focused on the empty bed at about chest level. Everyone was busy carefully checking equipment. All three of my ER nurses were there, and a respiratory therapist and lab technician stood by. A cardiac defibrillator was plugged in, and monitor leads were laid out and organized so they could be quickly attached to the patient. A laryngoscope and several sizes of endotracheal tubes lay on a toweled tray near the head-end of the stretcher for my use. An IV bottle hung from a pole, ready to go, with the end capped and the flow pinched off. An oxygen hose was plugged into the receptacle on the back wall and ready for use. I circled around this treatment area and double-checked every piece of equipment. I asked if we had obtained any more information from the ambulance crew about this patient.

One of the nurses spoke up. "The crew told me on the initial radio call, Doctor, that the young woman had some kind of rare heart condition and was scheduled for surgery next month in Maryland."

"Thanks, Linda. Do we know anything else?"

Linda wrinkled her brow as she thought for a moment. "They said her husband had called the ambulance and that he had been performing CPR on her in their bed when they arrived. That's all I can tell you."

I could have called the ambulance crew back on the radio to ask questions, but I knew they were busy and it wouldn't likely change our protocol when they arrived. I never liked to talk to the ambulance crews on the radio anyway. The sound of the siren in the background always unnerved me a bit, and I wanted to be calm when they rolled in.

A number of things were going through my head that I didn't like about this case already. The young age of the patient was the first thing bothering me. Most patients presenting with cardiac arrest are in their 50s or older. I hated to lose any patient, but losing a young person always seemed much more tragic and weighed heavily on me for a long time afterwards.

Another worrisome factor with this emergency was the time involved from the moment of cardiac arrest until advanced treatment at the hospital would be initiated. I had no way of knowing if her husband had been trained in CPR or whether he was performing it correctly. The ambulance crew was all-volunteer and had to be called from their homes, get out of bed, dress, and then make the run to the patient's home in Coeur d'Alene. In this case, the crew on duty lived in Post Falls—10 miles away—and had dispatched from there. The response and transport time might be approximating an hour. In the case of cardiac arrest, time is not our friend.

In 1980, EMS systems were just developing and acquiring adequate funding, improved equipment, standardized training programs, and advanced qualifications for first responders. Our ambulance crews were devoted volunteers but were trained only as basic emergency medical technicians; we had no paramedics trained to insert an endotracheal tube, start an IV, administer emergency drugs, or perform cardioversion with a cardiac defibrillator.

As we waited at the hospital for the ambulance to arrive, I thought about all these things going against us, and I concluded this patient would likely be beyond the point of resuscitation by the time she got to us.

In my early days in medicine—as a medical student and intern—cardiopulmonary resuscitation (CPR) was relatively new. I recall how a cardiac arrest, even in a hospitalized patient, was a scene of utter chaos. Several medical students, residents, and staff physicians often responded to a "Code Blue," which was announced over the public address system. When arriving at the scene, it was always hard to tell who, if anyone, was in charge. Orders were shouted by different individuals who were apparently flying by the seats of their pants as they thought of different things to try out. Successful outcomes were few in those days.

By the late 1970s, cardiopulmonary resuscitation had come a long way. All four on our team of emergency room physicians at Kootenai Memorial had completed a course and been certified in Advanced Cardiac Life Support. The physician in charge of a cardiac arrest now followed a standard protocol that provided a decision tree, at least through the initial phases of treatment. A much calmer atmosphere prevailed as a result of the protocol; fewer people were in the room and everyone attending the patient was well trained and practiced. When the ambulance finally arrived that night and the stretcher rolled in with a seemingly lifeless body on it, a calm, controlled atmosphere prevailed. Everyone in the room had a critical job to do and quietly went to work.

83

One EMT performed cardiac compressions as the wheeled stretcher was rolled in, only pausing his efforts momentarily as we quickly lifted our patient onto the ER gurney. The second EMT, at the patient's head, moved with us, with one hand squeezing air into her lungs with an Ambu bag as his other hand expertly held the bag's mask tightly against the woman's face.

The body we flopped onto the gurney showed no sign of life. The patient's skin was as pale as the sheet she was lying on, and her lips and fingernail beds were cyanotic. She was a small woman; in fact her body was so diminutive it resembled that of a child. I doubt she weighed more than 100 pounds.

The mantra, A-B-C, went through my mind: airway—breathing—circulation, as I moved to the head of the gurney. The lightbulb on the laryngoscope lit up as I unfolded its gently curved blade. I nodded to the EMT squeezing the Ambu bag, and he removed the mask and bag. I quickly extended the patient's neck, opened her mouth, and slipped the blade of the scope over the top of her tongue and down her throat until I could see the vocal cords. I picked out an appropriately sized endotracheal tube and slid it carefully between the cords until the inflatable balloon on the tube was positioned just below them. I inflated the balloon with a syringe, taped the tube to the side of her face, and mated the Ambu bag to it. The respiratory therapist, who was standing by, connected an oxygen tube to the Ambu bag and took over squeezing it to provide artificial respiration. I checked both lungs with my stethoscope to be sure the tube was positioned correctly and inflating both sides. I had taken care of A and B, but C (circulation) was always the hardest one. I stepped back for a moment and took a deep breath.

I moved down the gurney toward the patient's lower extremities where there was less activity and felt for a femoral pulse. The femoral artery is a large vessel that is close to the surface and normally has an easily palpable pulse; I couldn't feel one.

The monitor was hooked up, and the IV, which had already been started by one of the nurses, was dripping. As I looked at the monitor, any hopes I held for saving this young woman's life sank as I muttered, "Oh crap! Straight line."

I ordered two 50cc ampules of sodium bicarbonate be given by IV push followed by 1cc of aqueous epinephrine (adrenaline) and 0.5mg of atropine. I then watched the monitor closely, hoping to see something other than a flat, straight line. There was no change.

I reviewed the protocol and decision tree in my head and announced to the crew we would next attempt defibrillation. As I placed the flat paddles on our patient's bare chest, I ordered "clear" in a loud voice. The mechanical resuscitative efforts were momentarily interrupted as everyone stepped away from the gurney in order to avoid an electrical shock. When I simultaneously pushed two red buttons, one on each paddle, her lifeless body jerked spasmodically as all of her muscles contracted. When I released the buttons she flopped back down onto the gurney. The flat pattern on the monitor remained unchanged. The crew immediately moved back in and resumed CPR.

I knew defibrillation would only work if the heart was in ventricular fibrillation. The electrical shock would not normally start a heart that was in true standstill, but it was possible there might be a fine fibrillation I couldn't detect on the monitor. If that were the case, the procedure might work.

I repeated the dose of epinephrine and then shocked her again with the defibrillator. There was still no change. It appeared this was true cardiac standstill.

The next step was one I always disliked doing: an intra-cardiac injection of epinephrine. I put a long cardiac needle onto a syringe and shoved it at an angle through the skin below the breastbone, up under the xiphoid process at the lower end of the sternum and, hopefully, into the left ventricle of the heart. When I drew back on the plunger of the syringe and aspirated blood effortlessly, I knew I was at least in one of the four chambers of the heart. I detached the blood-filled syringe and handed it to the lab tech with an order for arterial blood gases. I attached another syringe containing 1cc of epinephrine and injected the medication directly into the heart chamber. I checked the monitor—still nothing. I pulled out the needle, and one of the nurses slapped a Band-Aid on the tiny hole in the skin.

We had now reached a decision point that often occurred in the process of a resuscitative effort: do we keep going or do we "call it?" Whenever this juncture was reached in the treatment of a cardiac arrest, I always hoped to get some support and feedback from my crew that would help me arrive at the proper decision. That never happened. I looked at my team, hoping to detect which direction each person was leaning. I didn't like this role of "playing God" in the slightest. Everyone in the room fell silent, stared right back at me, and waited for me to decide whether to continue what seemed to be a losing battle or end it, right there and then, by calling our patient's time of death.

We had been rotating the physically exhausting job of performing chest compressions, but everyone was getting tired. We had been working hard on this patient for more than 30 minutes, and the ambulance crew, taking turns with the ER nurses, had been performing CPR considerably longer than that. We all wanted this to be over. I had followed the recommended protocol and had reached the end of the decision tree.

I walked back up to the head of the gurney and pulled up the woman's eyelids. Slipping my penlight out of the breast pocket of my white coat, I shined its bright light directly into her eyes. The pupils did not react. The loss of this most basic neural reflex was considered an accepted sign of irreversible brain damage. I looked at the nurse who was recording each event with clipboard and pen in hand, and I told her to record the time and note the pupils as "fixed and dilated." This is frequently the last thing written on a patient's chart. I doubt if anyone in the room would have argued with me at that point if I had called our efforts to a halt. Before making that irreversible decision, though, I needed to go to the waiting room and talk to the husband. I wanted to know what her "rare" heart condition was and what kind of surgery she was scheduled for next month in Maryland, a piece of information we had obtained from the EMTs on the ambulance radio call earlier that night.

84

I learned that our patient's name was Robin Bevis, her husband was Mike, they were newlyweds, and the couple had gotten married only two months earlier. Mike told me Robin had an unusual heart condition known as idiopathic, hypertrophic, subaortic stenosis. I was familiar with this type of cardiomyopathy, commonly referred to as IHSS, although I had never actually seen a patient with this rare condition. The long name refers to a thickening (hypertrophy) of the heart muscle tissue just below the aortic valve (subaortic) in the heart resulting in narrowing (stenosis) of the arterial outlet of the left ventricle. The cause is unknown (idiopathic). When the ventricle in a heart with this condition contracts to pump blood to the body through the aortic valve, the hypertrophied muscle below the valve contracts as well, narrowing the outlet even more. So the heart is really working against itself each time it contracts, and cardiac output is diminished.

The prognosis for IHSS is poor. The afflicted patient will eventually develop an enlarged heart and die of heart failure. Prior to this time, there had been no known satisfactory treatment, but the National Institute of Health in Bethesda, Maryland, had recently developed a surgical procedure that involved opening the heart and reaming out the thickened muscle to relieve the partial obstruction. They had only performed about 80 of these risky operations, but early results were encouraging. Robin had been seeing a cardiologist, Dr. Terry Judge, in Spokane, and he had gotten her on the surgical schedule at NIH for the experimental procedure. A date had been set for open-heart surgery, and Robin and her husband had already purchased airline tickets to fly to Bethesda.

I questioned Mike about Robin's symptoms related to her condition, and he reported she had been getting progressively limited in her physical activities due to generalized weakness and shortness of breath. He told me their mailbox was at the street in front of their house and that Robin had to stop several times to rest whenever she walked down their short driveway to retrieve the mail. Her symptoms had been recently getting much worse.

Mike said he had been awakened in his sleep that night when Robin made a strange gasping noise. The unusual sound woke him, and he found her unresponsive and without any detectable pulse. He dialed the operator and requested an ambulance immediately. He then started CPR. He told me he had just completed a Red Cross CPR course the week before and hoped he was doing it correctly.

I quickly reviewed Robin's past medical history with Mike, made some brief notes, and wrote out a list of the medications she was taking. She had been on diuretics (water pills) for shortness of breath, and I suspected her cardiac arrest might be related to a serum electrolyte imbalance, most likely potassium or calcium.

I explained to Mike, honestly and candidly, that his young wife had not responded to our resuscitative efforts, that she had signs of permanent and irreversible brain damage, and I made it clear she would not likely survive. I felt he needed to be told this grim prognosis sooner than later. Mike appeared to be in a state of shock, and I wasn't sure how much I said even registered. He didn't plead with me or beg that we keep up our efforts. He just put his face in his hands and was unable to continue any further conversation. I told him we wouldn't stop our efforts until we were sure nothing else could be done.

I patted Mike on the shoulder and said I would come back out and report any significant change. As I headed back to the treatment room, I thought about the fact that, with each passing minute without a heartbeat, the likelihood of a successful resuscitation diminished. At that point, we were approaching two hours from the time of the arrest at their home.

85

When I got back into the room, nothing had changed. The lab tech was back with the arterial blood gas results. The oxygen saturation was pretty good, indicating my team was doing a great job with the CPR. The blood pH level indicated, as expected, that our patient was in severe metabolic acidosis from the marginal perfusion of her organs with oxygenated blood. We had only partially treated it with the sodium bicarbonate we had administered. I ordered another two 50cc ampules. I knew I needed to be careful with this; she needed the bicarb, but she didn't need the big sodium load she was absorbing with every dose.

I was looking at the monitor when the second ampule was injected into the IV line and saw a single electrical pattern, known as a QRS complex, move across the screen from left to right. Then another one floated across the screen a few seconds later. Everyone on the team was suddenly riveted to the monitor screen, and the room became completely quiet except for the beep associated with each random blip on the screen. I was excited to see a rhythm developing—a slow, irregular, and random rhythm, but it was something.

I opened the top drawer of the crash cart and removed another long cardiac needle from its sterile packaging and injected another cc of epinephrine directly into the left ventricle of the heart in the same manner I had done earlier. To my complete and utter surprise, a pattern of sinus tachycardia with a rate of 110 complexes per minute immediately appeared on the monitor. Other than being a little fast (tachycardia), it looked like a completely normal pattern. The room got noisy for a few seconds as everyone on the team voiced exclamations of surprise and amazement. I removed the needle.

I asked the attendant doing chest compressions to stop for a few seconds. I put my hand over the femoral artery, in the groin area, and felt for a pulse. Everyone in the room was staring at me as I concentrated intently on what I was feeling or not feeling with my fingertips.

"Resume cardiac compressions," I ordered, "there is no pulse."

I had never before had a case of electromechanical dissociation (EMD) during a resuscitation, but I recognized immediately I was dealing with one now. Simply stated, this condition is when the heart muscle is receiving organized electrical impulses, but the muscle fails to contract and produce a cardiac output and thereby a pulse. The outlook is grim, with a mortality rate of over 90 percent.

I had been taught in my Advanced Cardiac Life Support class there was no treatment for EMD, but it was suggested intravenous calcium chloride be administered. It was pointed out that evidence of the effectiveness of calcium for EMD was purely anecdotal. No studies had ever demonstrated calcium was of any value for this condition, but, since the calcium ion has such an integral role in muscle-fiber contraction, as every medical student learns in physiology class, it remained on the list as a last resort to reestablish cardiac contractions. I was now flying by the seat of my pants.

"One amp of calcium chloride by IV push," I ordered. I waited a few seconds and asked that chest compressions be momentarily stopped as I again felt for a femoral pulse. I thought I felt the artery give a single weak thump against my fingertips. I actually wondered if I wanted to feel a pulse so badly I might have imagined it or, possibly, I had felt my own pounding pulse in the tips of my fingers.

"Resume chest compressions," I requested, "and give another amp of calcium chloride." I waited a few seconds, as I had before, and asked that compressions again be stopped for a moment as I once more felt for a femoral pulse.

"Stop CPR, please; I've got a pulse—a strong pulse."

The atmosphere in the room was electric. We were all excited with this reward for our efforts, but none of us was exactly jubilant. The patient had made no spontaneous respiratory efforts and exhibited no sign of brain activity. The pulse rate was slightly fast and agreed with the rate on the monitor of 120 beats per minute. I put a blood pressure cuff on my patient's arm and got a reading of 120/70—completely normal.

I asked one of the nurses to call Dr. Jim Patacky, the cardiologist on call, and tell him we had an admission to the CCU for him and he needed to get to the hospital ASAP. "Tell Dr. Patacky I will keep her in the ER until he gets here," I instructed. I asked one of the crew to continuously monitor her pulse and returned to the waiting room to talk to Mike Bevis.

The sun was shining through the window of the call room when Jim Arthurs arrived for his shift to relieve me. I had slept for a couple of hours and was happy no other patients presented on my shift after I got Robin admitted to the hospital. I showered and dressed in my civvies. Instead of heading for the parking lot that morning, I walked down the hall toward the double doors leading into the rest of the hospital.

Robin's room was directly across from the Coronary Care Unit's nursing station. As I stood behind the desk, I looked through a wall of glass into her room and could see her lying in bed. No one else was in the room. The nurses told me her husband had gone home to make phone calls to relatives, and that Robin's mother was on her way from Seattle and should arrive by early afternoon. I studied her chart for a couple of minutes, and then walked into her room.

A mechanical respirator stood at the bedside and was connected to the endotracheal tube I had inserted. I watched her chest wall rise and fall beneath the blanket as the respirator cycled, assuming the function of breathing for her. I picked up her wrist, as an almost unconscious reflex, and palpated a strong, regular pulse. I only stayed in the room a couple of minutes. I felt the weight of extreme fatigue and sadness as I walked out of the hospital and headed for the parking lot. I wondered if my team and I had done Robin any favors by resuscitating her. I suspected Dr. Patacky and the family would be required to make some tough decisions over the next few days.

I was off work the next three days in a row. I spent some of my free time at the airport giving a couple of flight lessons. I was distracted and had a hard time enjoying my time off. At night, I slept fitfully and couldn't stop thinking about Robin Bevis in that hospital room, being kept artificially alive. I resisted calling the CCU or making a trip in to check on her, but I started anticipating my next shift in the ER, which would serve as an opportunity to check on her status.

I went into work a little early and proceeded directly to the CCU, where I saw there had been a significant change in Robin's condition. She remained in a deep coma, and the hospital still had her on the critical list, but that morning she had started making some spontaneous respiratory efforts. The respirator was switched from the "continuous" mode to the "demand" mode, which meant she was now triggering the machine to cycle as it then assisted in inflating her lungs. Spontaneous respiration is a basic brain stem reflex, and this was evidence it was resuming function—a positive sign.

I worked my 24-hour shift and stopped by the CCU before leaving to go home. Robin's vital signs remained stable, her heart rhythm was normal, and she was still triggering the respirator, but she remained in a profoundly deep coma.

After another three days off, I returned to work for my next scheduled shift and was happy to see Terry Phillips, my favorite critical care nurse, sitting at the desk. As I approached her, she gave me a big smile. I was confident Robin Bevis was in good hands with her on duty, as Terry was the most competent RN I had ever met over the course of my career. She was incredibly intelligent and could sort out, diagnose, and treat complicated heart rhythms that would challenge almost any experienced cardiologist. Besides all that, Terry was a wonderful person. Everyone loved her. She was from England and spoke with a delightful British accent that was a treat to my ears. Terry was probably in her late 40s, seemed rather matronly in demeanor, was always cheerful, and had a hilarious sense of humor. I had never seen her look quite as happy as she did that morning, and I wondered what was going on.

"Terry, I know you love me, but I have never seen you so happy to see me," I quipped.

"Good morning, Dr. Crawley. I've heard you have an interest in our patient, Robin Bevis. I think you need to go into her room for a visit this morning."

The drapes were pulled across the glass window of Robin's room, and I couldn't see her from the nurses' station. "Is it okay to go in now?" I asked Terry.

We both walked into the room and I was so overwhelmed I couldn't speak for a moment. Robin Bevis was sitting up in bed, her endotracheal tube had been removed, she had a breakfast tray in front of her, and she was eating a poached egg.

87

Robin didn't have any detectable neurologic deficit after she awoke from the coma other than a loss of some recent memory, which included complete amnesia for the events of the previous two months. This was interesting, since she had gotten married during that time and was somewhat shocked to hear Mike Bevis was no longer just her boyfriend—he was her husband. Robin's mother, Lynn Lancaster, brought a book of wedding pictures to her hospital room to convince Robin she was no longer a single woman. Robin viewed the pictures with dismay.

Dr. Patacky coordinated with Dr. Judge, Robin's cardiologist in Spokane, and they contacted the cardiac surgery department at NIH. They arranged for Robin to be moved to the top of the list for the experimental IHSS repair procedure. Dr. Patacky asked me if I could make arrangements for a transcontinental air ambulance flight. I decided I would do better than that; I would fly her to Bethesda myself with my own critical care team from the ER.

I had no trouble getting two of the regular ER nurses to volunteer their time and services for the trip. Mark and Linda were both RNs whom I worked with regularly and had a lot of confidence in. The three of us spent an afternoon making a list of medical equipment and emergency drugs we would take on the plane. The Kootenai Memorial Hospital Administrator, Joe Morris, agreed to supply us with everything we needed. We would have a flying intensive care unit.

At the airport, I scheduled the charter flight in the only pressurized twin-engine airplane available—the Cessna 414. Al Hall, the chief pilot, would be the official pilot in command for the flight, and I would serve as copilot and be available to move to the cabin if any problems developed with our patient. We had the mechanics carefully check over the aircraft and asked them to remove two seats and secure a stretcher in the resulting space.

The flight to Bethesda was long and tiring, taking the entire day to get there. Six of us made the trip: Robin and Mike Bevis, Linda and Mark (my two nurses), Al Hall, and I. Robin wanted to dress in regular clothes for the trip, but I insisted she wear a hospital gown and robe. In the event of an emergency, we didn't want to be fumbling with buttons or zippers trying to get her quickly undressed. She sat in one of the regular passenger seats for the entire flight, since she had trouble breathing when lying flat. The stretcher was only there to be used if, heaven forbid, she needed CPR again.

We made two fuel stops, which also served as restroom breaks. We walked Robin slowly into each air terminal and one of the nurses helped her use the bathroom. She had an IV bag of saline connected and running at a slow drip. It was there as an immediate route for any emergency drugs that might need to be administered.

Robin looked pale and very frail that day. I prayed she would survive the arduous trip. Al Hall let me fly the entire route from the left seat, and I was exhausted when I landed the airplane at our final destination. I couldn't imagine how Robin must have felt in her tenuous state.

An NIH ambulance met our flight at Dulles International Airport in Washington, D.C. The tension of the day dropped away when we said goodbye to Robin and her husband on the tarmac and the ambulance doors closed. We made it! I had done all I could, and my job was over. We spent the night at a nearby hotel and departed for Coeur d'Alene the following morning.

Robin's open-heart surgery was performed in Maryland on April 15. Dr. Patacky came by the ER during my shift a couple of days later to tell me Robin had survived the operation, and her doctors at NIH reported she was doing well post-op.

July 2, 1980

Our oldest daughter, Jill, and I were walking through the parking lot of Rosauer's Grocery in Coeur d'Alene after picking up a few party supplies for Jill's ninth birthday, which was the next day. We were approaching our car when I heard someone hollering, "Dr. Crawley....Dr. Crawley." I turned and saw a young woman with a big smile on her face riding toward us on a bicycle. She stopped a few feet away. I must have had a blank look on my face because she said, "You don't recognize me, do you? I'm Robin Bevis."

I introduced Robin to Jill, and then we chatted for a few minutes. When she finally pedaled off on her bike, Jill looked up at me and said, "Dad, why are you crying?"

Robin Bevis – Two months after open-heart surgery

June 1980

August 2015

Robin Bevis, now age 60, is alive, well, and physically active. She and Mike still live in the Pacific Northwest. They have been married for over 35 years and are enjoying a happy retirement life together.

Calcium chloride, which I had injected as a last-resort effort to save Robin, is no longer listed as an emergency drug for cardiac arrest—even if it involves electromechanical dissociation—and it has been removed from hospital crash carts. It was never scientifically proved to be of any therapeutic value.

Dr. Crawley and staff—

Wishing you and the wonderful emergency room staff a Merry Christmas and happy New Year.

Thank you for making ours possible!

Mike and Robin Bevis

88

The air ambulance flight to Bethesda gave my multi-engine flight time a nice boost. The Piper Tomahawk ferry flights and the instructing I was doing had pumped up my total flight time, but I wasn't sure how I was going to get more of the coveted multi-engine time; West Aire had very little charter business. That situation changed in 1980 when the company was purchased by a new owner and became Empire Airways. Since I had been working for West Aire at the time as a flight instructor, I got scooped up in the deal and "inherited" by Empire Airways. They seemed to accept me as a professional pilot, regardless of the fact I was also an emergency room physician. For a long time, I had hoped someone would take over West Aire and turn it into a viable air service. It had finally happened, and I was excited about it.

Mel Spelde was one of three investors in this enterprise and served as the president and general manager of the newly christened Empire Airways. When I met Mel, I liked him right away. He was a tall, thin fellow in his late 30s with a gregarious personality. He walked with long, purposeful strides and seemed to have boundless energy. He was an excellent pilot, held a Commercial Pilot certificate, and was also a certified Flight Instructor. The new owners kept Al Hall on as chief pilot. I was happy about that decision because I held him in high regard. Mel and Al quickly became good friends.

Mel was a shrewd businessman and started building the operation, mainly by bidding on and being awarded government flying contracts. He frequently bid a contract requiring a certain type of aircraft and specific pilot qualifications, even when he had no idea where he would find the airplane or the appropriately qualified pilot. He always said he would worry about those details when he was awarded the contract. It was gutsy and a little crazy to do business that way, I thought, but he always made it work out.

I had enough total flight time to start flying some of those contracts. Over the next few years, I was a pilot for the U.S. Forest Service, the Bureau of Land Management, and Washington Water Power. All three of these involved backcountry mountain flying in single-engine aircraft.

The USFS flights were mostly regular fire-patrol routes, and I always had a Forest Service spotter with me in the right seat. I also occasionally ferried Forest Service personnel. The Forest Service

353

administers their own checkrides to contract pilots, and I was required to take their written test and then regularly scheduled flight tests. I was awarded a qualification card, but special endorsements on the card were required for landing at backcountry unpaved airstrips. To get the backcountry strip endorsement, I had to fly with a USFS check pilot into each special strip that required it. Some of those mountain airstrips were one-way, due to obstructing terrain, and required a landing approach from one direction and a takeoff departure in the opposite direction. A few of these were "no go-around" airfields, meaning that once you descended below a certain altitude, you were committed to land, since a go-around for another try was impossible due to rising terrain. Those airstrips were especially sporting. I didn't mind the one-way fields, despite the fact most of them were quite short, but I didn't like the idea of no go-around. I generally begged off on those assignments and let one of my fellow aviators who enjoyed that type of challenge take it.

The BLM flying involved aerial inspection, and sometimes photography, of certain tracts of federal land or could involve simply ferrying personnel. Those flights were never particularly difficult or challenging.

The Washington Water Power contract was the most demanding of all. It was known as "power-line patrol" and involved aerial inspection of high-tension electrical wires. It was low and slow flying. A power company technician always rode along on these flights and had a UHF radio he used to call in repair crews on the ground. He wanted me to stay within 50 feet of the lines so we could see broken glass insulators on the cross-trees. We also looked for downed lines and tree branches touching the cables. This required a lot of fancy maneuvering at times, like when a line was strung over the top of a ridge and then dropped into a valley on the other side. Sometimes, in these situations, it wasn't possible to stay as close to the wires as the technician would have liked me to do. Whenever I was doing power-line patrol, I felt as though my head had to be on a swivel at all times—it was risky business.

One summer, I piloted several "bug patrols" with a U.S. Forest Service entomologist. This was another low-level operation in which the scientist mapped areas of insect damage to coniferous trees as we flew slowly up and down creek drainages in the Coeur d'Alene Mountains. I also spent a week doing a bug-patrol survey in the rugged terrain of Glacier National Park in northern Montana. The entomologist and I were based at the Kalispell Airport for that operation, an assignment involving the highest and most rugged mountain flying I had ever done.

One of my more interesting charters for the Forest Service was an operation to try to catch cedar tree rustlers who were cutting down giant cedars illegally in the Idaho Panhandle National Forest. The thieves were hauling the valuable logs out and selling them to various lumber mills for thousands of dollars. The Forest Service had been unable to apprehend the group and suspected they had been conducting all of their activities at night. I got the call for this flight just after midnight, and I arrived at the Coeur d'Alene Airport at about 3:30 AM to fuel and preflight an airplane. My assignment was to land on an unimproved grass strip near Priest Lake at first morning light to pick up an armed special agent. I had to time my night departure out of Coeur d'Alene to land on the strip as early as possible, but the airstrip was unlighted, so I needed just enough natural light to see the runway. The landing area in the forest was a narrow grass strip, which had been cut out in a dense stand of Ponderosa Pine and Douglas Fir, just to the west of the central portion of Lower Priest Lake. The sun hadn't risen when I arrived at the airstrip, but there was just enough light to pick out the narrow runway carved into the forest below and land.

It all seemed very clandestine as I bumped to a stop in the dim morning light. A shadowy figure dressed in dark-green fatigues emerged from the trees and walked quickly toward the airplane. As he got closer, I saw a holstered pistol on his belt and a gold badge on his chest. He got into the plane with the engine idling and the propeller still turning, and we took off immediately. The Forest Service agent directed me to the general area where he thought the cedar trees were being harvested. We found the culprits at work but stayed pretty high and didn't stick around because of the worry of small-arms fire. The agent called in pre-positioned law enforcement officers on the ground and told them which roads to block. We solved the mystery of how they were getting the logs down the highway without being caught: they were using closed moving vans instead of standard logging trucks. It was a fun little charter that made me feel like I was part of a secret mission in a James Bond movie.

Empire's multi-engine charter business started to pick up. The company employed another young part-time pilot, Ken Frank, who had about the same flight hours and experience as I. When both of us had over 300 hours of multi-engine time, Mel and Al started sending us out together on charters in the Cessna 414. We alternated each leg as pilot in command with the other acting as copilot, switching cockpit seats as our roles changed. After flying a few trips together, we both broke through the 500-hour mark for multi-engine time. We each then started flying multi-engine trips solo, as pilot in command.

After that, I started flying for Transtector Systems (an electronics manufacturer), Idaho Forest Industries (a local lumber company), and the Nez Perce Indian tribe. These trips were all in sophisticated, pressurized twin-engine aircraft.

Once more, I wasn't sure where all of this was taking me.

89

In the fall of 1981, I found out several U.S. Navy reservists lived in Coeur d'Alene and served as so-called "weekend warriors" at NAS Whidbey Island one weekend a month. The Navy Reserve unit on the base would send a C-118 (Douglas DC-6) to Coeur d'Alene and Spokane on Friday of a scheduled drill weekend to pick up reservists and then fly them back home on Sunday evening. Five years had elapsed since I was released from active duty as a naval flight surgeon, and I had started to miss some elements of military service life, especially the aviation part. If I transferred from the Inactive Ready Reserve to the Ready Reserve, it would mean I would be gone from home one weekend a month and be required to serve two weeks of active duty each year. With such a convenient transportation arrangement for weekend duty, I was interested. I discussed it with Martha, and, as always, she said she would support my decision—whatever it might be.

I thought about the pros and cons of become a drilling ready reservist. I was excited at the thought I might get assigned to a reserve squadron in which I could once again log some stick time in military aircraft. Another advantage was a small monthly paycheck. If I got a DIFOPS (duty involving flight operations) billet and logged a minimum of four hours of flight each month, I would also receive flight pay (known as hazardous duty pay). Our personal monthly income was still barely keeping up with our household expenses. Just as worrisome was the fact I hadn't been able to save anything for retirement yet, and any extra money would help. If I were to stay in the reserves for at least 20 years, I would be eligible for reserve retirement pay and medical benefits. The only disadvantage I could think of was I could be activated and put in harm's way if the country went to war. I accepted the risk by rationalizing that, in the event of another major war, I would likely be called to duty anyway—whether I was a drilling reservist or not.

I made some phone calls to the air station and found there was an open flight surgeon billet in a reserve anti-submarine patrol squadron. The unit was the training squadron for the P-3 Orion, a four-engine turboprop based on the venerable Lockheed Electra airframe. I took the open position and dusted off my old uniforms. I rode over on the C-118 for the next drill weekend, December 11, 1981, to take a physical and complete the paperwork.

My squadron was designated VP-0122 and was the Replacement Air Group (RAG). As soon as aviators finished training and qualified in the aircraft, they moved on to the operational sister reserve squadron of P-3's, which was VP-69. My duty involved performing flight physicals at the naval hospital on Saturday and Sunday mornings and then spending time in the squadron spaces in the afternoon. I also generally got my flight time in the afternoons by going on training flights in the P-3. Other duties included treating flight crews for minor illnesses and deciding whether an individual was fit to fly, serving on Human Factors and Pilot Disposition Boards, giving lectures to the crews on safety and aeromedical topics, and convening an occasional medical board to determine fitness for duty and/or continued military service. Since I was dealing with a population of young, healthy individuals, there wasn't much in the way of real medicine involved. The work was mostly administrative.

Most of the squadron's reserve naval aviators were commercial airline pilots in real life. I enjoyed being around those guys and envied their lifestyles. Their flying careers typically took them away from home for several days at a time, but they then had a few days off in a row. Having 15 or more days off each month was not uncommon. The pilots all looked physically fit, well-rested, and suntanned. A few of them drove fancy sports cars up from Seattle on the duty weekend. When not in uniform, they all wore nice clothes and had money in their wallets. For the pilots who were married, I suspected their wives weren't constantly worried about their grocery budgets like Martha was at our house.

Over the next few months, I began to compare my life with the lives of my squadron-mates. I often arrived at the drill weekend worn out from a 24-hour ER shift. When I looked in the mirror, I saw a pale and sickly looking person staring back at me. My clothes were old, and when my elbows wore holes in the sleeves of my shirts, I had Martha cut the sleeves off and hem them so I could wear them a few more years as short-sleeved shirts. My Navy uniforms were old and worn, and I had lost weight, so they no longer fit me well. I rarely had more than a few dollars in my wallet. Our family car was the same 10-year-old, lime-green station wagon we had owned since my intern days.

I envied my new airline pilot friends for their lifestyles, but I was mostly jealous that they got to go to work and get paid for flying big airplanes all over the world. I found myself wishing I could go back in time and choose my career path over again; I would have become an airline pilot.

The other reserve flight surgeons serving with me were physicians who had private practices around the Pacific Northwest. Some of these officers were attached to operational squadrons based at Whidbey, as I was, and some of them were attached to the Medical Reserve Unit at Whidbey Island Naval Hospital. All of these guys were highly intelligent and incredibly interesting people. Clint Furuya was an ENT doctor from Bellevue, Washington. Tony Bartley was a family physician from nearby Oak Harbor. Lee Harmon was an ophthalmologist from Arlington, Washington. Gil Vorhoff was an anesthesiologist from Tacoma. Rob Barnes was an infectious disease specialist from Bellingham. Bill Farr was an ophthalmologist from Portland. Bruce Noonan was an ophthalmologist from Seattle. Jim Stewart was a psychoanalyst from Bellingham. All of these accomplished fellows had successful practices and didn't need to be doing this, but they enjoyed it for various reasons and knew they were serving their country. We all became good friends over the next several years. We usually went to lunch together on Saturday and Sunday, and we sometimes regrouped for dinner at the O' Club on base or at one of the restaurants in Oak Harbor. I tried to split my social time with my doctor friends and my pilot friends in the squadron.

My Navy Reserve duty added a new dimension to my life, and I looked forward to putting on my uniform and heading off to Whidbey for duty on my assigned weekend. My new part-time job was interesting and stimulating; I acquired a whole new circle of friends, and it made me feel patriotic to be serving my country.

90

By the end of 1981, I began to feel as if I was developing burnout as an emergency room physician. The 24-hour shifts, which allowed me to enjoy several days off in a row, made my body feel like it was on a rollercoaster ride. I became tense and irritable, was continuously fatigued, and at times I felt physically ill. I was still in my mid-30s, but at one point I told Martha I thought if I were to continue doing what I was doing, I didn't think I would live another five years. That scared her.

Some mornings when I arrived home after a 24-hour shift, I walked in the door, looked into Martha's eyes, and burst into tears. I couldn't seem to treat my patients and deal with their families without sharing the emotions of their personal tragedies. I wondered how some of my colleagues seemed to stay objective and detached in similar situations. It was hard to tell what they were feeling inside, though, and maybe most them were suffering too. I probably hid my anguish at work as well as they did, but when I got home, I frequently couldn't hold it all in anymore.

I no longer looked forward to the high-energy drama of the ER, and instead I found myself sometimes worrying about what would come through the double doors next. I was tired of all the blood and gore, the crushed and deformed limbs, the ruptured internal organs, the massive head injuries, and I didn't want to see any more deaths. I became disgusted with caring for drunks in the middle of the night. I often had to tie them down with restraints to treat their injuries as they vomited, spat on me, and even occasionally struck me with a closed fist. I found I was developing negative feelings toward a significant segment of the patients I treated and becoming cynical toward humanity in general. I was progressively unhappy, and I even started dreading going in for my shift.

Martha was worried about me, and my unhappiness was affecting her happiness. I wasn't sure how much the kids were aware of, but it was probably affecting them too.

I talked to my physician friends at Whidbey Island about my problem, and most of them seemed to think I was just having a midlife crisis. When I got home and told Martha that, she said they were all wrong and she thought it was time to get out of medicine and find a career I really liked. She said, "Why don't you become an airline pilot? I know you would be happy doing that. It's obvious aviation is your first love."

I admitted to Martha that was my dream career but explained to her I had missed my chance for it. I knew airlines only recruited young, qualified pilots who would serve for a 30- to 40-year career. I had never heard of a pilot being hired by an airline if he or she was over 30. I would have to find some other career that might bring me satisfaction.

After that discussion, the ideas started coming fast and furiously. I had a new plan for my future almost every month. In each case, I enthusiastically described my new chosen "path du jour" to almost everyone I knew. After a while, I think I was the butt of a lot of jokes in the doctors' lounge at the hospital, where physicians gathered for coffee every morning. When I came in, I often heard, "So, Dave, we were just talking about you. What are you going to be this month? Have you decided what you are going to do when you grow up?" I tried not to show embarrassment or let their comments bother me, but I think they all thought I was going a little crazy.

I applied for a plastic surgery residency position at the University of Kansas School of Medicine, where I had gone to med school. I flew to Kansas City, and the chairman of the department interviewed me. I had decided beforehand that, if he offered me the slot, I would accept. When he did offer me the position, I told him I needed to go back home and think about it. Before leaving Kansas City, I went driving around with a realtor and looked at houses we might rent while I was in training for the next six to eight years. I called Martha and told her to hire a realtor and put our home in Coeur d'Alene up for sale. When I got home, there was a "For Sale" sign in the front yard. A couple of days later, I told Martha I had changed my mind—I wasn't going to become a plastic surgeon. We took the sign down.

I next started looking for summer dude ranches for sale. I told Martha I had decided that if we could somehow borrow the money to buy one, it would be a fun family business all four of us could participate in and enjoy. I found a remote lodge located on the Middle Fork of the Salmon River in Central Idaho that was for sale. Martha put her foot down at that idea. She had supported me in almost every decision so far, but at that point, even Martha thought I was getting a little crazy.

Next I decided I wanted to be a lawyer. Martha was skeptical about that idea too, but she said, "If that is what you think you really want, go for it." I took the LSAT exam. My test score was mediocre, but I applied anyway and was accepted to Gonzaga University Law School in Spokane. I went to the first day of classes and, by the end of the day, I was asking myself, "What am I doing here?" I quit at the end of that first day. My fellow physicians in the doctors' lounge were filled with glee when they heard about it. They couldn't wait for my next career-change announcement.

91

After the law school fiasco, Martha suggested we get away for a few days without the kids. She thought a vacation out of town might give me a chance to relax and possibly gain some perspective on what was happening. We left the kids with a babysitter and drove up into Canada. We stayed for a few days at the beautiful Chateau Lake Louise and then a couple of more days at the magnificent Banff Springs Hotel. Both of these castle-like lodges are located in Alberta's Canadian Rockies.

During the day we hiked mountain trails to teahouses above Lake Louise, crossing bubbling streams on rustic log bridges. It was early fall, and the leaves of the deciduous trees—maple and alder—had already started turning a brilliant yellow and orange. The sky was clear and sunny, the air pure and crisp; it was the perfect atmosphere in which to start calming my anxieties. At Banff we explored more mountain trails and walked the shores of the rushing Bow River. In the evenings we dined in the grand dining rooms at both resorts.

By the time we got back to Coeur d'Alene, I had convinced myself I had probably just been overworked, suffering from burnout, and that a vacation was all I needed to get rested and back on course. I decided I would stop bouncing around with a crazy career idea every few days and just settle back into my job in the ER. We had just added a fifth physician to fill in part-time, and that added flexibility to everyone's schedule. I cut back a little bit on my shifts and started flying more. The vacation effect was short-lived though, and it wasn't long before I had reverted back to my former tense, irritable, and gloomy self.

The one bright light in my life at that time, apart from my dear wife and family, was my monthly Navy Reserve weekend. I had developed a close friendship with Dr. Jim Stewart, the psychoanalyst from Bellingham. Jim and I didn't have an official doctor-patient relationship, but he was a wonderful listener, and I correctly concluded he must be an excellent psychiatrist. Our conversations were all on a social basis, but whenever we were together, he patiently listened to the whining complaints about how unhappy I was at work and how stuck I felt in my career. I got to the point where I could hardly wait for my scheduled drill weekend so I could talk to him. If it turned out, for one reason or another, we weren't scheduled on the same weekend, I was down in the dumps for the next month.

Jim finally recommended I seek psychiatric counseling on a professional basis and referred me to a colleague who was in practice in nearby Spokane. I scheduled a visit with the doctor he recommended and had an initial one-hour consultation. At the end of our session, he told me I was a "perfect" candidate to join a weekly group-therapy session he conducted. He said I would fit right in because all the members of the support group were physicians who hated practicing medicine and were learning to cope. He asked me if he could schedule me for the next session. I had to do something, so I agreed, even though learning to just cope didn't sound to me like a viable solution.

When I got home from Spokane and told Martha all about my consultation with the doctor, she was adamantly set against it. She said, "David, cancel the new appointment. You don't need a psychiatrist, you need to change careers." She then handed me a book she had bought that very day called *Pathfinders,* written by Gail Sheehy. "Read this book; maybe it will help," she suggested.

I started reading the book right away. It was a collection of stories about people who had grown unhappy or felt unfulfilled with something in their lives—usually having to do with their careers. Each of the individuals described in the book had arrived at a crossroads. Those who took the plunge to change their lives and pursue a dream ended up at the top of the happiness scale, and Ms. Sheehy dubbed them "pathfinders." The individuals she interviewed who decided to plod along in their old lives, avoid the risks involved in changing, and tried to just make the best of things, scored toward the bottom of the charts.

As I read the book, I found many of the subjects in her study described feelings of unhappiness and despair identical to what I was currently experiencing. I picked up a yellow highlighter and starting marking the passages that mirrored what I was going through. I began wondering if I might be able to summon up the courage to dramatically change careers and find the path to happiness as these "pathfinders" had done.

Some interesting changes were occurring in the airline industry at about that same time. Since the Airline Deregulation Act of 1978, all the rules had changed. New major airlines were popping up right and left, and old established airlines were going under. After many years of stagnant growth, passenger volume was growing rapidly. The newly established airlines were all hiring pilots, as were the old flagship carriers. Each company hurried to expand its fleet in an attempt to survive in this hotly competitive new environment.

My airline pilot buddies in the squadron told me the airlines were all having trouble finding qualified applicants who were under age 30. After the Vietnam War ended, military pilot training had been cut way back, and many pilots who left the military after the war found other jobs. Pilots with civilian pilot backgrounds and enough experience to be hired for commercial airline jobs were typically older. The result of all this was the airlines were raising their hiring-age limits for new pilots and starting to hire older candidates. One of my friends advised me his company, Northwest Airlines, had recently hired a couple of pilots in their mid-30s— I was 38 at the time.

My squadron mates, who were enjoying my dream career, encouraged me to apply for an airline job. I started thinking about this night and day. I had spent nine years of my life training to be a physician, and I would have to turn my back on that huge investment. I knew no airline would consider me a viable candidate as long as I was still practicing medicine. This realization meant having to quit my job as an emergency room physician and start flying full-time before they would take me seriously. I knew I had reached a major crossroads, just as the people in the book had, but could I summon up the courage to jump off the cliff and join the ranks of Sheehy's pathfinders? My pilot friends didn't see the risk, assuring me that if things didn't work out, I could always go back to being a physician. I knew, though, that once I turned my back on my medical career, there would be no going back. I could only go forward after that.

✈ 92 ✈

August 27, 1983

The Captain Whidbey Inn

Coupeville, Washington

Jim Stewart and I sat at a table next to a window in the dining room of the historic lodge at 11:30 AM on a rainy Saturday. We ordered lunch and each sipped a draft beer as we waited for our food. We were the first patrons to arrive, so the small dining room was empty except for our table. We watched, through rain-streaked windowpanes, as a flock of hungry seagulls circled over Penn Cove and dove into the water upon spotting a possible meal. The birds were hunting in waters that are home to one of the most well-known seafood delicacies on the West Coast—the Penn Cove Mussel.

Jim and I were on the island for our weekend Navy Reserve duty. We had finished the morning flight physicals and slipped off base for an early lunch.

"Okay, Dave, you can't just say you are unhappy practicing medicine. Be precise. Tell me specific things you don't like about it, and maybe we can get to the bottom of this."

I looked out at the swooping birds and took a sip of beer as I thought about that. Looking back at Jim, the first thing that came out of my mouth was, "Well, for one thing, I don't make enough money."

Jim looked me in the eye and said, "How much is enough?"

I closed my eyes and pondered that question for a minute. I was earning about $60,000 per year in the ER. Would $100,000 be enough? No, it would not, I concluded. Would $200,000 be enough? No, I didn't think so. I jumped, in my mind, to $1,000,000 per year. If I earned that much from practicing medicine, would I then be happy?

A light bulb snapped on in my head. I suddenly realized I wouldn't be happy practicing medicine for any amount of money. Money wasn't the problem.

What seemed like a simple question from my friend the psychiatrist resulted in an astonishing revelation. It unveiled a frightening and threatening thought: I had clearly picked the wrong career. What a time to be discovering that! I had struggled through a significant portion of my 38 years studying and training to be a physician, and I had, since then, become progressively disenchanted and unhappy with my life. Now I questioned why I had chosen medicine in the first place. It seemed like the wrong fit. I didn't want to practice medicine anymore for any amount of money. This sudden enlightenment hit me like a ton of bricks. Could I summon up the necessary courage to dramatically change careers in midlife, and, equally important, would a career change make me happy?

The decision I had been trying to make for so many months was suddenly crystal clear: I had to go for it.

Jim saw what was happening to me and right then and there knew he had put into motion something big, but he wasn't sure whether he had initiated something very good or something very bad.

When I went to my room that night at the BOQ, I read a few more pages from *Pathfinders*. I suddenly put down the yellow highlighter and closed the book firmly. I didn't need to read any more. I felt a new confidence I hadn't been able to muster up before.

The following week, Martha and I went out to dinner at The Cedars Floating Restaurant on Lake Coeur d'Alene. We sat at a small table next to the window and, with the light of an outdoor flood, watched a misty fog swirling just above the surface of the dark water. We each sipped a cocktail and discussed our future. If I decided to go for an airline career, I wanted to be sure she understood all the changes it would trigger in her life and the lives of our two girls. If this was going to work, she had to be 100 percent onboard. The transition would be difficult, I knew, and my ultimate goal was anything but assured. I had much to do before an airline might even consider me a candidate worth interviewing. I had to start flying full-time. I needed to log more total hours and gain experience in more complex aircraft, I needed to take and pass the FAA written test for a Flight Engineer Certificate, and I needed to attain an Airline Transport Pilot Certificate (ATP). This new path wasn't going to be easy for Martha either; she would have to go back to work full-time to help support our family during the transition.

Martha was so relieved to see the dramatic change in me that, after dealing with my increasing depression for so long, she gave me her full support. I gave notice of my resignation at the Emergency Room the following morning.

93

When I quit my job at the ER, Empire Airways had no full-time pilot positions open and no immediate hiring plans, so I was still a part-time employee. I decided I would just show up at the airport at 7:00 AM every day and be available for any flights that came up. Whenever one of the full-time pilots was unavailable for a trip, I got assigned to it. When I wasn't flying, I snooped around the office and found administrative tasks that needed attention and volunteered to tackle them.

I started perusing *Commerce Business Daily*, a publication which contained solicitations for government contract proposals. I circled any aviation contracts that were within Empire's capabilities and might be profitable to the firm. I placed these documents on Mel's desk for his review and later assisted in preparing formal bids for any contracts in which he was interested.

I also went on an organizing frenzy around the office. I cleaned out files, straightened up bookcases, and updated the pilot navigation charts to the latest revisions. I set up the flight bags so they were area-specific and affixed geographic identification tags on each. A pilot could then easily identify and grab the correct bag of charts for a flight within the state or a flight across the country.

My purpose in assuming these responsibilities was primarily to stay busy and keep from getting bored while waiting for a flight assignment, but I also hoped Mel would take note of my efforts and realize he needed me as a full-time employee.

Martha quickly landed a full-time job as a teacher in a Catholic grade school in Spokane, but her salary was a paltry $9,000 per year. I only got paid for actual flight time, and I wasn't flying much. I hoped something would change soon.

Despite our financial worries and my uncertain future as a professional pilot, I was much happier than I had been in many years. I told Martha how different it was to go to work and be around normal, happy people doing normal things, instead of being surrounded by the mayhem of a hospital ER. My cynicism for humanity in general melted away. Martha was happier because I was happier, and our kids seemed happier too.

I hadn't been skulking around the office for too many days when I got my big break. The opportunity wasn't for a full-time pilot position, but it would provide steady income for the next six weeks. The National

Oceanic and Atmospheric Administration (NOAA) awarded Empire a contract for flight operations in support of a study being conducted on acid rain in the Eastern U.S. and Southeastern Canada. Mel and Al selected me as the contract administrator and pilot.

The aircraft specified in the contract was a Piper Navajo Chieftain, a 10-passenger commuter plane. Empire didn't have a Chieftain, but it didn't take Mel long to find one available for lease and get it flown to Coeur d'Alene. As soon as it arrived, Al took me out for an accelerated flight training course in the aircraft. I spent most of the first day with Al flying around on one engine, doing single-engine instrument approaches, and practicing other inflight emergencies. That plane was the largest twin-engine aircraft I had ever flown, but he signed me off for solo on the second day. The next day, I took off on a solo flight in the Navajo with a destination of Wright Field in Dayton, Ohio. By the time I landed in Dayton, I was starting to feel pretty comfortable flying the aircraft.

Over the next six weeks, I flew all over the Northeastern U.S. tracking weather balloons with a team of NOAA scientists and technicians monitoring sophisticated electronic equipment installed in the passenger cabin. The flying wasn't particularly difficult, but the hours were long because the balloons often stayed aloft for long periods of time. One day we started off at 6:00 in the morning with a balloon launch from Dayton, and, except for fuel stops, we didn't land back at Dayton until 5:00 the following afternoon—a span of almost 36 hours in the air. If I hadn't previously been conditioned for those kinds of hours as a physician, I am not sure I could have stayed awake that long. I reported my 36-hour day to Empire, and they dispatched a second pilot, Ken Stroud, to Dayton so we could alternate flying duties on the long days.

Although the flights were always lengthy, we frequently had several days off in a row. The weather had to be just right for a balloon launch; we would wait for days for a temperature inversion, little or no wind, and stagnant air. Until those conditions were forecast, we had to wait it out. I took advantage of my free time to prepare for the Airline Transport Pilot and the Flight Engineer Turbojet written tests. I purchased home-study courses and hunkered down to study in my room at the Dayton La Quinta Inn. I had brought my typewriter along on the trip, and I started drafting and typing an aviation résumé. Ken thought I was wasting my time.

When I felt as prepared as I would ever be for the tests, I rented an old beat-up Plymouth from Rent-a-Wreck to drive to the FAA office in Cincinnati for the scheduled exams. The junker car cost only $7 for the day, which nicely fit my meager budget. The paint on the car looked like it had been exposed to a lot of the acid rain the NOAA scientists were researching. On the day I left on the 60-mile drive, it was pouring rain with standing water on the freeways. Only one windshield wiper on the car worked, and it was on the passenger side. I sat straddling the middle of the front seat, so I could see where I was going, and I drove the car the whole way to Cincinnati from that awkward position. The car didn't steer well either, and I think that might have been due to the fact that no two tires on the car were the same size. The engine ran roughly, and blue smoke puffed from the corroded exhaust pipe. I somehow made it to the FAA office in time, took both tests, and happily passed with flying colors. When I walked out to the parking lot, I was relieved to see the skies had cleared and the rain had stopped. That was a good omen, I thought. I made it back to Dayton without incident but decided I would never Rent-a-Wreck again.

During the last two weeks of the acid rain study, we operated north of the U.S. border, and our team was based in Sudbury, Ontario. A well-known freelance photographer from New York City, Peter Kaplan, met us there and spent several days accompanying us as he documented our activities for an upcoming article in Life magazine. He was quite a character and fun to have along on the flights. Peter flew with us on our balloon sorties, and Ken and I went along with him for a shoot from a helicopter he had chartered. Peter stepped out of the helicopter's door and stood on the skid several times during the flight to capture the shot he wanted. He was totally fearless when it came to heights, but watching him do that caused chills to run up and down my spine.

When I finished the NOAA contract and got back to Coeur d'Alene, I scheduled my Airline Transport Pilot oral exam and flight test at the Flight Standards District Office in Spokane. I knew none of the major airlines required this certificate as a prerequisite for a pilot position, but the ATP is considered the PhD of aviation and would be a nice addition to my résumé. I took the exam's flight check in the Navajo Chieftain, since I had been flying it exclusively for the past six weeks. The examiner required that I fly the entire flight check under the hood with reference only to the instruments, and most of it was flown with one engine out. When I landed back in Coeur d'Alene that afternoon, I had a new credential to add to my résumé. Martha and I went back to The Cedars Floating Restaurant for a celebratory dinner that night.

The NOAA acid rain study crew and the Navajo Chieftain

Dayton, Ohio - Fall, 1983

374

94

Shortly after I returned from flying the NOAA contract, Mel called me into his office and delivered a double-whammy of good news. While I was back East, he made the decision to put me on the payroll as a full-time employee. My salary was small but would at least provide steady income. The other bombshell he dropped was that he had decided to start a scheduled intrastate commuter airline. He had already leased a Cessna 441 Conquest, a high-performance twin turboprop, and was looking for a second one to add to the fleet. The aircraft would be operated with a crew of two pilots and carry nine passengers and their luggage. The first planned route was a twice-daily roundtrip from Coeur d'Alene to Boise.

I had kept my major airline aspirations a guarded secret, so Mel had no idea how well the commuter airline flying fit into my career plans. I quickly completed training on the Conquest and got my route check as a first officer; it was my first turboprop, and I loved flying it. The plane was a hot little performer and could climb directly to 35,000 feet, even when near maximum gross weight. It was fast for a propeller aircraft, cruising at close to 300 knots true airspeed.

By early summer, I was able to add the title commuter airline captain to my résumé, and I started filling out applications for employment at all of the major airlines, whether they were actively hiring or not.

On my Navy drill weekends that summer, I started hanging out less with my fellow physicians and more with my airline pilot friends. They all told me I needed to find a key person at each airline who could recommend me and call attention to my application so it would wind up in the right hands. Several of those guys wrote letters for me, but most of them admitted they probably were not in positions to have much influence. I had to find someone within one of the airlines who had real clout and might be able to make something happen for me. I spent my Navy weekends at Whidbey that summer beating the bushes in search of that key person.

Commander Dave Wilder was the commanding officer of the transport squadron, VR-61. I had recently been transferred from the P-3 training squadron to serve as flight surgeon for his squadron of DC-9's. At the time, Dave was a Boeing 757 captain for Northwest Airlines. He agreed to write a letter of recommendation for me to the Personnel Department at Northwest, where I had an application on file. His letter made it sound like I could walk on water and was almost embarrassing for me to even read, but I had high hopes that this was just the kind of boost I needed. Although I never received a response from Northwest Airlines, I have never stopped appreciating Dave Wilder's gracious efforts on my behalf.

One Sunday morning in mid-June, I was performing flight physicals at the naval hospital when someone started pounding on the door to my exam room and shouting my name. I thought it was either some hysterical patient having a panic attack or the building was on fire. I cracked open the exam room door and found Lieutenant Commander Bill Fitch, a P-3 naval flight officer, standing there wide-eyed and excited.

"Doc, do you know who is in the waiting room for a physical this morning?" Of course, I had no idea, but it was apparent Bill couldn't wait to break the exciting news to me.

"Bill, calm down," I said. "I'm in the middle of an exam here. Can you wait until I'm through?"

"Doc, you don't understand. Steve Drennon is out here. He's the chief flight engineer at Alaska Airlines and he's on their Pilot Selection Board." That got my attention.

I told the pilot I was examining to stay where he was and that I would be right back. I walked out to the waiting area's counter where the patients' medical records were stacked in the order they were to be seen. I found Steve Drennon's folder near the bottom of the pile and carried it back to my exam room before it could be picked up by one of the other flight surgeons performing pilot physicals.

My heart was beating rapidly with excitement as I finished up the exam that had been in progress when Bill had so awkwardly interrupted. I then picked up Steve Drennon's folder, now in my possession, and casually carried it back into the waiting area.

"Lieutenant Commander Drennon," I calmly called out as I scanned the seating area, "You're next." An officer stood up with a look of surprise on his face. Many of the patients sitting there were aware he was one of the last to arrive in the waiting room. He glanced around and saw a few hostile stares. He returned their glares with an innocent smile, shrugged his shoulders, and followed me down the hall and into the exam room.

Alaska Airlines was considered a regional airline at the time due its relatively small size, but it did have a fleet of large turbojet aircraft— Boeing 727s and a few 737s. The company had fewer than 300 pilots on its payroll and only about 17 airplanes. I had sent an application to Alaska with the idea I could get some experience in large passenger aircraft and then possibly get hired by one of the larger flagship carriers. Alaska was a well-run company and profitable. It would be a great place to start my new career.

I immediately found Steve Drennon to be a warm, likeable person and I thought we hit it off well. He patiently and compassionately listened to my life story and promised to look over my application. I just happened to have with me a Xerox copy of my Alaska application and my résumé, and he left the exam room with those documents in hand.

Steve and I stayed in touch over the next few weeks. I worried over the fact I hadn't flown any large, heavy aircraft, but he told me that was not a problem. Apparently the airline had hired quite a few pilots in the past with only light-aircraft experience. He thought I was qualified and had at least a chance of getting hired. In our phone conversations, he assured me he had brought my application to the attention of the director of Personnel and the vice president of Flight Operations and that I could expect a phone call any day to start the multi-tiered personal interview process.

When I came home from flying each evening, I started asking Martha the same question: "Did Alaska Airlines call today?" As days—and then weeks—passed, it became kind of a joke. Martha would tease me and say, sometimes before I even asked, "Let me think a minute….no, I don't think they called today."

One evening I came in after a particularly long, hard day and Martha said, "Aren't you going to ask your question today?" She had a glowing smile on her face and announced, "The answer is 'yes,' they did call today."

95

August 6, 1984
10:30 AM

Alaska Airlines Corporate Headquarters

Seattle, Washington

"So, Dr. Crawley, after all that education and training to become a physician, why do you now think you want to be an airline pilot?" Larry Hogan, the vice president of Flight Operations was directing the interview.

Mr. Hogan sat at one end of a long, polished walnut table in a richly paneled conference room, and I sat at the opposite end. Steve Drennon, the airline's chief flight engineer, was on Mr. Hogan's right, and Captain Bruce Calkins, the chief pilot, was seated to his left. Captain Calkins was in full uniform. Larry Hogan wore a brown suit with a vest. Second Officer Drennon was dressed in a conservative navy-blue suit, white dress shirt, and dark blue tie with a thin red stripe; my attire was so similar to his that it looked like the two of us had gone shopping at Nordstrom together.

The question of why I'd decided to switch careers came as no surprise. It was the one question I was sure would be asked. I knew I would need to put a good spin on my response if I had any chance of successfully navigating this intensive, multi-tiered interview process. I sat up straight in the chair and tried to look calm and in control as I met Mr. Hogan's gaze. I had been briefed that he would be asking most of the questions and that he liked having full control of the selection of pilot candidates for the airline. I was also told he was not a pilot and that he carefully considered and respected the opinions of the two pilot interviewers with us in the conference room.

Larry Hogan looked like a typical businessman in his brown suit, white shirt, conservative tie, and vest. I guessed him to be in his early to mid-50s. His brown hair was thin and combed over to one side; he had rather plain facial features and a soft voice with a flat tone and little inflection. He didn't make me feel threatened or intimidated, but he exhibited no friendliness or warmth and his gaze was intense. His cold manner unnerved me a bit, but I tried my best to remain calm and relaxed.

379

Captain Calkins was a big bear of a man, with dark, bushy hair and eyebrows, and a large head. In fact, he was so big that his uniform looked like it was about ready to split at the seams. Even so, he had soft eyes and a friendly manner, and just looking at him gave me some slight relief from the tension I felt.

I glanced over at Steve Drennon. Although we had just recently met, he was batting for me. He had personally gone to the Personnel Office at Alaska Airlines and pulled strings to set me up for the interview process. Steve was a people person, with a cheerful disposition and a friendly open manner. He was a straight-shooter, and I knew I didn't have to worry about him in this interview.

Steve gave me a reassuring little nod, a slight smile, and a wink. That helped.

"I love airplanes and I love to fly, sir."

"I'm sorry, Doctor, I don't understand. Don't you love medicine?"

I lied in answering that one. These guys didn't need to know how disenchanted I was with my life as a doctor and how truly depressed I had become. "Yes, sir. I enjoy being a physician," I replied. There was stone silence as Mr. Hogan thought about this for a minute. The silence of the room made me feel the need to add something to my answer. "I'm a very dedicated doctor, sir, and I'm good at what I do. In fact, there are some extremely satisfying moments in medicine, but when I'm flying an airplane, I feel much happier and fulfilled than when I am doing anything else."

"That may be true, Doctor, but you have to understand our concerns. We spend a lot of money on initial and recurrent training for the aircraft you will fly. The pilots we hire have to meet all of our minimum requirements, which include certain FAA certificates, medical standards, and flight hours; each candidate must also hold a college degree, and background checks must reveal the highest level of moral standards. You wouldn't be in this room if you didn't meet all of our minimum requirements, but we also need to be sure we are hiring a person who is anticipating a long career at Alaska Airlines."

"Mr. Hogan, you don't need to address me as 'Doctor.' I'm a pilot and I am applying for a position as a flight officer. Please call me David." I paused to think about what I wanted to say next.

I knew in advance this concern would come up, and I had all but memorized an answer I hoped would be satisfactory. Now, sitting in the hot seat, it seemed a little weak, and my brain was going at warp speed to come up with a convincing assurance that flying was a permanent career change and something I had thought about and worked toward for a long time. The three of them were looking at me, waiting for me to continue.

"Sir, it was a long, difficult path earning all the FAA certificates I now hold. I started flying in 1973, and I attained these certificates and ratings and accumulated all of my flight hours over an 11-year period. During 10 of those 11 years, I was also practicing medicine full-time. I have accumulated 2,500 hours of total flight time, most of which were commercial flying hours. I haven't practiced medicine for over a year and have been flying full-time during that time frame. You must realize how much dedication, perseverance, and direction it took to accomplish this."

Mr. Hogan leaned back in his chair a bit and glanced at Captain Calkins, who hadn't uttered a word yet. He then cleared his throat and thoughtfully answered. "So you're telling us you're not doing this on a whim."

I had just thought about saying exactly that, but it might have sounded a little flip or disrespectful coming from me. I was glad he was the one who said it and glad it didn't sound like a question. I thought maybe he got it. At least I hoped he did. I was starting to feel pearls of perspiration rolling down the sides of my chest from my armpits.

He then moved on and began questioning me about my flying experience. He wanted to know which of the major airports in the country I had flown in and out of, what were the largest and most complex aircraft I had piloted, and whether or not I had any jet time. This line of questioning opened the door for Steve and Captain Calkins to step in and start asking a few questions.

Steve knew I had little jet time, and that experience was as a copilot on a corporate Lear Jet and a Cessna Citation. He wasn't concerned about that and knew Captain Calkins wasn't worried either, but he wanted to make sure Larry Hogan knew it wasn't a big issue.

"Dave, which is more difficult and demanding to fly: the Lear Jet or the twin turboprops you flew as a captain for the commuter airline in Idaho?" Steve knew exactly how I would answer his question.

I didn't have to think about that one. "I thought the training, check-out, and actual flying of the Lear and the Citation were easier and less demanding than the two high-performance twin turboprops I operated—the Cessna 441 Conquest and the Piper Cheyenne IIIA. The propellers on these aircraft add another layer of complexity to the aircraft systems and another set of emergency procedures to learn. Also, much of my single- and multi-engine time was single-pilot IFR in every type of weather conditions imaginable. The Lear Jet and Citation flying, requiring a minimum crew of two, was definitely less demanding."

"So you don't feel your limited experience in jet-powered aircraft will cause you any difficulty in your initial training at our airline? Is that what you are saying?" Steve was not really questioning this; his question was again for Larry Hogan's ears.

Before I could answer, Captain Calkins seemed to suddenly come to life, speaking his first words since the interview began. He said, "Steve, you know as well as I do we have a number of 727 pilots whose only experience before they got here was flying single-engine aircraft as bush pilots in Alaska. They all did fine in initial training. The doctor here has some good experience under his belt, and I think he'll do fine."

I was happy to have Captain Calkins entering into the conversation, as he seemed to be aligned with Steve and on my side. But that was the only comment he made from the moment I entered the room until I left. He didn't ask me a single question. He was on his way out on a flight as soon as the interview was over, and I saw him checking his watch every few minutes.

After that, the atmosphere in the room turned a little more casual. Mr. Hogan and Steve then asked me a few questions about my military service and my personal life. It seemed they were just trying to get to know me a bit and acquire a feel for what I was really like. I tried to be casual without letting my guard down and attempted to give honest and straightforward answers.

Before the interview, I had talked to several Alaska Airlines pilots whom I knew through my Navy Reserve unit at Whidbey Island and who had recently been through the interview process. I had asked if I could expect some technical aviation questions. They all told me they usually didn't do that in the interview process, but that I should be prepared in the event they did throw in some technical questions. So I had studied like crazy in case they asked me such questions as:

"What is the significance of the lift-over-drag ratio and what is L/D max?"

"What is P-Factor?"

"Can you explain the difference between indicated airspeed, calibrated airspeed, true airspeed, and groundspeed?"

"What kind of weather would you expect at the passage of a cold front?"

I was ready for these and any others I thought they might throw at me, but they didn't ask a single technical question.

The whole interview lasted about 30 minutes. I was told to go back out to the lobby and have a seat. One of them would be out in a few minutes and tell me what, if anything, was the next step for me in this process.

96

At the end of the day, I was finally told to go home and expect to hear something within the next week. I didn't know whether that was a good thing or a bad thing.

It was a long week, but I finally got a call and was asked to return to Seattle for completion of the screening process. This included an interview by the vice president of Personnel, a review of my high school, college, and medical school transcripts by a department head, a complete physical exam, and a flight simulator test.

A few days after I had returned home again, a secretary in the Personnel Department called to tell me I had passed everything and was in a pool of candidates for a possible future new-hire class. I called Steve Drennon to ask him what exactly this meant.

Steve said the company hadn't decided whether or not they needed to hire any more pilots that fall. If they started another new-hire training class, it would likely be a small one. The aviators for a new class would be chosen from the pre-selected pool. By that time, I was getting used to not knowing what to expect next, and I just went back to work at Empire and tried to concentrate on my flying and enjoy what I was doing. I had run out of excuses for my trips to Seattle by then, and one day I confessed to Mel my pursuits and ultimate goal. The news didn't seem to surprise him much, and he wished me luck.

Steve called me one evening during the last week of September with good news and bad news. The good news was the company had chosen 12 candidates from the pre-selected pool to start class in October. The bad news for me was that I wasn't one of those chosen for this last new-hire class of 1984. Steve said future hiring needs for the upcoming new year were unknown. I felt as though I was again on a never-ending rollercoaster ride and wondered if that was the way everyone felt about their lives.

The rollercoaster stopped for me during the last week of October. I was sitting in my high-rise hotel room at Caesar's Tahoe in the town of Lake Tahoe, California, when the phone rang. I had flown a group of Transtector executives from Coeur d'Alene to the beautiful resort town. I laid the book I was reading on the bed beside me and picked up the receiver. Steve Drennon was on the line. He said, "Jan Mae has been trying to get in touch with you. You need to call her right away."

Jan Mae was the secretary in Personnel at the airline who processed the pilot applications and set up the new-hire classes. When I called Jan, she told me one of the chosen candidates for the October class had gotten another offer and backed out. If I wanted the spot in the class, I was to immediately fax her a copy of my written resignation from Empire Airways.

I knew, when submitting a resignation from employment, a two-week notice was considered a minimum and 30 days more courteous and professional. It was Thursday, October 25, when I talked to Jan from my Lake Tahoe hotel room. I assured her I would be in Seattle for the first day of class on the following Monday, October 29.

I arrived back in Coeur d'Alene on Friday afternoon and proceeded straight to Mel's office. He took my announcement fairly well under the circumstances. Since I was already on the flight schedule every day the following week, I knew I was putting him in a bind. Mel would have to fly my scheduled flights until the company could hire and train a replacement pilot. I felt terrible about leaving him in such a lurch after all the opportunities he had provided for me and apologized profusely. Mel grumbled for a couple of minutes, and then he looked across his desk, smiled, and said, "Dave, your ship has come in. I am happy for you, and I wish you the best of luck."

On Monday morning, I walked out of my room at the Sandstone Motel in Seattle, crossed 188th Street, and headed for an aircraft hangar with "Alaska Airlines" painted on the metal side in giant letters. I was dressed in my navy-blue interview suit. I climbed the stairs to a second-floor classroom to begin training as a Boeing 727 flight engineer. I was the first new-hire to arrive for class that morning. I was 39 years old, the oldest pilot ever hired at the airline at the time, and the first medical doctor.

The training classroom was only on the second floor of the large building, but I felt as though I was on the top of the world that morning. My ship had finally come in.

Epilogue

I shall be telling this with a sigh somewhere ages and ages hence...

After commuting from our home in Coeur d'Alene to Seattle for my first year of employment as an airline pilot at Alaska Airlines, we made the decision, in the summer of '85, to move to the Seattle area where I would be based for the remainder of my career. The move was, at first, difficult for our two girls, Jill and Alice, as they were being pried away from the only life they had known. Both of them accepted it bravely, and they adapted quickly to a new house in a new city, new schools, and new friends. For Martha and me, it was all part of the new adventure, and before long, it seemed all four of us were happier than we had ever been. Life just got better and better from there.

I enjoyed a 21-year career as an airline pilot for Alaska Airlines. I went to work every day with a smile on my face. It fulfilled my dream in every way I imagined, and I never looked back on my career change with any regret.

I completed initial training at the airline in early 1985. I served as a flight engineer on the Boeing 727 for two years, first officer on the 727 for three years, first officer on the McDonald-Douglas MD-80 for three years, and I finally checked out in the left seat of the MD-80 in 1992. I flew as captain for the last 13 years of my career until hitting the mandatory retirement age of 60 in 2005.

Our airline's route system took me to interesting new places which were mostly in the western half of North America. In Alaska, I flew into Ketchikan, Sitka, Juneau, Yakutat, Cordova, Anchorage, Fairbanks, Nome, Kotzebue, and Prudhoe Bay. In the lower 48 states, I landed in Seattle, Portland, Reno, Spokane, Boise, San Francisco, Oakland, San Jose, Los Angeles, Ontario, and San Diego. My destinations in Canada included Vancouver, Calgary, and Toronto. South of the border flights were to Ensenada, Puerto Vallarta, Mazatlán, and San Jose del Cabo. I had overnight layovers in many of these cities and loved the opportunities to explore, meet new people, and enjoy local cuisine.

I continued to serve as a flight surgeon in the Navy Reserve throughout my career as an airline pilot. I retired from Alaska Airlines and the Navy in 2005.

> *...Two roads diverged in a wood, and I,*
> *I took the one less traveled by,*
> *And that has made all the difference.*

> Robert Frost

✈   ✈   ✈

The events described in this memoir are all true to the best of my recollection. Most of the dates and times are accurate, having been extracted from copies of military orders and civilian and military flight logbooks. The individuals introduced are identified by their real names in most cases, but a few names are fictitious.

In the cockpit at 35,000 feet on the 100th anniversary of
the Wright brothers' first flight at Kitty Hawk, NC

Final flight – June 26, 2005

389

Also by David B. Crawley

A MILE OF STRING

A BOY'S RECOLLECTION OF HIS MIDWEST CHILDHOOD

Readers' Reviews

A String of Tales From the Age of Innocence

For those of you who wish to take a journey back to the days when dreams were limitless in America, seen through the eyes of a young man, this is a book you will savor.

Remember When...

The experiences and descriptions remind us of the value of family life and relate a period in time unencumbered by the pace and noise of modern day technology. The world has changed in many ways and the wholesome adventures described in this book are a journey perhaps less likely for children born today.

A Sweet Tale

This sweetly told tale captures the flavor of a particular time and place now gone. As someone based in Kansas City who helps people write and edit their memoirs, I especially appreciate the glimpse into this city during an era that shaped the formative years of many of my local clients. Thanks for an enjoyable read, Dr. Crawley!

Great History and Life Lesson

Very good, enjoyed every word of it. Growing up in a farming community it was spot on......

391

Amazing Recall

Boyhood adventures well remembered. Wonderful and amazingly detailed recollection of childhood experiences in the 1950s, replete with "double feature" movies, parochial school misadventures, work responsibilities, summer camp fun, and, above all, the exploration, personal initiative and sheer freedom seldom allowed children in today's environment.

A Delightful Little Book

Anybody who grew up Catholic in the '50s and went to a parochial school in the Midwest will have a lot of memories rekindled reading this delightful and well written book. Chapeau, Dr. Crawley! We eagerly await the sequel.

A Mile of String, a Lot of Memories

I was six or seven years ahead of David at St. Agnes and did not know him. However, I knew some of the individuals or families and some of his teachers. Most of the places and some of his experiences such as the Kansas City Kansan paper route were also shared by me. Thank you for some chuckles and fond memories. These were good times in a good place.

Memories of My Childhood!

I truly enjoyed this book but because I grew up during this time frame and actually lived in this area that the book describes, it really resonated with me. I would think that most baby boomers could relate to this story. Dave has an incredible memory! Liked it a lot!

Better Than I Could Ever Put It

This book brings back both wonderful and not so wonderful childhood memories. Most were very good. It was a much simpler time for my generation for which I will always be grateful. I hope there is a sequel coming!

Made in the USA
San Bernardino, CA
05 March 2016